Medical Treatment

This practical and easily navigable book covers the gamut of issues that need to be understood to provide excellent medical care for those with ADHD. Outside of mental health professionals, those who most often treat ADHD are primary care providers such as family practitioners, pediatricians, nurse practitioners, physician assistants, and school personnel.

Based on clinical conversations with patients with ADHD and their families, this book provides concise, useful, up to date information of a practical nature for most, if not all of the problems, associated conditions and questions that arise when an individual has concerns about ADHD. Treatments discussed include a thorough review of medication options, with expected results and side effects, as well as other recommended treatments including a variety of therapeutic modalities, and a review of less commonly considered but important interventions regarding general health, sleep, diet, exercise, and school interventions.

Readers will gain an understanding of what ADHD is, practical reviews of the literature that will help in discussion with patients and their families the importance of intervention, and all the resources and options available to provide the best treatment strategies for anyone who has ADHD as well as the commonly associated conditions.

J. Dennis Odell MD, FAAP medical clinic director at the Center for Persons with Disabilities at Utah State University for 34 years, also private practice in general and developmental/behavioral pediatrics at Intermountain Budge Clinic from 1984 to 2020.

Medical Treatment of ADHD

A Practical Guide for Clinicians, Counselors, and Parents

J. Dennis Odell

Routledge
Taylor & Francis Group

NEW YORK AND LONDON

First published 2021
by Routledge
52 Vanderbilt Avenue, New York, NY 10017

and by Routledge
2 Park Square, Milton Park, Abingdon, Oxon OX14 4RN

Routledge is an imprint of the Taylor & Francis Group, an informa business

© 2021 Taylor & Francis

Library of Congress Cataloging-in-Publication Data
Names: Odell, J. Dennis (John Dennis), author.
Title: Medical treatment of ADHD : a practical guide for clinicians, counselors, and parents / J. Dennis Odell.
Description: New York, NY : Routledge, 2021. | Includes bibliographical references and index.
Identifiers: LCCN 2020015743 | ISBN 9780367494797 (hardback) | ISBN 9780367494780 (paperback) | ISBN 9781003046349 (ebook)
Subjects: MESH: Attention Deficit Disorder with Hyperactivity–diagnosis | Attention Deficit Disorder with Hyperactivity–therapy | Attention Deficit Disorder with Hyperactivity–complications
Classification: LCC RC394.A85 | NLM WS 350.8.A8 | DDC 616.85/89–dc23
LC record available at https://lccn.loc.gov/2020015743

ISBN: 978-0-367-49479-7 (hbk)
ISBN: 978-0-367-49478-0 (pbk)
ISBN: 978-1-003-04634-9 (ebk)

Typeset in Bembo
by Taylor & Francis Books

Contents

Illustrations

Figure

Tables

Contributors

Camille Odell MS, Department of Psychology, Utah State University, Logan, Utah. Program Director—Professional School Counseling Program

J. Dennis Odell MD, FAAP, Pediatrician specializing in developmental and behavioral pediatrics, Intermountain Healthcare Budge Clinic, Logan, Utah. Formerly director of Biomedical Division, Director Medical Clinic, Center for Persons with Disabilities, Utah State University, Logan, Utah

Martin Toohill Ph.D., Clinical Psychologist, and Coordinator, Psychological Services Unit, Center for Persons with Disabilities and the Sorenson Center for Clinical Excellence, Utah State University, Logan, Utah

George Wootton FNP, Clinician, Medical Clinic, Center for Persons with Disabilities, Utah State University, Logan, Utah

Preface

ADHD is very commonly diagnosed, and there is a wealth of published information on the subject. However, accessing practical and useful information can be overwhelming. I have spent the last 34 years working with children in a clinical setting who have attention deficit/hyperactivity disorder and related problems. There have been many thousands of children and their families who have come in with a litany of challenges and difficulties, and we have learned together how to understand the core problems, and best treatment approaches. This book is based on clinical conversations with these families and is an attempt to document some of the discussions that we've had in a way that will hopefully put this condition, and the challenges that arise because of it, in a meaningful perspective, and that will allow an understanding of the individual's personality, what is the motivation behind the behaviors of concern, and a sensible approach to intervention. It is also an attempt to provide concise, useful, up to date information of a practical nature for most, if not all of the problems, associated conditions and questions that arise when an individual has concerns about ADHD. This involves an understanding of not only what attention deficit/hyperactivity disorder really is, but also an understanding of the many conditions that may mimic or co-occur with ADHD. All of these need to be assessed to have a true understanding of the individual's difficulties and to produce a meaningful treatment program.

As such, I need to express my deepest thanks to all of the patients and families who have shared their experiences, frustrations and successes over the years for all they have taught me and for helping me understand and appreciate the incredible diversity of talents and strengths in dealing with everyday challenges. Likewise I need to thank our many incredible staff members, medical assistants and nurses who have with amazing patience, good humor and competence made our clinics joyful and fulfilling places to be a part of. Additionally I have had the privilege and opportunity to work with many very excellent coworkers, clinicians, researchers and colleagues who have shared their expertise and friendship over many years, and from whom I have learned so much. Lastly I would like to thank my wife Camille, for her patience, suggestions, editing, discussions and encouragement, without which, this work would not have been completed.

Part I
ADHD Defined

1 Introduction

An Overview of ADHD

J. Dennis Odell

Individuals who have ADHD (Attention-deficit/hyperactivity disorder) may be viewed in many different ways by the public at large. The hyperactive and disruptive behaviors of young children who have ADHD may be perceived as the result of misguided parenting, with the thought that a firmer parenting style with immediate consequences for incorrect behavior will result in better behavior. This is the "I would never let a child of mine get away with that kind of behavior" mindset. Some may view the student who can't remember assignments and who never get their homework turned in on time, with resulting poor grades, as unmotivated and lazy, and suggest that setting limits and taking away privileges will ensure better school performance. Comments like "I know he can do it, he just needs to try harder" or "when she tries, she does well, so it's just a matter of self-discipline, and then she will live up to her potential" describe these views. Parents may wonder why their parenting practices that worked well with other siblings don't seem to have an effect on their child with ADHD, or may wonder if they have done something wrong as parents that contributed to their child's difficult behavior or unexplained challenges. Peers may be put off by aggressive and hyperactive behaviors of their ADHD peer, and avoid establishing friendships with them in fear of their unpredictable and impulsive behaviors.

Professionals differ widely in their conceptions about ADHD. Some claim that ADHD is not a real disorder, but something created by physicians collaborating with pharmaceutical companies to profit by convincing the public that ADHD is a dreadful disorder that should be treated with their very expensive and profitable drugs. Or there may be the idea that the symptoms are very real, but explaining them by creating the vague category of ADHD with all its inconsistencies is misguided. Many who have dedicated their professional careers to studying ADHD will state, as quoted from Dr. Russell Barkley's encyclopedic tome on ADHD "it clearly represents a serious deficiency in one or more psychological adaptations that harm the individuals so afflicted, which is the very definition of a mental disorder".[1] Other professionals have questioned whether it should be termed a disorder. As quoted by Edward Hallowell in his book *Driven to Distraction* "there are advantages to having it, such as high energy, intuitiveness, creativity and enthusiasm, and they are completely overlooked by the 'disorder' model."[2]

Those who have ADHD may refuse to believe in ADHD entirely, or to accept that they have any problems whatsoever. They may blame others' unrealistic expectations or demands on the conflicts they are experiencing. Or they may feel that they have struggled for years and feel immensely relieved when they discover there is actually an identified condition that explains their challenges, and that it comes with very effective treatments. Most who are familiar with the term ADHD will share a degree of bewilderment about this "disorder", as there are so many conflicting views about it and the most appropriate interventions.

In the following pages, hopefully we can answer these questions and clarify current conceptualizations of ADHD, and come to an understanding of the broader complexity of ADHD, best evaluation practices, and treatment strategies.

ADHD Defined

David was 3 years old when he was first seen in our clinic. He was a first child, and his parents were at their wits end in trying to deal with his behavior. He was clearly very smart, but he was very disobedient, and was frequently getting into trouble. They reported that they had to keep all writing utensils away from him, as he would draw on walls, furniture, himself, the refrigerator. He climbed whenever he got a chance, and would hang off of second story railings, seemingly fearless of falling. He had fallen off of slides and playground equipment, resulting in 4 sets of stitches, and a broken wrist. He would never sit still at the dinner table, and ate on the run. Mealtime used to be a battle, but his parents finally gave up trying to get him to sit at the table. They never went out of the house with him because of his destructive tendencies in stores. He would run away, and they twice had to call the police to help locate him. They could not get babysitters, and his grandparents no longer cared for him in their home because they could not handle his behavior. They enrolled him in a neighborhood preschool, in hopes that behavior would improve in that setting, but he was expelled after 2 weeks. The preschool teacher apologized, and seemed embarrassed, but stated that his behavior was too disruptive for the others, and they didn't have enough staff to handle him.

He reached his developmental milestones at appropriate ages, and his medical history was very normal, with no evident explanation for his behaviors. His parents did report that there were 2 paternal uncles and a cousin who were diagnosed with ADHD. At first they assumed his behavior was just normal for a young child, but they became more concerned as they struggled to keep up with him. They had discussed his behaviors with his pediatrician, who witnessed much of this in her office. They were told this could be extreme "terrible twos and threes" and that he might improve a lot as he got older, but the pediatrician agreed the behaviors were challenging, and told them he likely did have ADHD. Behavior therapy was recommended and they arranged to see a child psychologist. They went to 12 sessions with him, and were able to find some strategies and interventions that were helpful in mitigating some of the most difficult behaviors. However, he remained very active and impulsive, and it was difficult and time consuming to continually try to manage his behavior, and they were getting exhausted.

When he was seen in the office, he was indeed everything they described. He was into everything he could reach, climbing onto tabletops, loud and boisterous. Although there were plenty of toys to choose from, he did not play with any particular one, but would bounce from one to the next, and within a short time the floor was covered with toys. Frequent parental attempts at redirecting his behavior were successful for only a limited time. He was cooperative for the exam, and very interactive and fun, but high energy. After a short period, he repeatedly tried to leave the room, and ultimately had to be taken out by one parent so we could have a discussion.

The above case scenario is the classic presentation for what has been known over the years as the hyperactive child, now termed Attention-deficit/hyperactivity disorder, or ADHD. ADHD is a complex neurodevelopmental condition that is far more than just hyperactive behavior and short attention span. It can present in many different ways, and symptoms evolve as the child gets older, so by no means does everyone with ADHD have exactly this history. In addition, ADHD usually comes with other associated but not universally present conditions that accentuate the challenges. To understand and effectively treat ADHD it is important to understand the varied problems that can occur and the background behind them. ADHD as currently defined has 3 core symptoms: hyperactivity, impulsivity and attention problems.

Hyperactivity

Hyperactivity is defined as nonproductive overactivity that is more than normal for age. Children who are hyperactive seem to be in constant motion throughout the day, and have a difficult time with quiet activities. Situations that require prolonged sitting are problematic, such as sitting still in the classroom, church services, long rides in the car and mealtimes. They may be unable to sit through a movie or television show. Hyperactivity typically changes as the child ages. Most 2 year olds are hyperactive, and this is normal developmentally. But by age 5 or 6, children should be much more able to sit still in certain environments, and it is this developmentally inappropriate level of activity that is considered part of ADHD. Hyperactivity often becomes less overt in adolescence and adulthood, but still may be manifest as general restlessness, overly talkative, and need for activity. To be classified as a symptom of ADHD, it has to be to a degree that is disruptive and significantly impacting the individual and those around him.

Impulsivity

Impulsivity is a trait where the individual will act on whatever they are thinking at the moment, and not be cognizant of consequences. They may have a hard time waiting their turn in line, or take things that belong to others. They may butt in on conversations and frequently interrupt. Children may put themselves or others in dangerous situations, not thinking about the consequences of their actions. Parents may wonder how their impulsive child will survive childhood because of frequent accidents or near accidents brought on by seemingly irrational decisions. Children who are impulsive may make friends easily, going up to strangers and sharing life stories, and being fearless in diving into situations. They may also lose friends quickly because their personalities can seem too much to handle. They may react to others with aggressive behavior such as kicking, hitting and biting, when frustrated. These are individuals who have difficulty delaying gratification. Decisions are often made without considering consequences, even when consequences are known. We all are impulsive at times, but just as with hyperactivity, symptoms of impulsivity in ADHD have to be to a degree that is developmentally inappropriate, and significantly negatively impacting the child.

Impulsive children are very challenging to parent because we usually shape behavior of our children based on consequences, such as reward or punishment. We tell them if they do something we ask, they will get a treat, or be able to do something they want, or if they don't do something we ask, we will remove a privilege. But the impulsive child doesn't respond quite so readily to our usual reinforcers, and we are left as parents wondering what to do, and why they keep misbehaving in spite of our best parenting efforts. From the child's perspective, when just caught doing something with a bad outcome, we will say (or yell) "didn't you know what was going to happen when you did that". The child will respond yes, but when asked "why then did you do what you just did", they will shrug their shoulders and say "I don't know". And from their perspective, that is what they experience and feel. They may be frustrated themselves, and think there is something wrong with them, because they are so often getting in trouble, and they don't know why.

Impulsivity doesn't magically disappear as children get older. Examples in older children or adults might include aggressively acting out towards others such as in road rage, or getting in fights at school. Even severe consequences such as attempting suicide when feeling particularly down, or getting into drugs or criminal activities may be a manifestation of an impulsive cognitive style. There is often a fearlessness component. Certain professions may attract individuals who are impulsive. A comment by one of the commentators for the winter Olympics that were held in British Columbia in 2010 brings this into perspective. He mentioned that athletes who participate in winter Olympic activities are often not like the rest of us (meaning most of the viewing audience). They thrive on danger and excitement. For example when skiing down an icy mountain at 100 miles an hour, they're often asking themselves "how do I go faster", when most of us would be asking ourselves "how do I not die". Many of these athletes in fact have ADHD, but likely if they were offered medication to treat their impulsiveness, they would decline, as it might take away their competitive edge.

Inattention

Inattention is a misnomer. Most individuals who are diagnosed with ADHD can attend very well to activities that they are interested in. The primary difficulty is in activities that require self-effort, especially those that are being required by others. This typically comes about in activities that are perceived as boring, such as schoolwork, homework and chores. From the perspective of the child, when they are in school, they spend the entire school day doing what their teacher instructs them to do and they have little choice in the matter. Additionally if their work is not completed at school, they must spend extra hours at home doing homework. There is typically not much reward for all of this effort other than the intrinsic joy of learning and doing a good job. And even if there are rewards in place, because of the impulsivity component, they may not help much to change behavior or performance. Individuals with attention problems may come across as being lazy or unmotivated. So it is very common for parents to state, for example, that their child can play for hours with Legos, building blocks, video games or building activities outdoors but when it comes to homework they may take hours to finish what should be a 15 minute task. There is often the appearance of being very disorganized and forgetful. Often, even when homework is done, it is not turned in. They frequently lose assignments, and have a hard time knowing what the assignments are and when they are due. Often adolescents with attention problems who are doing poorly in school are getting poor grades because their work isn't being done, not because they don't understand the material or necessarily do poorly on tests. They often appear to not be listening when spoken to, and are easily distracted. The best way to conceptualize the attention component of ADHD is that individuals with ADHD don't do boring well. And overall those with ADHD have difficulty with self-regulation.

Subtypes

ADHD comes in 3 main subtypes. Some children have all 3 symptoms and are diagnosed with ADHD-combined presentation. Some do not have significant hyperactivity or impulsivity and only have difficulties staying focused and are very easily distracted. These are diagnosed with ADHD-inattentive presentation, or commonly incorrectly termed Attention Deficit Disorder or ADD. Less commonly, some individuals have only the hyperactivity and impulsivity components but are able to attend well. They are diagnosed with ADHD-hyperactive/impulsive presentation.

By definition, symptoms need to have been present for at least 6 months, and at least some must have been present prior to age 12. Additionally, symptoms have to be to a degree that is felt to be developmentally inappropriate, and sufficient to significantly negatively impact the quality of life. Symptoms need to be present in more than one setting, such as home, school and work. ADHD symptoms are further subcategorized into level of severity. David in the above scenario would be classified as severe ADHD-combined presentation.

Who Decided the Criteria for Having ADHD?

There have been attempts at classifying diseases and disorders for centuries, in efforts to have a unified system of classification as a standard for all who provide healthcare and make diagnoses. Current diagnostic criteria for ADHD are delineated in the DSM-5.[3] The *Diagnostic and Statistical Manual of Mental Disorders* (DSM) is the definitive guide used by healthcare and mental health providers that classifies and provides the criteria for diagnosing mental health disorders. Because these disorders usually don't have underlying known causes, or specific medical tests that can be used for diagnosis, the DSM provides the best known descriptions on each condition, and specific criteria on how they are diagnosed and recognized. The first section of the DSM-5 is on neurodevelopmental disorders, which includes conditions such as autism, intellectual and learning disorders, communication disorders and ADHD. Other sections include sections on schizophrenia, mood disorders such as bipolar disorder, depression, OCD and anxiety, disruptive and conduct disorders, eating disorders, substance abuse disorders and others. It was originally published in 1952 and undergoes periodic revisions as more is understood about the various disorders. Each disorder is reviewed by experts and researchers in the field, who review the research and clinical information to help update and clarify diagnoses.

ADHD has gone by many other names over the years. It was not described in the first DSM edition. Prior to DSM terminology, it was known as minimal brain disorder or minimal brain dysfunction or simply hyperactivity. The DSM-II used the term hyperkinetic reaction of childhood. The DSM-III changed the name (and concept) to Attention Deficit Disorder with or without hyperactivity, and the current ADHD term was introduced in the DSM-IV.

ADHD through the Lifespan

ADHD is thought of as primarily a disorder whose symptoms begin in childhood. ADHD in toddlers and preschoolers will usually present with hyperactive and impulsive behavior. Prior to preschool, we don't expect children to do tasks that require sustained attention, and the ability to sustain attention developmentally improves through childhood. The ADHD-hyperactivity/impulsivity presentation is felt to be the least common presentation of the 3 subtypes, and often evolves into the combined type as children get into grade school. Combined type ADHD can be described as behaviors that are similar to 2-year-old behaviors, because most will have short attention spans, be impulsive and hyperactive. Just as a developmental exercise, I spent 30 minutes recording the unplanned and unsupervised activities of my then 2-year-old son, without intervening in his activities. He knew I was there, but was involved in my own project, so he was on his own as far as activities and entertainment. He rarely stayed with an activity for longer than a few minutes. He would start with one toy, play briefly and then move on to another. Eventually he got bored with the toys, started pulling children's books out of the bookshelves and leafing through them, then moved onto the kitchen, opening cupboards, pulling out plastic dishes and cups to stack and build with. Ultimately he ended up sitting and playing inside the dishwasher. At no time did he get into any trouble, nor did he clean up or put away any of his projects. None of this is age inappropriate hyperactivity or inattention, but would be considered normal behavior for a 2-year-old.

Rarely will a 2-year-old ever be diagnosed with ADHD, as the personalities and behaviors of 2-year-olds vary widely, and it is a tough call to know if those behaviors are out of the normal range for age. More often 2-year-olds will come to attention because of developmental delays and oppositional behavior. Part of routine screening at every well child check at the pediatric or family practice office is to ensure that the child is developing appropriately, and if not to guide the family to early intervention services. Generally if there are significant behavioral concerns, recommended treatment will be behavioral intervention from a child psychologist or therapist. In our general pediatric clinic, all parents of 2-year-olds are encouraged to attend two 1-hour behavior and mental health prevention sessions that are designed to help parents understand best parenting practices for dealing with typical 2-year-old behaviors, with the intent to prevent bigger problems later on. This has been well received by families, reinforcing the concept that mental health prevention services are as important as physical health prevention that is part of routine checkups and physicals.

As children age into the preschool phase, variations from normal developmental behavior become more obvious. Extreme hyperactivity becomes less age-appropriate. Severe temper tantrums, aggressive and violent behavior, inability to sit for very long at any given task such as meals or reading stories or to play without needing direct supervision can be signs of possible ADHD, as well as oppositional behavior. Additionally, difficulties with social interactions and motor clumsiness can be early signs of ADHD, but may also be related to developmental delays, or other conditions such as autism. Sleep problems, bedwetting (enuresis) and bowel problems (encopresis) are also very common at this age for any child, but especially for children with ADHD. Again behavioral and developmental interventions are the first choice for treatment, with medication considered only in the most severe cases when other interventions are ineffective. A good percentage of children who present with what seems to be ADHD symptoms in the preschool period no longer have symptoms in elementary school, whether due to appropriate interventions or to maturation.

As children age, our expectations change considerably. Starting at least in kindergarten and first grade, we expect children to be able to separate from the family and attend school and be involved in a learning environment with many other children and nonfamily adults. Activities in school are considerably different than what most children have experienced at home. Often nowadays, prior to the age of school entry, children are entertained by activities that grab their attention, such as television shows like Sesame Street, or tablets with video games and entertaining stories. Play is often loosely supervised and children are usually allowed to do whatever they want, as long as they don't get into trouble. In school, they now have to sit for many hours a day doing preplanned activities that they have very little choice in. These are typically not as entertaining or as fast-paced as they may be used to. There are also much more restrictive social requirements, with the expectation that they follow rules and get along with peers. For most children this transition happens smoothly, but in this environment ADHD symptoms may stand out quite a bit more, and previously unrecognized symptoms may appear. The great majority of those with significant ADHD symptoms will be diagnosed or at least develop concerns during the first few years of grade school, as they struggle with the transition from the home environment to school expectations. Additionally, other conditions such as anxiety, learning disabilities and social skills difficulties may become apparent, sometimes co-occurring with ADHD, and sometimes separate conditions that confuse the picture. In this age group school failure with or without behavior problems is the most common reason for evaluation for possible ADHD. By third grade, where fluent speech and reading skills are now the norm, many untreated children with ADHD will be floundering, especially those who have associated learning disabilities.

The next big challenging period comes with the transition from elementary school to middle school and early adolescence. This can be a very awkward time generally, dealing with rapid growth and physical and emotional changes. Girls will typically start into puberty 2 years before boys, causing a gender gap with physical and emotional maturity. Developmentally, young teenagers are starting to develop more of their own identity, and may begin to question authority and adult values. Social interactions become more complex with more language nuances such as the use of sarcasm and teasing. Experimentation with drugs and alcohol, pornography, gender identification issues and exploratory sexual activities may begin at this age. Overt hyperactivity often diminishes during adolescence, but defiant behaviors may become more prominent. Young adolescents are often incredibly self-conscious, and almost universally do not want to stand out as being different, and sometimes problem behaviors are manifestations of their attempts to compensate for self-perceived deficiencies and to appear normal. This can be a challenging time for those with ADHD. In elementary school, most children will have a single or few teachers, who know them well, and if problems surface, will quickly recognize them and communicate readily with parents. In middle school there is now a transition to higher-level expectations, with multiple teachers and much higher level need for organizational and study skills.

Middle schoolers are less likely to seek help from parents and teachers, and if problems do surface, they are less likely to be recognized until grades start to fall, or significant behavioral changes are noted. At this stage, anxiety and depression can surface, and those with more subtle learning disabilities may also start to struggle. Children with ADHD who were getting along well in elementary school may experience a significant drop in performance and be overwhelmed by the new expectations of middle school. On the other hand some with ADHD will find middle school to be exhilarating, where they no longer have to sit in a single classroom all day long, but now have multiple teachers, different classes with breaks in-between each period and some say in their curriculum. Nonetheless, they are still required to do what teachers and school authorities tell them to do all day long, plus usually homework after school, and their rewards for good performance are minimal. Especially for those with mild ADHD, significant problems may now appear during this time, and may go unrecognized, with behaviors attributed to adolescent hormones or lack of motivation.

High school is another time of change. By high school age, most adolescents have developed specific areas of interest and are starting to develop goals and have found a niche they are comfortable with. Grades now mean considerably more than they did in middle school, as they are used to determine acceptance into post high school education programs. This can be a significant motivator for some with ADHD and may be sufficient to stimulate more focused effort in academic performance. High school also allows students considerably more say in their curriculum, and extra-curricular activities are much more available with opportunities suitable to their interests. For better or for worse, most schools have a minimum grade-point average requirement to be able to participate in sports, so for those for whom sports is a major interest, this is another motivating factor. Any particular area of interest or expertise allows opportunities to collaborate and socialize with others with the same interests, so there are many more opportunities for favorable social interactions. Hyperactivity continues to decrease in severity, and by high school, many students may have found their own coping strategies to deal with attentional problems and academic struggles. For these reasons a significant number of high school students who have ADHD will do better, and some, who had ADHD when they were children, no longer have enough symptoms to warrant a diagnosis. These are some of those who may be perceived to have grown out of their ADHD.

Some however will continue to struggle. Depression and anxiety often become more pronounced during this age. People generally tend to migrate towards environments and peers where they feel most comfortable, and for some who don't feel like they fit in, they may migrate into problem environments. This may include problems with drugs, unplanned pregnancies and gang activity. The 3 most common causes of death in adolescence are unintentional injuries, especially motor vehicle accidents, suicide and homicide.[4] Adolescents with ADHD are at higher risk for all of these.

The great majority of research studies on ADHD have been in children, usually boys, until recently. Symptoms of ADHD evolve with age, and most who have ADHD diagnosed in childhood will not meet criteria for diagnosis by adulthood, although most will still have some symptoms of impairment, emphasizing that current criteria for older adolescents and adults may be less than optimal.[5] Lately there has been some evidence that for some, ADHD may not appear until a later age, or even adulthood.[6],[7] Many of these cases likely had ADHD symptoms at a younger age that were unrecognized or below threshold for diagnosis, but late onset ADHD without childhood symptoms appears to occur.[8]

ADHD symptoms in adulthood also may be compounded by other disorders such as substance abuse disorder, antisocial personality disorder, bipolar disorder, and other mood disorders. Diagnostically, this can be very challenging, as a life time of coping strategies and development of other disorders can obscure the core underlying problems. Clues to potential ADHD symptoms in adults who had not been previously evaluated or diagnosed include presence of symptoms as a child, with helpful information from parents and siblings, family history of ADHD and related problems, and unexplained academic failure. Just as in other transition periods, the post high school period is another major transition time, with expectations that the individual now has life plans and goals, and a means to accomplish them. For those in college who have gotten by with high adaptive skills, they may now flounder academically if their organizational and attention skills can't keep up with the much higher demands of college curriculums. Job expectations are also much higher with the profound consequence of getting fired if performance is deemed inadequate.

On the flip side, one major advantage for the ADHD individual after high school is that one can do whatever is interesting and motivating, and sometimes avoid activities that aren't. If math is not an interest or area of expertise, engineering and accounting careers can be avoided. If highly stimulating activities are desired, becoming a professional athlete, helicopter pilot or surgeon may be an option. When individuals with ADHD are involved in what they enjoy, the attention problems are far less of an issue, and environments that are perceived as boring and unstimulating to a certain extent can be avoided. For this reason, those who had ADHD as a child or adolescent may still have the core symptoms as adults, but they may not be causing as much difficulty because the environment has changed.

ADHD presents in many different ways, and one major factor affecting this is age and developmental stage. DSM criteria are primarily geared towards school aged children and adolescents, and may not accurately define those outside of that age range.[5] At all ages, developmental factors and the evolving course of ADHD symptoms need to be taken into account in the evaluation.

Is it Truly a Disorder or is it an Extreme Degree of Normal Behavior?

It is important to understand that ADHD is not a distinct disorder separate from what would be considered normal behavior. The medical model that we are used to for most conditions is based on a distinct abnormality that can be identified, often based on abnormal laboratory values or imaging tests such as x-rays, CAT scans or MRI scans or other specific medical tests. Conditions such as type 1 diabetes, tuberculosis, Down syndrome and cancer are examples of such conditions. One either has or does not have the disease or disorder, and there are generally straightforward tests that can be done to rule in or out each condition. ADHD used to be thought of as that type of disorder, and there was significant effort spent in trying to find the "cause" for ADHD. Some medical conditions however, including ADHD, are better conceptualized as existing on a continuum of symptoms, ranging from normal or neurotypical to borderline, mild, moderate or severe. Many mental health conditions, such as depression and anxiety, and many medical conditions such as obesity and hypertension are examples of this model. We all have blood pressure, and "normal" blood pressure is in a range that varies with age, gender, height and other factors. It is known that when someone has very high blood pressure the risk for having complications, such as strokes or heart disease becomes significant. Hypertension is defined based on blood pressure that is statistically higher than normal for a given size, gender and age, and is at a level where complications can be expected. For example a blood pressure of 140/90 would be considered mild hypertension for an adult and would warrant intervention. One could rightly ask does that mean a blood pressure of 139/89 is not a problem. Obviously the answer is no. So, blood pressure exists as a continuum ranging from low to normal levels, borderline, mild, moderate and severe. The higher the blood pressure the greater the risk of complications generally.

ADHD should be conceptualized in the same way.[9] Specific behaviors range from normal to some degree outside the normal range, and intervention is indicated only when that particular behavior is causing significant problems in the normal function of the individual. ADHD is not diagnosed based on the presence or absence of symptoms alone, but on whether those symptoms are significantly out of the normal range, and are causing difficulties. When we conceptualized ADHD as a distinct disorder like diabetes, the logical conclusion was that there must be a distinct cause or etiology for it. However, just like with hypertension, there are multiple different conditions that may lead to ADHD symptoms, some of which are more serious than others. Some who have mild ADHD symptoms without functional impairment may be considered to have more of an attention deficit/hyperactive-impulsive personality style rather than a disorder, and could be generally best thought of as having behavioral traits that are passed on genetically (like height or intelligence). However, ADHD symptoms tend to vary with age and environment, and those with mild or subthreshold symptoms may develop more difficulties as they age or in an environment that is more challenging.

When there are more severe ADHD symptoms there is a greater likelihood of having an identifiable cause. Children who were very premature, who are known to have suffered from brain infections like encephalitis or meningitis, or who have had severe head injuries, or been exposed to significant neurotoxins during pregnancy such as high levels of alcohol or drugs like cocaine or methamphetamine, have a very high risk of developing severe ADHD symptoms. But this should not lead to the conclusion that if one has ADHD that there is something pathologically wrong, for in most cases no cause can be identified.

Causes of ADHD

As mentioned above, much of the etiology of ADHD is genetically based, meaning that the traits that make up ADHD are passed on from genes from the parents. Multiple lines of evidence, including twin studies and adoption studies indicate a high degree of heritability.[10] In most cases there is no single genetic cause, but a collection of many different interrelated genes. A number of different candidate genes have been identified and found to be associated with ADHD, many related to neurotransmitters known to be involved in ADHD, such as dopamine and norepinephrine,[11] and others related to development of structures that affect neurotransmitter regulation that may help in understanding variable effects to medications.[12] Some specific genetic disorders can mimic or include ADHD symptoms, although collectively these are not common causes for most of those diagnosed with ADHD. These include Aarskog syndrome, Turner syndrome, Down syndrome, Klinefelter syndrome, Williams syndrome, fragile X syndrome, Angelman syndrome and others. These all have other features that suggest the diagnosis, and identifying potential medical reasons for ADHD is one of the reasons why a thorough medical evaluation is essential as part of the evaluation. Other conditions such as autism spectrum disorders, fetal alcohol syndrome and Tourette syndrome often include ADHD symptoms as part of the condition.

Additionally, environmental factors can lead to ADHD symptoms. As was speculated early in the last century, anything causing significant brain injury can lead to some symptoms of ADHD. Those who have suffered from brain infections such as meningitis and encephalitis, those who have had brain injuries, and those exposed to certain toxins in utero or after birth, such as certain drugs, tobacco and alcohol can all later exhibit severe ADHD symptoms. There are increased risks of ADHD and learning problems in those who were very premature,[13] or who had adverse pregnancy or delivery experiences, such as neonatal asphyxia.[14] All of that being said, most individuals diagnosed with ADHD do not have any of these in their history, and for the majority of them, ADHD is primarily a familial trait passed on from parents and ancestors.

What is passed on genetically does not appear in most cases to be certainty of developing ADHD, but rather to having a susceptibility to it. Specific genes code for specific proteins, but the production of those proteins is regulated by other factors. Genes provide the blueprint for the gene product (proteins), but they are not producing those products all of the time. At times genes are turned off or on, and may produce their product at different rates depending on the need. There are many different mechanisms that the cell uses to regulate gene expression, but suffice it to say that there are often environmental factors that influence gene regulation and expression. The biologic process that affects how genes are expressed and regulated is called epigenetics. This process may explain how environmental factors combine with genetic predisposition to result in the ADHD outcome, and why for example those with the same genetic makeup (i.e. identical twins) don't necessarily have the same outcome. A number of different genes have been identified that are potentially related to ADHD, but none of these accounts for more than a small percentage of the overall symptomatology. Much work is currently being done trying to identify specific genes that contribute to causing ADHD but it appears it is the interaction of multiple different genes, in association with environmental factors that leads to ADHD.[15] This appears to be the case with other disorders as well, such as autism, bipolar disorder and schizophrenia.

Studies looking at brain imaging, utilizing CT or MRI scans or other modalities have found various differences in those with and without ADHD, especially size differences in the frontal lobe and basal ganglion, and longitudinal studies have demonstrated delayed development of certain areas, especially the prefrontal cortex. A study looking at MRI changes with age demonstrated delayed thickening of the cerebral cortex, implying delayed maturation of brain development and connections between neurons in those areas. Peak cortical thickening occurred by age 7½ for the control group, but not until an average of 10½ in the ADHD group. The areas involved were those areas that had to do with many of the cognitive function processes that are problematic in individuals with ADHD, such as controlling impulsive thoughts, attention control, assessing consequences, and working memory.[16] Other MRI studies that have looked at brain maturation related to pruning of neuronal networks or eliminating neuronal connections that are not being used have also shown delays in the ADHD group.[17] These MRI findings are group differences however, and doing MRI scans on individuals being evaluated for ADHD is not usually useful. Evidence also points to relative deficiencies in neurotransmitter functioning in certain parts of the brain, especially dopamine and norepinephrine. Interestingly, although there is widespread concern that giving children medications to treat ADHD may be harmful for the developing brain, there is evidence that administering medicine may potentially lead to more normal brain development compared to those not treated, meaning it may actually protect the developing brain to a degree in those with ADHD.[18], [19]

Parents often express guilt when they are having a child evaluated for ADHD, feeling that there must have been something they did as parents that caused their child to have the disorder. They may feel this, even when they use the same parenting style for all of their other children who do not have ADHD symptoms. As reviewed above, parenting style is not evidently a cause of ADHD, and there is no place for guilt in looking for a cause for ADHD. There are certainly behavioral strategies that can help with parenting, but often the usual parenting styles that we all use for our children are less effective for dealing with behaviors of ADHD. This is in part because of the relative lack of response to typical reinforcers such as rewards and punishment. It can be interesting to hear of children's and adolescents' thoughts on their response to medication. Often we will hear from the individual with ADHD that the medicine doesn't seem to be helping much, but that now their parents and teachers are much nicer, they are getting better grades, and they have more friends.

Likewise, often we are asked if there are dietary contributions to ADHD symptoms. Is it due to too much sugar, too much junk food, perhaps milk allergies, gluten intolerance or chemicals or hormones in our diets? For many years the Feingold diet was widely used to treat those with ADHD, but it fell out of favor when research did not support the benefits of the diet. There have been many studies on special diets over the years, and for the most part, there are no convincing studies demonstrating a causal effect for any dietary components, although more recent studies are revisiting this question. A healthy diet with lots of fresh fruits and vegetables, limited junk food, and limited reliance on high sugar items is certainly appropriate for those with ADHD, as it is for all individuals, but the likelihood that it will make a big difference in ameliorating ADHD symptoms is small.

Another interesting potential cause of ADHD in rare cases is a reaction to streptococcal infections. There is a condition called PANDAS (pediatric autoimmune neurodevelopmental disorders associated with strep) that appears to cause some cases of Tourette syndrome, anxiety and ADHD. In a similar fashion to how rheumatic fever with its associated heart, joint and skin problems is caused as a consequence of exposure to certain strains of strep-tococcal bacteria, some who are infected with strep (strep throat or strep impetigo) can develop new onset of OCD, Tourette syndrome and possibly ADHD. Other infections such as mycoplasma or certain viruses have also been implicated in PANDAS. PANDAS causing ADHD is very con-troversial, but if there is a new or sudden onset of symptoms that were not previously present, and evidence of a recent significant infection, PANDAS should be considered.

Differential Diagnosis

Differential diagnosis refers to other conditions that may mimic a condition, or might be confused for the same thing. In the case of ADHD, there are many conditions that may look like ADHD that should be considered in the differential diagnosis. Many of these will be discussed in more detail in later parts of this book, as they may frequently co-occur, but a brief review is pertinent here.

Poor Parenting

A frequent question from parents is if the behaviors are just an extreme of normal behavior (usually referring to boys) that will go away when they get older. Or from other family members or observers, aren't the behaviors just a result of bad parenting, and with better techniques, the child wouldn't misbehave so much? Or is it possible that the behaviors are the result of abuse or neglect from a primary caregiver? There is no question that the above situations will affect a child's behavior. All the books on parenting exist and are utilized because we all assume that the best parenting practices will bring out the best outcomes in our children, and we want to optimize that, and surely poor parenting will adversely affect our children. But before we lay blame for ADHD on bad parenting, it is important to point out that behavioral traits in children can bring out seemingly nonproductive parent-ing styles. When reinforcers don't work the way they are supposed to, parents may just give up and let the child get away with bad behavior. Or they may become overly punitive, spanking or hitting or yelling, in frustrated attempts to control a wayward child. Or they may be perfect parents, and yet still experience extreme difficulty in reining in challenging behaviors. There is no question that optimal parenting strategies can help even the most dif-ficult behaviors, but many children have behaviors that are not easily treated with the usual parenting strategies that most of us are familiar with.

Numerous research studies looking into the various causes of ADHD demonstrate a very clear strong genetic basis for the development of ADHD. For example, adoption studies demonstrate that children with ADHD are far more likely to share symptoms with their biologic parents than with their adoptive parents.[20] Twin studies also demonstrate that much of the symptomatology of ADHD is inherited as opposed to environmental influences. In other words, children with ADHD are more similar to their biologic parents than adoptive parents. Identical twins are far more likely to share an ADHD diagnosis than fraternal twins.[21] A diagnosis of ADHD assumes that the individual has inborn, innate, elevated levels of hyperactivity, impulsiveness and/or inattention that are not caused by adverse environmental influences. But it is also recognized that adverse environmental influences exist, and will affect how symptoms are manifest.

Oppositional Defiant Disorder

There is a common stereotype of children with ADHD that they misbehave often, and that poor behavior is a hallmark of the disorder. To clarify, there is no willful disobedience or malicious intent as part of ADHD. If you ask a child with ADHD to go clean their bedroom, and they don't accomplish it, the reason is that they head to their rooms with the intent to do what they have been asked, but along the way are distracted by something else that turns their attention away from what they are supposed to be doing. When asked later why they didn't clean their rooms, they will innocently proclaim "I forgot". Some children will have no intention of doing what is asked of them because they do not want to. This is not ADHD, but oppositional behavior. While it is very common in children with ADHD (and all of us for that matter), it should not be considered as part of the core symptoms of ADHD, and many children with ADHD have no striking oppositional behavior at all.

Learning Disorders

Learning disorders refer to having difficulty learning in a specific area, such as reading, writing, and math. Like those with ADHD, children with learning difficulties may struggle academically, and be very frustrated in school. They may appear to be inattentive and easily distracted, and may have associated behavioral problems related to frustrations of underperforming. However, the inattentiveness associated with learning disorders is due to lack of comprehension of the task at hand, not to innate distractibility. Most of us in an environment where we don't understand what is being discussed will eventually give up and lose interest, and someone observing this may conclude that we are lacking the ability to focus. With learning problems, the apparent distractibility is only seen when associated with the area of learning difficulty, and not in other aspects of life. The global inattentiveness seen in ADHD is not present in those with learning disorders. However, to complicate matters further, learning disorders are very common in those with ADHD, and both need to be considered in any evaluation for ADHD.

Intellectual Disorder

Like those with learning disorders, those with cognitive difficulties when placed in an environment beyond their abilities may have a hard time staying focused. Again, the symptoms are only present in those environments, and would not be expected to be present in non-academic settings. Symptoms of hyperactivity and impulsivity, if present, would have to be more than expected for cognitive level to qualify as ADHD symptoms.

Auditory Processing Disorders

Auditory processing disorder refers to having difficulty processing information that is presented by sound. It is not due to a hearing problem, but to problems in the network of nerves that have to do with making sense of sounds. Individuals so affected may have difficulties following oral instructions, or may appear to not listen well. They may struggle to hear when there is a lot of background noise, having difficulty discriminating between important sounds and those that need to be screened out. They may appear to be inattentive. It may adversely affect how they interact with others. It is a diagnosis made by audiologists, and is not universally recognized as a valid diagnostic entity, nor is it listed in the DSM-5. Nonetheless, it is commonly diagnosed, and there are specific interventions that are often recommended as part of educational accommodations. Those with auditory processing dysfunction may appear to have ADHD, and in fact there is a lot of overlap of symptoms. And like so many of the disorders discussed here, it is very common to have both. Many of the treatments recommended for auditory processing difficulties are also very helpful for those with ADHD.

Language Disorders

Like with those with auditory processing disorders, individuals with difficulties with receptive language (understanding spoken language), or pragmatic language problems (understanding how to use language to effectively communicate), or with expressive language problems (being able to say what you are thinking), all may mimic some of the symptoms of ADHD. They may flounder academically in a similar fashion to those with learning disabilities, and may develop secondary behavioral problems that go along with frustration such as anxiety, oppositional or acting out behavior. And of course if there is a primary hearing problem, this will lead to the same set of symptoms if not recognized. It is essential in any ADHD evaluation to be sure there are no hearing or vision problems.

Mental Health Conditions

Many mental health conditions such as anxiety, depression, obsessive compulsive disorder, bipolar disorder and disruptive mood dysregulation disorder may present with symptoms that can be confused for ADHD. If a teacher is talking about fractions, or Greek history, and a student is severely depressed, he or she will be having thoughts internalized to their own sadness rather than being interested in the topic at hand, and may appear to be inattentive. Each of these comes with some emotional dysregulation that can manifest as behavior problems that can be seen also in ADHD.

Associated Conditions

To truly understand ADHD it is important to understand that it rarely comes in isolation. ADHD is frequently associated with other conditions that must be assessed for and taken into consideration in order to understand the behaviors of concern and treatment modalities. There are four very common associated conditions. Learning disabilities are seen in a large percentage of children and adults with ADHD. Individuals with learning disabilities have difficulty learning in a specific area. Common examples would be reading disabilities such as dyslexia, speech and language problems, written language difficulties, mathematics and motor coordination difficulties. Any or all of these can be seen in individuals with ADHD. Second, mood disorders, and anxiety are also very common. These can be primary mood problems that are independent of the ADHD, or can be secondary due to the challenges that occur from dealing with ADHD symptoms. These include such common conditions as anxiety disorders, depression, obsessive-compulsive disorder and sometimes bipolar disorder. A third very common associated condition is oppositional defiant disorder and related problems. Oppositional behavior refers to the attitude of "I'm not going to do it, and you can't make me." This is often mistakenly thought of as part of ADHD, but it is not, and is seen only in about a third of individuals diagnosed with ADHD. Lastly, autism spectrum symptoms are very common in those diagnosed with ADHD. Often these are not enough to warrant a full diagnosis of autism, but can lead to difficulties with interactions with peers. Typically these individuals have a hard time understanding how their behaviors are perceived by other people, and will often do things that drive others away. Often this includes a very poor sense of personal space, and behaviors that others perceive as obnoxious or too much. In addition to these four, there are other symptoms that are common as well. These include a variety of sleep disorders, enuresis (bedwetting) and encopresis (bowel accidents), eating disorders, common tics and Tourette syndrome. Recognizing the possible presence of any or all of these is important in the assessment of any individual with ADHD. Often times all of these conditions have a genetic predisposition, so it is very helpful to review family history for potentially related conditions.

Appendix

DSM-5 Attention-Deficit/Hyperactivity Disorder Diagnostic Criteria

A A persistent pattern of inattention and/or hyperactivity-impulsivity that interferes with functioning or development, as characterized by (1) and/or (2).

1. Inattention: Six (or more) of the following symptoms have persisted for at least 6 months to a degree that is inconsistent with developmental level and that negatively impacts directly on social and academic/occupational activities.

Note: The symptoms are not solely a manifestation of oppositional behavior, defiance, hostility, or failure to understand tasks or instructions. For older adolescents and adults (age 17 and older), at least five symptoms are required.

a   Often fails to give close attention to details or makes careless mistakes in schoolwork, at work, or during other activities (e.g., overlooks or misses details, work is inaccurate).

b   Often has difficulty sustaining attention in tasks or play activities (e.g., has difficulty remaining focused during lectures, conversations, or lengthy reading).

c   Often does not seem to listen when spoken to directly (e.g., mind seems elsewhere, even in the absence of any obvious distraction).

d   Often does not follow through on instructions and fails to finish schoolwork, chores, or duties in the workplace (e.g., starts tasks but quickly loses focus and is easily sidetracked).

e   Often has difficulty organizing tasks and activities (e.g., difficulty managing sequential tasks; difficulty keeping materials and belongings in order; messy, disorganized work; has poor time management; fails to meet deadlines).

f   Often avoids, dislikes, or is reluctant to engage in tasks that require sustained mental effort (e.g., schoolwork or homework; for older adolescents and adults, preparing reports, completing forms, reviewing lengthy papers).

g   Often loses things necessary for tasks or activities (e.g., school materials, pencils, books, tools, wallets, keys, paperwork, eyeglasses, mobile telephones).

h   Is often easily distracted by extraneous stimuli (for older adolescents and adults, may include unrelated thoughts).

i   Is often forgetful in daily activities (e.g., doing chores, running errands; for older adolescents and adults, returning calls, paying bills, keeping appointments).

2. Hyperactivity and impulsivity: Six (or more) of the following symptoms have persisted for at least 6 months to a degree that is inconsistent with developmental level and that negatively impacts directly on social and academic/occupational activities:

Note: The symptoms are not solely a manifestation of oppositional behavior, defiance, hostility, or a failure to understand tasks or instructions. For older adolescents and adults (age 17 and older), at least five symptoms are required.

a   Often fidgets with or taps hands or feet or squirms in seat.
b   Often leaves seat in situations when remaining seated is expected (e.g., leaves his or her place in the classroom, in the office or other workplace, or in other situations that require remaining in place).
c   Often runs about or climbs in situations where it is inappropriate. (*Note:* In adolescents or adults, may be limited to feeling restless.)
d   Often unable to play or engage in leisure activities quietly.
e   Is often "on the go," acting as if "driven by a motor" (e.g., is unable to be or uncomfortable being still for extended time, as in restaurants, meetings; may be experienced by others as being restless or difficult to keep up with).
f   Often talks excessively.
g   Often blurts out an answer before a question has been completed (e.g., completes people's sentences; cannot wait for turn in conversation).
h   Often has difficulty waiting his or her turn (e.g., while waiting in line).
i   Often interrupts or intrudes on others (e.g., butts into conversations, games, or activities; may start using other people's things without asking or receiving permission; for adolescents and adults, may intrude into or take over what others are doing).

B Several inattentive or hyperactive-impulsive symptoms were present prior to age 12 years.

C Several inattentive or hyperactive-impulsive symptoms are present in two or more settings (e.g., at home, school, or work; with friends or relatives; in other activities).

D There is clear evidence that the symptoms interfere with, or reduce the quality of, social, academic, or occupational functioning.

E The symptoms do not occur exclusively during the course of schizophrenia or another psychotic disorder and are not better explained by another mental disorder (e.g., mood disorder, anxiety disorder, dissociative disorder, personality disorder, substance intoxication or withdrawal).

Specify whether:

314.01 (F90.2) Combined presentation: If both Criterion A1 (inattention) and Criterion A2 (hyperactivity-impulsivity) are met for the past 6 months.

314.00 (F90.0) Predominantly inattentive presentation: If Criterion A1 (inattention) is met but Criterion A2 (hyperactivity-impulsivity) is not met for the past 6 months.

314.01 (F90.1) Predominantly hyperactive/impulsive presentation: If Criterion A2 (hyperactivity-impulsivity) is met but Criterion A1 (inattention) is not met over the past 6 months.

Specify if:

In partial remission: When full criteria were previously met, fewer than the full criteria have been met for the past 6 months, and the symptoms still result in impairment in social, academic, or occupational functioning.

Specify current severity:

Mild: Few, if any, symptoms in excess of those required to make the diagnosis are present, and symptoms result in only minor functional impairments.

Moderate: Symptoms or functional impairment between "mild" and "severe" are present.

Severe: Many symptoms in excess of those required to make the diagnosis, or several symptoms that are particularly severe, are present, or the symptoms result in marked impairment in social or occupational functioning

Reprinted with permission from the *Diagnostic and Statistical Manual of Mental Disorders*, Fifth Edition, (Copyright © 2013). American Psychiatric Association. All Rights Reserved.

Bibliography

1. Barkley RA. *Attention-Deficit Hyperactivity Disorder a Handbook for Diagnosis and Treatment.* 4th ed. (Barkley RA, ed.). Guilford Press; 2015.
2. Hallowell E, Ratey J. *Driven to Distraction.* Pantheon Books; 1994.
3. American Psychiatric Association. Taskforce on DSM-5. *Diagnostic and Statistical Manual of Mental Disorders,* 5th ed.; 2013.
4. Heron M. Deaths: Leading causes for 2015. *Natl Vital Stat Rep.* 2017;66(5):1–76. doi:10.1016/S0140-6736(15)00057-4.
5. Faraone SV, Biederman J. Can attention-deficit/hyperactivity disorder onset occur in adulthood? *JAMA Psychiatry.* 2016;73(7):655–656. doi:10.1001/jamapsychiatry.2016.0400.
6. Agnew-Blais JC, Polanczyk GV, Danese A, Wertz J, Moffitt TE, Arseneault L. Evaluation of the persistence, remission, and emergence of Attention-deficit/hyperactivity disorder in young adulthood. *JAMA Psychiatry.* 2016;73(7):713–720. doi:10.1001/jamapsychiatry.2016.0465.
7. Caye A, Rocha TBM, Anselmi L, et al. Attention-deficit/hyperactivity disorder trajectories from childhood to young adulthood evidence from a birth cohort

supporting a late-onset syndrome. *JAMA Psychiatry.* 2016;73(7):705–712. doi:10.1001/jamapsychiatry.2016.0383.

8. Chandra S, Biederman J, Faraone SV. Assessing the validity of the age at onset criterion for diagnosing ADHD in DSM-5. *J Atten Disord.* February2016. doi:10.1177/1087054716629717.

9. Levy F, Hay DA, McStephen M, Wood C, Waldman I. Attention-deficit hyperactivity disorder: a category or a continuum? Genetic analysis of a large-scale twin study. *J Am Acad Child Adolesc Psychiatry.* 1997;36(6):737–744. doi:10.1097/00004583-199706000-00009.

10. Faraone SV, Perlis RH, Doyle AE, et al. Molecular genetics of attention-deficit/hyperactivity disorder. *Biol Psychiatry.* 2005;57(11):1313–1323. doi:10.1016/j.biopsych.2004.11.024.

11. Akutagava-Martins GC, Salatino-Oliveira A, Kieling CC, Rohde LA, Hutz MH. Genetics of attention-deficit/hyperactivity disorder: current findings and future directions. *Expert Rev Neurother.* 2013;13(4):435–445. doi:10.1586/ern.13.30.

12. Bruxel EM, Salatino-Oliveira A, Akutagava-Martins GC, et al. LPHN3 and attention-deficit/hyperactivity disorder: a susceptibility and pharmacogenetic study. *Genes Brain Behav.* 2015;14(5):419–427. doi:10.1111/gbb.12224.

13. Franz AP, Bolat GU, Bolat H, et al. Attention-deficit/hyperactivity disorder and very preterm/very low birth weight: a meta-analysis. *Pediatrics.* 2018;141(1). doi:10.1542/peds.2017-1645.

14. Getahun D, Rhoads GG, Demissie K, et al. In utero exposure to ischemic-hypoxic conditions and attention-deficit/hyperactivity disorder. *Pediatrics.* 2013;131(1):e53 LP–e61. http://pediatrics.aappublications.org/content/131/1/e53.abstract.

15. Nigg JT. *Getting Ahead of ADHD.* Guilford Press; 2017.

16. Shaw P, Eckstrand K, Sharp W, et al. Attention-deficit/hyperactivity disorder is characterized by a delay in cortical maturation. *Proc Natl Acad Sci.* 2007;104 (49):19649–19654. doi:10.1073/pnas.0707741104.

17. Shaw P, Malek M, Watson B, Sharp W, Evans A, Greenstein D. Development of cortical surface area and gyrification in attention-deficit/hyperactivity disorder. *Biol Psychiatry.* 2012;72(3):191–197. doi:10.1016/j.biopsych.2012.01.031.

18. Frodl T, Skokauskas N. Meta-analysis of structural MRI studies in children and adults with attention deficit hyperactivity disorder indicates treatment effects. *Acta Psychiatr Scand.* 2012;125(2):114–126. doi:10.1111/j.1600-0447.2011.01786.x.

19. Spencer RC, Devilbiss DM, Berridge CW. The cognition-enhancing effects of psychostimulants involve direct action in the prefrontal cortex. *Biol Psychiatry.* 2015;77(11):940–950. doi:10.1016/j.biopsych.2014.09.013.

20. Sprich S, Biederman J, Crawford MH, Mundy E, Faraone SV. Adoptive and biological families of children and adolescents with ADHD. *J Am Acad Child Adolesc Psychiatry.* 2000;39(11):1432–1437. doi:10.1097/00004583-200011000-00018.

21. Thapar A, Stergiakouli E. An overview on the genetics of ADHD. *Xin Li Xue Bao.* 2008;40(10):1088–1098. doi:10.3724/SP.J.1041.2008.01088.

2 Historical Perspective

J. Dennis Odell

To understand our current concept of ADHD, it is helpful to review how ADHD has been understood and treated in the past. The question of whether ADHD is a modern disorder or whether it has existed for a long time is rendered somewhat difficult because our society, and indeed concept of childhood is so very different now than it was even a century ago. Public education for all only really began in the last century. Prior to that it was sporadic, and often available only to those who could afford it. Up until the early 1900s, children were often expected to work, either on the farm, or in factories, and education was available only when it didn't interfere with work activities. Even the awareness of seemingly obvious problems such as child abuse didn't reach national consciousness until 1962 with the concept of the battered child and the development of national child protective services. Our school and instructional system has also evolved greatly, from the most common one room school houses where all ages were taught in the same room, to age based grades and progressing with same age peers. Children prior to 1900 were not necessarily seen as being in a separate developmental stage, but as a resource to aid in family economic survival. Also child survival rates were quite low until the advent of good sewage, clean water, and good healthcare, especially the availability of vaccines, but also of antibiotics after WWII. So descriptions of child behavior prior to modern times must take into account the very different culture of childhood then as compared to what we are used to today.

Accurate descriptions prior to several hundred years ago are hard to come by, as modern medicine didn't start to appear until the 19th century. Most of the advances in health in the 19th century occurred because of improvements in public health and nutrition, such as effective sewage systems, and improvements in diet and startling discoveries about the causes of many diseases. It wasn't until the mid-1850s that the concept of handwashing to prevent transmission of disease was realized, first reported by the Hungarian physician Ignaz Semmelweis, but widely ignored for many years. Louis Pasteur, Robert Koch and Joseph Lister revolutionized medical care with their discoveries and work on microorganisms causing disease and infection in the 1860s and 1870s. The dentist, William Morton first used ether to provide pain free surgery in 1846. Although Edward Jenner first demonstrated vaccine efficacy for smallpox in 1798, widespread use of vaccines for other diseases did not occur until the early 1900s.

Behavioral problems in the 1800s were often, perhaps correctly so, attributed to poverty, poor nutrition, and poor upbringing, as these were rampant. Our current conceptualization of ADHD was formalized in the late 1960s. But there are medical reports of ADHD-like symptoms long before that, and much speculation on historical figures, such as the apostle Peter (impulsive), Mozart and Einstein. Although suggestive descriptions of ADHD behavior occurred in literature, and even in medical descriptions as far back as ancient Greece, the first known modern medical description available was from a German textbook by Melchior Adam Weikard in 1775, describing children and adults with difficulties with attention, distractibility, impulsiveness, overactivity and lacking in persistence.[1]

The first report of a disorder that appears to be similar to what we now know of as ADHD was by a Scottish physician named Sir Alexander Crichton in 1798. In writing about attention and its diseases, he reports variabilities in attention, and describes different aspects of difficulties with attention, including distractibility, fidgetiness and mental restlessness.[2] Another commonly cited example is the story of Fidgety Phil, a character in one of a series of cartoons about children's behaviors, written by the German physician Heinrich Hoffmann in 1845. These were published in the book *Struwwelpeter*, a group of entertaining children's stories and pictures depicting a variety of problematic childhood behaviors and their consequences.

The Story of Fidgety Philip
"Let me see if Philip can be a little gentleman;
Let me see if he is able to sit still for once at table."
Thus spoke, in earnest tone, the father to his son;
And the mother looked very grave to see Philip so misbehave.
But Philip he did not mind His father who was so kind.
He wriggled and giggled,
And then, I declare, swung backward and forward
And tilted his chair, just like any rocking horse;-
"Philip! I am getting cross!"
See the naughty, restless child, growing still more rude and wild,
Till his chair falls over quite. Philip screams with all his might,
Catches at the cloth, but then that makes matters worse again.
Down upon the ground they fall, glasses, bread, knives forks and all.
How Mamma did fret and frown, when she saw them tumbling down!
And Papa made such a face! Philip is in sad disgrace.
Where is Philip? Where is he? Fairly cover'd up, you see!
Cloth and all are lying on him; He has pull'd down all upon him!
What a terrible to-do! Dishes, glasses, snapt in two!

Here a knife, and there a fork! Philip, this is naughty work.
Table all so bare, and ah! Poor Papa and poor Mamma
Look quite cross, and wonder how they shall make their dinner now

In more modern times, in 1902 a British physician named Sir George Frederic Still described children who had features of what we now know as ADHD. Still recognized two distinct groups of children, one who had a history of physical illness that was felt to be associated with the behavioral symptoms, and the other who had similar behavioral problems but no evidence of any physical disease. Although the children he described were a mix of different behavioral disorders, his descriptions often fit with current descriptions of children with ADHD, oppositional defiant disorder and conduct disorders. He also pointed out the strikingly higher prevalence in boys than girls, and the early age of onset of symptoms. He distinguished between those whose symptoms appeared due to improper upbringing, from those who had more typical childhood experiences. He surmised that there was a biologic basis for these behaviors, either genetic or due to illness or injury.[3]

In the early 1900s, clinicians noted an association between significant birth injuries or illnesses and later difficult behaviors, leading to the idea that severe behavioral problems in children may be due to underlying brain damage. From 1917 to 1930 there was a worldwide epidemic of encephalitis, a condition causing inflammation of the brain. The mortality rate from this disease was very high, and many of the children who survived the disease developed a number of problems including severe hyperactive behavior, attention problems, personality changes and learning difficulties. They suffered from what was termed post encephalitic behavior disorder, which gave further evidence to a link between brain damage and childhood behavioral problems. At that time, the general consensus was that hyperactive and impulsive behavioral problems were caused by some form of brain damage. There was also the notion that mild, often unrecognized brain damage could lead to behavioral problems later on, giving rise to the term minimal brain damage, which was felt to be one end of the spectrum of brain damage that resulted in symptoms ranging from severe cerebral palsy and mental deficiency, to milder hyperactive behavior and learning problems.[3],[4]

In the early 1930s, two German physicians, Franz Kramer and Hans Pollnow described a condition they called hyperkinetic disease of infancy that was not due to encephalitis residual effects. These were children who were very overactive, unable to sit still, constantly moving. Often the excessive motor activity was of a nonproductive nature, such as climbing onto furniture, switching lights on and off, throwing objects, and activities were typically not sustained.[3]

By the 1960s, there were concerns about this conceptualization because evidence of brain damage was often lacking. The terminology was changed to reflect the thinking that this was more of a functional rather than anatomical problem, and the term was changed to minimal brain dysfunction, and included the core symptoms of what we now call ADHD, hyperactivity, impulsivity and attentional difficulties. Clinicians at the time were trained to look for "soft neurologic signs" that might demonstrate an underlying neurologic cause for the symptoms. These are minor neurologic abnormalities that are not associated with specific neurologic disorders, but that were thought to indicate subtle underlying neurologic problems. Examples include difficulty with rapid finger movements, overflow movements (movements of other parts of the body at the same time as the part that is intending to move, such as the left hand performing the same movement when only the right hand movement was intended), spooning of the fingers when hands are outstretched, and many others. They are usually normal in young children, but resolve with age, but when persistent in older children they are considered abnormal, and have been associated with ADHD, learning problems and development delays. CT scanners did not become available until the late 1970s, so brain imaging was not an option. However, although more common in children with ADHD, they are also common in many without any symptoms, and the interest and utility for soft signs has waned.[5]

More specific definitions have evolved in the years since then, as delineated in the *Diagnostic and Statistical Manual*, editions II through the current 5. The original DSM made no mention of an ADHD type disorder. The minimal brain dysfunction concept persisted into the late 1970s, but the DSM-II, published in 1968, used the term "Hyperkinetic Reaction of Childhood", and it was felt that the symptoms of the disorder improved or resolved by adolescence. It did not delineate criteria for diagnosis, or age. Descriptions at that time emphasized the hyperactivity, but over the ensuing decades the difficulties with inattention and impulsiveness became more apparent. In the third edition of the DSM, published in 1980, the definitions were more precise, with specific symptoms required for diagnosis. The disorder was named attention deficit disorder (ADD), with subtypes with and without hyperactivity, although it was not clear whether these were two manifestations of the same disorder, or two separate conditions.[6] The terminology remains confusing, as at present often ADHD inattentive type is referred to as ADD.

As evidence of effective treatment with stimulant medications was observed, medication use became much more widespread, and with it a backlash against stimulant medication use for children. ADHD and its controversies became much more newsworthy and in the public eye. With that came an explosion of research studies on all aspects of ADHD that continues to this day. Other medication options deemed to be safer than stimulants, and non-medication treatments were widely sought, and various remedies including special diets, herbal supplements and specialized neuro-feedback techniques started to become available. In parallel developments, educational mandates for those with disabilities helped to provide services for students with learning disabilities and ADHD, and behavioral approaches to modifying behavior and parent training strategies became available and more widely utilized. Diagnostic tools, especially well normed and valid behavioral questionnaires, improved the reliability of diagnoses and helped in identifying additional disorders.

In 1987 the APA published a revised and updated version of the DSM, called the DSM-III-R, and changed the name to ADHD, and fine-tuned diagnostic criteria, reflecting an updated understanding of the disorder. The inattentive subtype was eliminated, as there were too many controversies, and not enough research to support its inclusion, and the requirement that symptoms be developmentally inappropriate was added. Now labelled Undifferentiated Attention-deficit Disorder, they called for more research to determine its validity. [7]

In 1994, diagnostic criteria and conceptualization were again updated and published in the DSM-IV. The inattentive subtype was brought back, and subtypes were defined to include combined type with all 3 major symptoms, inattentive type predominant with only inattention symptoms, and hyperactive-impulsive type. Reflecting the feeling that ADHD always starts in childhood, symptoms had to be present before age 7, and had to be in multiple settings.[8] Conceptualization of ADHD, its primary deficits, potential causes, optimal treatment modalities, natural course, age of onset and persistence have continued to evolve. Availability of techniques such as microarrays to detect genetic contributions and neuroimaging to evaluate brain structure and function have added much, as have now available long term outcome studies.

The most recent iteration of the DSM, edition 5 was published in 2013, and reflects current concepts, including again a merging of ADHD into one type with 3 different presentations, and later possible onset (or recognition) of symptoms.[4] It is still thought of as a disorder with onset in childhood but the requirement of age of symptom onset has been increased to 12 years. The recognition that ADHD subtypes are not permanent and that one can evolve through different ADHD subtypes is also new with the DSM-5. Recognition of the evolution of symptoms developmentally and especially into adulthood is also ongoing.

Research into the core difficulties causing ADHD symptoms suggests that the inattention symptoms of ADHD are related to problems with executive function skills. These refer to cognitive functions that are necessary for self-management, for goal directed planning and organization, motivation and self-monitoring. Executive function is mediated in areas throughout the brain and at least part of the difficulties in ADHD may be attributed to inefficiency of communication between different neural networks that regulate executive function.[9] Additionally problems with self-restraint and behavioral disinhibition may underlie the symptoms of hyperactivity and impulsivity.[4] Newer technologies including genetic, imaging such as fMRI and continued study of long term outcomes ensures that the conceptualization of ADHD will continue to evolve.

History of Stimulants

Amphetamine was first synthesized in 1887 by a Romanian chemist named Lazar Edeleanu, but was largely ignored until rediscovered and marketed as Benzedrine in 1932 by the drug company Smith, Kline and French (SKF), as an adrenaline analog. It was used initially as a decongestant and to treat asthma, and it was found to be helpful for depression (chronic exhaustion), but worsened anxiety. It started to be used recreationally because it produced feelings of euphoria, energy and initiative, and was nicknamed pep pills. It was used during WWII to help with battle exhaustion, and widely used and abused after World War II. Methamphetamine was produced in Germany for the same purpose, and has been credited with aiding in the success of the German Blitzkrieg, but it was abandoned because of its associated reckless behavior and abuse potential.[10] Because of societal backlash and widespread concerns of abuse, governmental regulation led to the passage of the Controlled Substance Act in 1971, and amphetamine preparations were labelled as schedule-II drugs, recognizing their potential for abuse.

In 1937 Dr. Charles Bradley was serving as the medical director of the Emma Pendleton Bradley Home in Rhode Island. He was a Harvard trained pediatrician. The school opened in 1931, founded by his great uncle as a means to treat their daughter Emma, who suffered post encephalitis disabilities, and others like her, and was one of the first centers designed to evaluate and treat children with behavior disorders, as opposed to mere custodial care or training schools. Children there underwent evaluations that included pneumoencephalography (air injected into the spinal column to outline brain structures by x-ray). This was a painful procedure, and Bradley attempted to alleviate the post procedure pain by administering Benzedrine, theorizing that it would stimulate production of spinal fluid. It did not help the pain, but teachers noted significant improvement in academic performance and behavior. This was during a time when behavior and psychologic interventions were the mainstay of treatments for behavioral problems, and it was generally believed that behavioral problems did not have a biological basis.

His original studies were published in 1937, and were based on treatment of 30 children with behavioral disorders. This was followed by a larger study of 100 children, published in 1941. They were observed in the home setting for a week, followed by a week of treatment, and then another week off medication. He noted increased motivation, less irritable behavior, and more socially appropriate behavior. Results were quite variable however, and did not help all of the children, presumably because of varied diagnoses. [11] In spite of his and colleagues' publication of their dramatic results, general use of stimulants for ADHD did not occur until 25 years later. Methylphenidate was first synthesized in 1944 and marketed as Ritalin by Ciba-Geigy in 1954, and has been one of the main medications used to treat ADHD since. There are now multiple stimulants on the market for ADHD, but all are derivatives of either amphetamine (the original Benzedrine) or methylphenidate. Since 2000, the main advance in ADHD medication options has been the development of longer acting stimulant preparations, and the development of some non-stimulant options (atomoxetine and guanfacine).

Bibliography

1. Barkley RA, Peters H. The earliest reference to ADHD in the medical literature? Melchior Adam Weikard's description in 1775 of "Attention Deficit" (*Mangel der Aufmerksamkeit, Attentio Volubilis*). *J Atten Disord.* 2012;16(8):623–630. doi:10.1177/1087054711432309.
2. Martinez-Badia J, Martinez-Raga J. Who says this is a modern disorder? The early history of attention deficit hyperactivity disorder. *World J Psychiatry.* 2015;5 (4):379–386. doi:10.5498/wjp.v5.i4.379.
3. Lange KW, Reichl S, Lange KM, Tucha L, Tucha O. The history of attention deficit hyperactivity disorder. *ADHD Atten Deficit Hyperact Disord.* 2010;2(4):241–255. doi:10.1007/s12402-010-0045-8.
4. Barkley RA, ed. *Attention-Deficit Hyperactivity Disorder: A Handbook for Diagnosis and Treatment.* 4th ed. Guilford Press; 2015.
5. Fellick JM, Thomson APJ, Sills J, Hart CA. Neurological soft signs in mainstream pupils. *Arch Dis Child.* 2001;85(5):371–374. doi:10.1136/adc.85.5.371.
6. Carlew A, Zartman A. DSM nosology changes in neuropsychological diagnoses through the years: a look at ADHD and mild neurocognitive disorder. *Behav Sci (Basel).* 2016;7(1):1. doi:10.3390/bs7010001.
7. American Psychiatric Association, ed. *Diagnostic and Statistical Manual of Mental Disorders III-R.* 3rd rev. ed.; 1987.
8. American Psychiatric Association, ed. *Diagnostic and Statistical Manual of Mental Disorders-IV.* 4th ed.; 1994.
9. Cortese S, Kelly C, Chabernaud C, et al. Toward systems neuroscience of ADHD: a meta-analysis of 55 fMRI Studies. *Am J Psychiatry,* 2012; (October): 1038–1055. doi:10.1176/appi.ajp.201211101521.
10. Durham B. Benzedrine sulphate used in war operations. *Laurier Mil History Arch.* 2014.
11. Strohl MP. Bradley's Benzedrine studies on children with behavioral disorders. *Yale J Biol Med.* 2011;84(1):27–33.

3 Long Term Consequences of ADHD

J. Dennis Odell

What are the consequences of ADHD? What kind of problems do children with ADHD face, and do they ever grow out of it? Is there any harm in just monitoring the symptoms to see if they go away, and look at evaluation and treatment if behaviors don't improve? We have avoided having our child evaluated for ADHD because we have heard such bad things about medicines for ADHD and want to avoid medication for our child. We just want the best for our child, to have a normal life and be successful in school and be happy and successful as an adult. But how will this ever happen given how many problems we're having now? What can we do as parents, educators, therapists to help with the problems we are having now, and improve long term success? These are some of the questions that often come up in addressing concerns about children with ADHD. To do so, we will need to review in some detail some of the long term studies that have been done to address these questions.

While this chapter may seem to paint a rather grim picture of long term problems in those with ADHD, it is meant to point out potential problems that can occur. It should be noted that ADHD generally is a rather mild disorder relative to some potential medical or psychiatric conditions (cancer, diabetes, schizophrenia, bipolar disorder), and that there are effective treatments and preventive measures available for ADHD and all of its potential complications. If anything, because it is relatively mild, it can be easily overlooked or ignored, despite the fact that intervention can make a big difference. In this discussion, I will admit to having a huge bias regarding the necessity for accurate assessment and early intervention for any problems associated with a diagnosis of ADHD. I have talked to many adolescents and adults who have expressed that they wished their difficulties related to ADHD had been addressed earlier, so they could have been spared years of anguish and struggles. Many carry the baggage of problems that were never or improperly treated as children. And, I have the strong impression that early intervention makes a big difference in preventing problems later on, and the earlier the identification and treatment, the less difficult the intervention, and the better the outcome. Many problems that stem from ADHD surface as defensive or maladaptive behaviors that are the child's attempts to deal with frustrations brought about by the ADHD symptoms in the first place, and the longer these persist, the harder they are to remediate. For the most part research bears this out.

To address the reasons for recommending early identification and aggressive early intervention, let us review what we know about long term outcomes for children who have ADHD. There have been a number of research studies looking at the natural outcome of ADHD as well as the results of different treatment modalities, but most have been relatively short term studies. There have, however, also been some very good long term studies, and a few of these will be reviewed here. Before reviewing outcome data, it is important to emphasize the challenges that come with trying to study long term outcomes of children with ADHD. These studies are incredibly difficult to do, requiring initial assessment and treatment protocols that will hold up over time, and then monitoring the results of the initial subjects over many years. Keeping track of these subjects over a long period of time is extremely challenging, having the funding and staff to continue such research is a never ending trial, and losing track of some of the original subjects is to be expected, either from moving away, subjects dropping out of the study, or especially with longer term studies, death. Given these challenges, the fact that there are any such studies is remarkable, and in fact there have been a number.

Interpreting the results is also challenging. Usually, research studies in this area are looking at group results, comparing results in a group of individuals with ADHD to individuals who don't have ADHD. Especially when looked at over time, it is difficult to sort out all of the different variables that may affect outcome. The ideal study would look at a group of young children all of whom had very typical ADHD without any associated problems, or subgroups of children with ADHD who had very similar initial profiles, and comparing these to a similar group of children who have no ADHD, and then following them over the lifetime. Or, in the case of treatment studies, one has to compare groups who received the same types of treatments to similarly diagnosed children who did not receive treatment, or received a different kind of treatment. These children would hopefully be raised in similar environments and have similar opportunities, and then years later outcomes would be assessed and the differences measured. The problem of course comes in sorting out other variables that might affect outcome, because everyone has different experiences in the home, parenting styles, educational opportunities, socioeconomic status, and other mental or physical health problems, any of which can affect the outcome. Results of outcome studies need to be interpreted with these factors in mind. Any research study will try to minimize confounding variables as much as possible, and the use of statistics in analyzing the data can sort much of this out.

It should also be noted that these studies generally examine group differences, meaning for example that a larger percentage of individuals with ADHD will exhibit a certain outcome compared to those who don't have

ADHD. This indicates a risk for individuals with ADHD to have that particular outcome but by no means ensures it. We are all of course unique, and no group study can address an individual's specific set of conditions. ADHD rarely comes in isolation and the list of potential associated problems is long. Long term studies typically will combine everyone who has ADHD, regardless of associated problems, and almost all of the long term studies look at outcomes for those with what is now combined type ADHD, not subtypes such as inattentive type. But it is clear that often the associated problems can be part of the reason resulting in a particular outcome. For example early outcome studies indicated that a significant percentage of children with ADHD developed antisocial behavior as adults. Later studies however found that this was partially due to or aggravated by associated conduct disorder and bipolar disorder.[1] Also, as previously reviewed, the criteria for diagnosing ADHD have evolved over the years, and over the length of time of most of these studies, criteria for diagnoses will have changed. The main benefit from these studies is showing potential risks for particular problems associated with ADHD, as well as guiding treatment strategies. Being aware of potential problems can help in designing preventive measures at an early age. Outcome studies show that a certain percentage of children with ADHD will develop challenging problems as teenagers and adults, but by no means all. One should not assume bad outcomes for all children with ADHD. The trick is to determine how those with good outcomes achieved them, and to implement measures at an early age that will provide the best opportunities for achieving long term goals. There is ample evidence that interventions for children with ADHD are effective in improving long term prognosis.

Outcome Studies

The Montreal Study

Early studies looking at outcomes were mostly retrospective studies, looking at populations of adults with particular problems, and then looking back at their childhood histories to see if there was an association with hyperactivity in childhood. One of the first prospective studies, identifying a group of children with ADHD and then following their outcomes as they grew older, was a study from Montréal Children's Hospital. The original study group consisted of 104 hyperactive children who were diagnosed between 1962 to 1965, and were ages 6–12 at the time of initial assessment. To be included in the study, the children had to have symptoms of restlessness and poor concentration with symptoms present both at school and at home, and had to have IQs above 85. This was before DSM-III, but in retrospect it was felt that all of the children had what the DSM-III called ADD with hyperactivity, and most also had significant behavior or conduct problems. The study group varied considerably as far as presence of other associated problems such as learning disabilities. Additionally there was a control group of 45 children who did not have ADHD and had no history of academic difficulties or behavior problems.

Follow-up was done 10 years and again 15 years after the initial assessment. They found that two-thirds of the study group still had some symptoms of ADHD in adulthood. There was a trend towards greater drug and alcohol use and antisocial behavior in the hyperactive group. Overall, the ADHD group completed less education and were more likely to leave school. Self-esteem and social interactions were lower, and they were more likely to have other problems such as anxiety and physical complaints. They were less likely to have favorable work experiences as adults. Suicide attempts were also more common in the hyperactive group.

One of the interesting follow-up questions for the hyperactive group was "what had helped them most during their childhood". The most common response was that someone, usually a parent or teacher, believed in them, and for some turned their lives around. Another common helpful factor was being able to develop a special talent. They did not find that stimulant treatment in childhood predisposed to greater drug and alcohol use in adulthood. They also did not find any long term differences in height, weight, pulse rate or blood pressure. Factors that predicted increased likelihood of problems in adulthood included lower IQ, initial degree of aggressive behavior and antisocial behavior. Those treated with stimulant medication seemed to do better in such areas as fewer car accidents, more positive childhood experience, better social skills and better self-esteem. One of the most important findings from these studies at the time was the realization that for many with ADHD, symptoms didn't disappear by adulthood, and there often were persistent problems and difficulties in many different areas.[2]

The MTA Study

The Multimodal Treatment of Attention Deficit Hyperactivity Disorder study (MTA) was a cooperative group study sponsored by the National Institutes of Health and the Department of Education in 1992 that was originally designed to answer questions related to long term treatment strategies for children with ADHD. However the subjects have been followed for many years since the conclusion of the original study and have yielded much valuable information on long term outcomes of children with ADHD. Most previous studies had primarily looked at short term treatment benefits, generally no more than 4 months.

The sample of children studied were ages 7–9 who were in grades one to four, had a diagnosis of ADHD combined type using DSM-IV criteria, and who also had a range of associated conditions that was meant to represent children normally seen in a community setting. The children were divided randomly into 4 different treatment categories that included medication management, behavioral treatment, combined behavioral and medication treatment, or standard community care, and the initial study followed outcomes for 14 months. Children were evaluated from 6 different sites, and the initial group included 579 children. Medication used was methylphenidate, given at breakfast, lunch, and half the dose in the afternoon. Behavior management included a combination of parent training, child focused treatment and school-based intervention which was fairly intensive initially but eventually tapered over the 14 months. The community care group received treatment from their community providers rather than the study providers. This group was meant to compare the intensive interventions of the first 3 groups with the typical standard of care in the community at that time. Two thirds of the community care group was treated with any of a number of different medications and some also received behavioral therapy and mental health services. This study was very well designed and carried out, and implemented by some of the most experienced experts in the field. The initial results were published in the *Archives of General Psychiatry* in 1999 [3] with additional information available at the NIH MTA website (The Multimodal Treatment of Attention Deficit Hyperactivity Disorder Study (MTA): Questions and Answers; Revised November 2009).

There were 3 questions that were addressed in the initial study. The first question was whether medication and behavioral treatments were comparable in improving ADHD symptoms. The results showed that there was clear benefit of medication treatment over behavioral treatment. The second question was whether combination treatment was significantly better than medication or behavioral interventions alone. Somewhat surprisingly, the results indicated that combination treatment was not significantly better than medication alone for ADHD symptoms, but both were better than behavior management alone. The third question was how the study interventions compared with typical community care, and the results showed that medication management and combination medication and behavioral interventions were both superior to community care results for ADHD symptoms. Combination treatment resulted in much better outcomes for associated conditions including oppositional behavior, social skills difficulties, parent–child relations, reading achievement scores and anxiety and depression. Importantly, all 4 groups showed improvement in ADHD symptoms over the 14 months, but greater improvement was seen in the medication only group and the combination group. Although the results were similar between the medication and combination groups for ADHD symptoms, effective medication dosages in the combined group were lower than the medication only group, suggesting that there were advantages in the behavioral component in reducing dosage of medication needed. In comparing medication management between the medication group and the community group who were administered medications, the medication management group were monitored quite a bit more closely, parents received a lot of training and information about medication, and dosages were often significantly higher than comparative doses in the community group (meaning community dosing was often sub therapeutic), accounting for some of the greater improvement in outcomes. Overall, all children improved over the 14 months in core symptoms, and although medication seemed to make the biggest difference, children's responses varied considerably, and some children showed great benefit in each treatment group.

In an analysis of other subgroups, it was found in those with ADHD and anxiety disorders, that the behavior management arm was as effective as medication management and combination, and all gave better results than community care. Some 34% of the initial sample of 579 children were deemed to have an anxiety disorder. Overall, combination treatment showed greater improvement over medication management for participants who had ADHD and anxiety. There was some initial concern that children with ADHD and anxiety would not respond as well to stimulant medication, but this was not the case in the study. They also looked at those who also had oppositional defiant or conduct disorder, and found results similar to the original findings.[4]

This study originally looked at treatment outcomes, but has been valuable over the years as researchers have looked at a number of different parameters regarding outcome of ADHD. A follow-up analysis was done 8 years after the initial assessments to determine long term effects of the original treatment modalities. Although most of the children (now adolescents) maintained improvement over their original symptoms, there were no longer differences between any of the groups. After the initial 14 month study, the treatment of all of the children was turned over to community providers. Many were no longer taking medication, and the powerful effects of medication initially were not sustained over time. The study group was compared with age matched controls, and as a group fared less well than the control group in most measures.

Predictors of better outcome in adolescence included lower severity of ADHD symptoms at initial diagnosis, absence of conduct and severe behavioral problems, higher IQ, social advantage and the strength of the response to treatment. The results showed that in spite of significant interventions after initial diagnosis, and continued community treatment subsequently, a portion of adolescents continued to have significant challenges, emphasizing the need for continued close monitoring over time, and perhaps the need for more school and community supports besides relying on medication alone.[5]

A study published in 2016 looked at adult outcomes 16 years after childhood diagnosis. They were able to collect data for up to 16 years for 476 of the original 579 children diagnosed with ADHD and from 241 age and gender matched classmates, and looked at those whose ADHD had resolved, those who still had ADHD and those who never had ADHD.

A number of categories showed distinct differences between those with and without ADHD. Educational achievement was significantly better for those who did not have ADHD, with 37% obtaining a bachelor's degree compared to 8% of those with persistent ADHD. 16% of those with ADHD were receiving public assistance compared to 3.2% of those without. There were 3 general patterns of outcomes, the most common being that the group without ADHD had the best outcomes compared to those with ADHD, and those who had ADHD but whose symptoms had resolved had intermediate outcomes. This included obtaining a bachelor's degree, job stability, income, receiving public assistance and risky sexual behavior. In the second pattern, the group without ADHD and those whose symptoms had resolved did not differ but both functioned better than those who had persistent ADHD. This included emotional lability, mood disorders and substance use disorders. Lastly was a group where no differences were noted among the 3 groups and this included number of jobs held, alcohol use, and jail time.[6]

Other studies were cited that showed significant risk for educational, occupational and emotional problems and mood disorders for adults who were diagnosed with ADHD as children. Factors that had to do with persistence of ADHD included initial severity of symptoms, parental mental health and parenting practices, as well as presence of conduct disorder and major depression. The authors emphasized the importance of early intervention and continuous treatment as needed to provide the best outcomes. [6]

There are a number of take-home messages from the MTA study.

1   Having ADHD in childhood carries a significant risk of long term difficulties in adolescence and adulthood.
2   Treatment interventions clearly help, but even with intensive early treatment, long term problems can resurface after treatment has ended.
3   Initial dramatic responses to medication may not be sustained over time.
4   Medication management is far more effective when monitored very closely with frequent office visits and optimization of medication dosages.
5   Intensive treatment with stimulant medication does carry a risk of slight decrease in height over time.
6   Combined medication and behavior intervention over time gave the best likelihood of good outcomes by adulthood.
7   Parent factors such as parenting practices and parental depression have a significant impact on outcomes by adulthood and should be a target of intervention.
8   When parents showed large improvements in reducing negative and ineffective discipline through behavior interventions, their child's social skills improved and disruptive and aggressive behavior normalized, emphasizing the merit of parent interventions.

9   Multimodal behavioral intervention including working with parents, the individual and in the school settings provides the best opportunity for long term improvement and in some cases normalization of symptoms.

10   Co-occurring conditions matter as far as long term outcome and need to be targeted in the initial treatment plan. Co-existing anxiety disorder is far more effectively treated with a behavior management component in addition to medication. Co-occurring conduct problems increase the likelihood of poor outcomes as adults and need to be addressed early.

BGALS

The great majority of long term studies involved primarily males with ADHD combined type. Very few studies have looked at outcomes for females, and also haven't compared subtypes of ADHD. Since there are group differences in developmental outcomes based on gender, such as increased anxiety and depression in girls and increased conduct disorder and antisocial behavior in boys, a long term outcome study of girls diagnosed with ADHD as children was done at University of California at Berkeley to help address these issues, and included a subset of girls with inattentive type ADHD. The study is known as BGALS for Berkeley Girls with ADHD Longitudinal Study. The original sample included 140 girls aged 6–12 years, and 88 age and ethnicity matched controls. Forty-seven of the original group had the inattentive subtype of ADHD (ADHD-I). At 10 year follow-up, most of the subjects who had ADHD-I no longer met criteria for that diagnosis, either no longer having enough symptoms to warrant that diagnosis, or now meeting criteria for ADHD-combined type (ADHD-C). Similarly many in the ADHD-C group no longer had ADHD-C or shifted to the other subtypes. This lack of persistence of ADHD diagnosis has been reported in other studies as well. Because symptoms of ADHD are moderated by developmental changes, this is not unexpected, and led to a reassessment of criteria for diagnosing ADHD in adults and changes in the DSM-5. Even though many no longer met ADHD criteria, there was continued impairment at 10 year follow up in multiple areas. Areas of problems included increased risk for depression, anxiety, oppositional defiant disorder, and poor academic achievement. There were no major differences in outcomes between the 2 ADHD groups, except the ADHD-C group was much more likely to attempt suicide and self-injury, whereas the ADHD-I group had rates similar to the control group.[7]

Another follow-up was done at 16 years after initial assessment, and in general the above results continued to be valid. Seventy-four percent of the girls who had childhood ADHD still had ADHD as adults, and overall had increased risk for most adverse measures. A portion of the initial group (26%) no longer had ADHD symptoms as adults, and generally they fared much better than the group that still met ADHD diagnostic criteria, and in most areas had no increased risk compared to the control group who did not have childhood ADHD. They still retained increased risk for unplanned pregnancy, increased body mass index, and lower educational achievement. In the all-female group, ADHD was not associated with substance use, driving outcomes or worse employment opportunities. Childhood ADHD, whether the diagnosis persisted or not, was a risk factor for lower educational achievement.[8]

Other Studies and Outcomes

1. Self-esteem and social function: In a review of studies looking at social function and self-esteem outcomes for those with ADHD, the majority of studies reported significantly higher problems in both areas. Social function outcomes tended to be worse in childhood, becoming less prevalent with age, whereas poor self-esteem was highest in adults and less prevalent in children and adolescents. In looking at treatment response, there were beneficial results for most individuals in both categories, whether treatment was pharmacologic, behavioral or both. In a significant percentage of individuals, treatment results approached the same level as compared to controls with no ADHD.[9]

2. Education: Besides behavioral concerns, educational and academic concerns are the most common reason for evaluation for ADHD. In addition to the core symptoms, associated problems including especially learning disabilities, but also mood disorders and disruptive behaviors significantly impact the ADHD child's educational experience. It is therefore logical to assume that academic struggles and decreased academic performance compared to non-ADHD groups is seen in adolescents and adults, and this is indeed born out in long term studies. A larger percentage of ADHD children will need special education assistance or may repeat a grade in school. A larger number drop out of school or fail to finish high school and the numbers who have enrolled in and completed college education courses are diminished. Associated conduct disorder increases the risk of dropping out, but attention problems alone contribute to educational underachievement. [10] Again because of the large mix of presentations, having ADHD is no guarantee of later academic problems, but the risk is large, and emphasizes the need for long term monitoring and intervention.

3. Work experience: Those with ADHD as children ranked significantly lower than control groups in occupational status in adulthood, and work performance is rated lower than for control groups without a history of ADHD. Also socioeconomic status is lower as a whole. This is especially so for those where ADHD symptoms persist into adulthood and much less so for those who are treated and have diminished ADHD symptoms. They also were more likely to be unemployed or to have had multiple jobs, again with improved outcome with treatment. However, those who found a good fit in their employment with their interests report having a better

outcome and job satisfaction. Often those work experiences involved more stimulating environments, more physically demanding and more hands on type environments.[11]

4. Drug abuse: In a review (meta-analysis) of relevant studies on ADHD, those who had ADHD as children were twice as likely to use nicotine than those without childhood ADHD and three times as likely to report nicotine dependence in adolescents and adulthood. Alcohol use was not increased, but they were almost twice as likely to abuse or be dependent on alcohol. Risk of marijuana use and cocaine use and abuse were increased. Substance abuse risk was 2 1/2 times higher than in those without ADHD.[12] Co-occurring conduct disorder, anxiety and depression increases the risk, emphasizing the need for mental health intervention when present. Reasons for increased substance abuse are speculated to be in part due to the impulsivity and poor judgment that can come with ADHD, but may also be due to self-medicating. Additionally with an increased risk of school failure and potentially dropping out of school, adolescents with ADHD may migrate socially to groups of peers more likely to abuse drugs. There is general concern that early treatment with stimulant medication increases the risk of later substance abuse, but in fact studies have shown that there is no increased risk of later substance abuse, and the risk in some studies has been reported to be reduced, with earlier age of treatment associated with less likelihood of substance abuse as adolescents and adults.[13]

5. Obesity: Individuals with ADHD have a higher likelihood of being overweight or obese with approximately 70% increase in adult prevalence of obesity, and 40% in children. In studies of obese adults, there are also significantly higher rates of ADHD compared to those with normal weights. Hypothesized causes for obesity in the ADHD individuals have included abnormal eating patterns, decreased physical activity, sleep disruption and genetic factors. Associated conditions also may play a role. The question of whether treatment of ADHD moderates these effects is at present unanswered.[14]

6. Growth: Studies are mixed on whether ADHD, and especially treatment, is associated with decreased height as an adult. A longitudinal study looking at 340 childhood ADHD cases and 680 controls concluded that neither ADHD nor treatment with stimulants was associated with differences in peak height velocity or final adult height. However delayed age of peak height velocity was associated with stimulant medication use.[15] On the other hand, long term follow-up of children in the MTA study showed up to a 1 inch decrease in adult height compared to those who were not treated.[16] As previously mentioned, the Montréal study did not detect long term differences and height,[2] nor did a long term study of children in New York.[17] Although results are mixed, it appears that if there is height suppression, it is relatively mild. Nonetheless, monitoring growth and weight are part of the reasons for frequent monitoring of medication effects.

7. Motor vehicle accidents: As reviewed by Barkley, adverse events associated with driving are a significant risk for those with ADHD. This includes an increase in motor vehicle accidents, traffic citations especially for speeding and reckless driving, and involvement in crashes resulting in injuries. Some of this is due to the increased risk of ADHD itself with impulsiveness and inattention to details. But also driving under the influence of alcohol or drugs, texting, and even road rage are increased risk factors.[18] Treatment with stimulant medication appears to improve driving performance and risks of adverse driving events.[19]

Summary

It is clear that ADHD diagnosed in childhood carries a risk for significant life challenges over the lifespan. These include educational success and achievement, job success and satisfaction, social and relationship issues, increased risk for drug and alcohol abuse, growth and obesity concerns, risky driving practices, depression and suicide risk and others. Those with commonly associated conditions such as conduct and mood disorders carry an even higher risk. However, most studies have shown that appropriate interventions, including medication and appropriate behavioral and mental health interventions can significantly decrease and sometimes normalize those risks and outcomes. Early and accurate assessment and intervention appears to provide the best outcomes.

Bibliography

1. Wilens TE, Biederman J, Mick E, Faraone SV, Spencer T. Attention Deficit Hyperactivity Disorder (ADHD) is associated with early onset substance use disorders. *J Nerv Ment Dis*. 1997;185(8).
2. Weiss G, Hechtman LT. *Hyperactive Children Grown up: ADHD in Children, Adolescents, and Adults*. Guilford Press; 1993.
3. Group TM cooperataive. A 14-month randomized clinical trial of treatment strategies for Attention-Deficit/Hyperactivity Disorder. The MTA Cooperative Group. Multimodal Treatment Study of Children with ADHD. *Arch Gen Psychiatry*. 1999;56(12):1073–1086.
4. The MTA Cooperative Group. Moderators and mediators of treatment response for children with Attention-Deficit/Hyperactivity Disorder. *Arch Gen Psychiatry*. 1999;56(12):1088. doi:10.1001/archpsyc.56.12.1088.
5. Molina BSG, Hinshaw SP, Swanson JM, et al. The MTA at 8 years: Prospective follow-up of children treated for combined-type ADHD in a multisite study. *J Am Acad Child Adolesc Psychiatry*. 2009;48(5):484–500. doi:10.1097/CHI.0b013e31819c23d0.
6. Hechtman L, Swanson JM, Sibley MH, et al. Functional adult outcomes 16 years after childhood diagnosis of Attention-Deficit/Hyperactivity Disorder: MTA results. *J Am Acad Child Adolesc Psychiatry*. 2016;55(11):945–952.e2. doi:10.1016/j.jaac.2016.07.774.

7. Hinshaw SP, Owens EB, Zalecki C, et al. Prospective follow-up of girls with attention-deficit/hyperactivity disorder into early adulthood: Continuing impairment includes elevated risk for suicide attempts and self-injury. *J Consult Clin Psychol.* 2012;80(6):1041–1051. doi:10.1037/a0029451.

8. Owens EB, Zalecki C, Gillette P, Hinshaw SP. Girls with childhood ADHD as adults: Cross-domain outcomes by diagnostic persistence. *J Consult Clin Psychol.* 2017;85(7):723–736. doi:10.1037/ccp0000217.

9. Harpin V, Mazzone L, Raynaud J-P, Kahle J., Hodgkins P. Long-term outcomes of ADHD: A systematic review of self-esteem and social function. *J Atten Disord.* 2016;20(4) doi:10.1177/1087054713486516.

10. Barkley RA, Fischer M, Smallish L, Fletcher K. Young adult outcome of hyperactive children: Adaptive functioning in major life activities. *J Am Acad Child Adolesc Psychiatry.* 2006;45(2):192–202. doi:https://doi.org/10.1097/01.chi.0000189134.97436.e2.

11. Lasky AK, Weisner TS, Jensen PS, et al. ADHD in context: Young adults' reports of the impact of occupational environment on the manifestation of ADHD. *Soc Sci Med.* 2016;161:160–168. doi:10.1016/j.socscimed.2016.06.003.

12. Lee SS, Humphreys KL, Flory K, Liu R, Glass K. Prospective association of childhood attention-deficit/hyperactivity disorder (ADHD) and substance use and abuse/dependence: A meta-analytic review. *Clin Psychol Rev.* 2011;31(3):328–341. doi:10.1016/j.cpr.2011.01.006.

13. Chang Z, Lichtenstein P, Halldner L, et al. Stimulant ADHD medication and risk for substance abuse. *J Child Psychol Psychiatry.* 2014;55(8):878–885. doi:10.1111/jcpp.12164.

14. Cortese S, Tessari L. Attention-Deficit/Hyperactivity Disorder (ADHD) and obesity: Update 2016. *Curr Psychiatry Rep.* 2017;19(1). doi:10.1007/s11920-017-0754-1.

15. Harstad EB, Weaver AL, Katusic SK, et al. ADHD, stimulant treatment, and growth: A longitudinal study. *Pediatrics.* 2014;134(4):e935–e944. doi:10.1542/peds.2014-0428.

16. Swanson JM, Arnold LE, Molina BSG, et al. Young adult outcomes in the follow-up of the multimodal treatment study of attention-deficit/hyperactivity disorder: Symptom persistence, source discrepancy, and height suppression. *J Child Psychol Psychiatry.* 2017;58(6):663–678. doi:10.1111/jcpp.12684.

17. Biederman J, Spencer TJ, Monuteaux MC, Faraone SV. A naturalistic 10-year prospective study of height and weight in children with attention-deficit hyperactivity disorder grown up: sex and treatment effects. *J Pediatr.* 2010;157(4):635–640, 640.e1. doi:10.1016/j.jpeds.2010.04.025.

18. Barkley RA. *Attention-Deficit Hyperactivity Disorder a Handbook for Diagnosis and Treatment.* 4th ed. (Barkley RA, ed.). Guilford Press; 2015:289–291.

19. Chang Z, Quinn PD, Hur K, et al. Association between medication use for attention-deficit/hyperactivity disorder and risk of motor vehicle crashes. *JAMA Psychiatry.* 2017;74(6):597–603. doi:10.1001/jamapsychiatry.2017.0659.

4 ADHD Predominantly Inattentive Presentation

J. Dennis Odell

Lennie was 16 years of age when first seen in our clinic. His mother reported that she had concerns about Lennie since he was preschool age. At that time, he was struggling to learn his colors and letters. He reportedly worked very hard, and received a lot of extra help from teachers and parents, but in spite of this, he was near the bottom of his class academically. He struggled academically throughout elementary and middle school, and in high school was failing many classes. There were never any behavior concerns, but teachers expressed concerns that he often appeared to space out and not attend to discussions in the classroom. He took hours to finish homework that for most students was taking less than an hour, and homework always required parental supervision. He struggled with spelling and handwriting was difficult to read. At times he would become oppositional when pushed to do schoolwork. He tended to be very quiet and he was kind to peers and respectful to teachers and adults. He was well liked by peers, but had very few close friends.

After struggling in elementary school, his parents transferred him to a charter school with smaller class sizes and more individual attention in hopes that he would do better in that environment, but he struggled there as well, and his teachers reported that he wasn't getting work turned in and was floundering in class. At that time, he was evaluated by his primary care pediatrician and was diagnosed with ADHD-inattentive type. He was started on low dose stimulant medication, which helped considerably. He also received extra help at school, and did much better that year. Homework was completed much more quickly, and handwriting became legible. However the improvement was not sustained, handwriting again became difficult to read. He enjoyed football, but was kicked off the team because of his grades. Lennie reported that the medication helped him socially, helped him pay attention better, and helped him work more efficiently. He stated that he had a hard time taking notes. He felt like he understood the school material just fine, but took a long time to get his work done, and just couldn't keep up. He reported concerns with difficulties with memorization but stated that he worked hard. He reported difficulty concentrating and paying attention in school, and felt confused and was easily distracted.

His hobbies included music, and his parents reported that he was very good at the piano and trumpet. He loved sports, especially football and basketball. His parents described him as very bright and with a very fun personality.

Medical history was remarkable for some developmental delays. He did not walk until 24 months of age, and was 8 years old before being able to ride a bicycle. There were no speech delays. He had his tonsils and adenoids removed at age 8, but had no other significant health problems. He had some difficulty with coordination, which persisted into adolescence.

Family history was positive for an uncle who was treated for ADHD as a child, and seemed to have a similar personality to Lennie's. There was no other history for ADHD, learning disabilities, developmental delays or related problems. He was the oldest of 4 children, and the others were doing well with no reported problems behaviorally or academically.

Physical examination was unremarkable. He was extremely pleasant and was readily engaged in the discussion. In spite of his years of struggling, he had no evident negative behaviors, nor any depression or anxiety symptoms, but seemed sincerely interested in finding solutions to his challenges.

Initial testing included behavioral questionnaires that were completed by his parents, himself and two teachers that knew him well. All reported high levels of inattention, but no one reported any concerns about behavior, mood problems such as anxiety or depression, or problems with social interactions. A continuous performance test was administered and his scores on the attention component were quite low, but he exhibited no impulsivity or hyperactivity.

He was diagnosed with Attention deficit/hyperactivity disorder-inattentive type predominant, with concerns about possible learning disabilities. His stimulant medication dose was increased, and testing for learning disabilities was arranged. On IQ testing, his full scale score was 102 (very normal), but the processing speed subscale was 75. Achievement test scores for reading, math and language were all in the normal range, except his reading comprehension and written language scores were well lower than his IQ score, but not low enough to qualify for extra help at school. At present he is doing fairly well, but continues to struggle academically in spite of putting in hard work. There is a disconnect between his IQ and achievement scores and the amount of work he puts in, compared to his grades and academic success.

ADHD-predominantly inattentive presentation (ADHD-I) has been formerly known as ADHD predominantly Inattentive Type, or ADD without hyperactivity, and is now commonly, although incorrectly, referred to as ADD. It is characterized by being easily distracted, unorganized, frequently off task, forgetful, and having extreme difficulty with tasks that seem mundane or boring. Again these need to be to a degree that is significantly impacting the individual in more than one environment. It is a diagnostic class that remains an enigma. The disorder was first described in the DSM-III in 1980, called Attention Deficit Disorder (ADD) without hyperactivity, and was considered a subtype of ADD that included difficulties with focusing and inattention, but without the hyperactive and impulsive symptoms. At the time there was very little research on ADD without hyperactivity, and the inclusion in the DSM was based on clinical evidence that some children with ADD were not hyperactive.[1] Although the inattentive subtype was not included in the next DSM version (DSM-III-R), subsequent editions have conceptualized ADHD as having subtypes including the inattentive subtype, as research has demonstrated two distinct areas of difficulty in ADHD, hyperactivity/impulsivity and inattention. However, most of the research on ADHD up until recently has been focused on ADHD with hyperactivity, and was done primarily in children and adolescents. Conclusions about outcomes, associated conditions and best treatments were primarily applicable to the combined ADHD category. Questions remain about the validity of ADHD-I as a subtype of ADHD as opposed to a separate disorder entirely, about the core deficit causing the attentional difficulties, long term outcomes and associated problems, and best treatment practices.

Even within the inattentive category, reviewing research is made difficult, because it likely includes a heterogeneous group. Technically, one is diagnosed with ADHD-I if they meet criteria for the inattention component, and do not have enough symptoms to meet criteria for the hyperactivity and impulsivity component (see appendix chapter 1). For each component, one must have 6 of the 9 symptoms present to warrant a diagnosis, or 5 of 9 if the individual is 17 or over, reflecting the fact that symptoms may become less obvious or lessen with age. As children age, the hyperactivity tends to diminish as part of the normal developmental course. So, an adult who had ADHD-C as a child, but whose hyperactivity and impulsivity lessened with age, might now be diagnosed with ADHD-I because he/she no longer has enough hyperactive and impulsive symptoms to fulfill criteria for that category. Or a child might be diagnosed with ADHD-I if they meet criteria for the inattention component, but had fewer than 6 of the symptoms of hyperactivity and impulsivity (sub-threshold ADHD-C). Or, they might have ADHD-I if they have symptoms that meet inattention criteria, but have no hyperactivity or impulsivity. Until recently, in ADHD research, all of these types of ADHD-I have been combined, making it difficult to interpret conclusions.

There is another category that is often diagnosed as ADHD-I that has been termed sluggish cognitive tempo (SCT). Although not formally recognized as a distinct diagnosis, there is evidence that it is a distinct entity separate from traditional ADHD-I.[2] Rather than symptoms of disorganization, careless mistakes, and distractible behavior, they tend to be slow at processing information. There is not yet specific criteria for SCT, but the core features are daydreaming, trouble staying awake and alert, mentally foggy, easily confused, stares a lot, spacey, lethargic, underactive, slow-moving and sluggish, difficulty processing questions and explanations accurately, drowsy or sleepy appearance, apathetic and withdrawn, lost in thoughts, slow to complete tasks and lacks initiative or sustained effort.[3]

While SCT is felt to be a distinct disorder from ADHD-I, it frequently overlaps with and co-occurs with it, and it may be formally diagnosed as ADHD-I. Those with SCT tend to be daydreamers, spacey, and have difficulty staying alert in situations that are perceived as boring. They are typically underactive, slow moving, may appear drowsy and take a long time to complete tasks, not because of distractibility, but because of slow processing. They may be able to do a task well, but need an excessively long time to complete it. They may appear unmotivated or lazy, lack initiative and give up easily, and may seem generally uninterested in pursuing interests. While these symptoms describe many who have been diagnosed with ADHD, they are distinct from the symptoms that define inattention in ADHD. While SCT is not currently recognized as a specific disorder, there are now diagnostic tools to help recognize it. Russell Barkley, who has been one of the foremost advocates for recognizing and researching SCT, has developed a formal rating scale called the Barkley Sluggish Cognitive Tempo Scale (BSCTS) that is available for use in children and adolescents.[4] It is likely that in the future, SCT will be recognized formally as a distinct disorder from ADHD, but one that commonly co-occurs, in a manner similar to anxiety and depression.

In assessing for ADHD-I, it is best to identify which of the above presentations is most likely occurring. Also, other disorders may mimic ADHD-I. Some individuals may appear inattentive because they actually hyperfocus on an area of interest to the exclusion of all else (as is often the case in those with autism or Asperger Syndrome). Anxiety and depression both have as part of their core symptoms difficulty with focus and attention. Just as those with autism and Asperger's syndrome may appear inattentive because they are hyperfocusing on something else, those with anxiety and depression may be so focused or even obsessed with their own fears or sadness that they may be unable to attend to a discussion on a topic that seems relatively unimportant or trivial, and may appear to be off task. Children with severe allergies or with chronic pain or other medical problems may be unable to focus because of the overwhelming medical symptoms. Those with hearing or vision deficits, auditory processing difficulties or sensory processing dysfunction all may appear to have attentional difficulties. We have seen patients diagnosed with ADHD-I who had hugely enlarged tonsils and such severe sleep apnea, that they were chronically sleep deprived. The attention problems resolved with tonsillectomy.

Depending on the underlying cause of the inattention symptoms, associated conditions will vary. With the sub-threshold ADHD-C, or ADHD-C where the HI symptoms have diminished, the association with oppositional behavior, conduct problems, substance abuse and antisocial personality disorder is strong. On the other hand these are not associated with sluggish cognitive tempo, and may even decrease the risk for these disorders, but rates of anxiety and depression are higher.[1] And SCT and ADHD, especially ADHD-I frequently coexist.

Treatment for ADHD-I is typically similar to treatment of ADHD in general, although there is debate about whether stimulant medication effects are more dramatic in those with the combined type of ADHD.[5] In our clinical experience, it seems the likelihood of dramatic improvement in symptoms with stimulant medications or other ADHD medications is less in those with ADHD-I than those who have a hyperactivity and impulsive component. Some studies have found equal responses to medication regardless of subtype.[6] Clearly assessing for associated conditions is critical for optimal treatment, especially for symptoms of anxiety, depression and learning disabilities that are common in those with ADHD-I. Additionally, implementing non medicine approaches is critical.

When the symptoms of ADHD-I are predominantly due to sluggish cognitive tempo there appears to be a decreased likelihood of a good response to stimulant medications.[7] There are few studies looking at medication responses to SCT, but it appears treatment response is generally poor to traditional ADHD medications. While stimulant medications may provide some benefit, as in the case above, generally the positive effect is not as dramatic as for those who have ADHD, unless they have ADHD as an associated condition. One study suggested atomoxetine may be beneficial.[8] Some have argued that diagnosing SCT is just another excuse to add more children to the long list of disorders that can be medicated. However, it appears the majority of those with SCT are likely already diagnosed with ADHD-I, and this gives a potential explanation for why typical ADHD medications may be ineffective in this subgroup. In addition to medication, other modalities should be explored, including accommodations in the classroom (504 plan), social skills training, cognitive behavior therapy, and even occupational therapy. Given the current level of research, there will likely be more specific research based recommendations forthcoming.

Bibliography

1. Milich R, Balentine A, Lynam D. ADHD Combined Type and ADHD Predominately Inattentive Type are distinct and unrelated disorders. *Clin Psychology: Science and Practice*. 2006;8. doi:10.1093/clipsy.8.4.463.
2. Becker SP, Leopold DR, Burns GL, et al. The internal, external, and diagnostic validity of Sluggish Cognitive Tempo: A meta-analysis and critical review. *J Am Acad Child Adolesc Psychiatry*. 2016;55(3):163–178. doi:10.1016/j.jaac.2015.12.006.
3. Barkley RA. *Attention-Deficit Hyperactivity Disorder a Handbook for Diagnosis and Treatment*. 4th ed. (Barkley RA, ed.). Guilford Press; 2015.
4. Barkley RA. *Barkley Sluggish Cognitive Tempo Scale-Children and Adolescents (BTCTS-CA)*. Guilford Press; 2018.

5. Beery SH, Quay HC, Pelham WEJ. Differential response to methylphenidate in Inattentive and Combined Subtype ADHD. *J Atten Disord.* 2017;21(1):62–70. doi:10.1177/1087054712469256.

6. Barbaresi WJ, Katusic SK, Colligan RC, Weaver AL, Leibson CL, Jacobsen SJ. Long-term stimulant medication treatment of attention-deficit/hyperactivity disorder: Results from a population-based study. *J Dev Behav Pediatr.* 2014;35 (7):448–457.

7. Froehlich TE, Becker SP, Nick TG, et al. Sluggish Cognitive Tempo as a possible predictor of methylphenidate response in children with ADHD: A randomized controlled trial. *J Clin Psychiatry.* 2018;79(2). doi:10.4088/JCP.17m11553.

8. Wietecha L, Williams D, Shaywitz S, et al. Atomoxetine improved attention in children and adolescents with attention-deficit/hyperactivity disorder and dyslexia in a 16 week, acute, randomized, double-blind trial. *J Child Adolesc Psychopharmacol.* 2013;23(9):605–613. doi:10.1089/cap.2013.0054.

Part II
Associated Conditions

5   Learning Disabilities

J. Dennis Odell

Learning difficulties are extremely common in individuals with ADHD, and one of the chief reasons that families seek help. These may be due to diagnosable learning disabilities or disorders, or may be due to less severe difficulties, that in combination with ADHD may render learning particularly difficult in the usual school environment. Estimates on the prevalence of co-occurring ADHD and learning disabilities vary widely, but suffice it to say that it is extremely common to have both, and learning disabilities should be considered in any child who is diagnosed with ADHD. Common areas of difficulty include reading, math, and written language, but also motor skills and communication disorders. Learning disabilities may be conceptualized as having difficulty in a particular area of learning. Learning difficulties may mimic ADHD symptoms. If we are involved in a task that we do not understand or that is overly difficult, any of us may appear to be off task. For example, a third-grade child with a reading disability may appear to have difficulty staying focused when given a reading task, when the problem is actually difficulty in doing the task itself or understanding the material. So this child could have a primary reading disability, ADHD, or very commonly could have both.

Stefanie was 9 1/2 years of age and was seen originally with concerns about academic struggles and difficulty focusing. She was in fourth grade and was receiving resource help. First concerns were in first grade with reading problems, and she had received resource help since that time. Her teachers and parents had concerns about attention problems, but these were initially attributed to her reading difficulties. Behavior was not a concern except she could get defiant when pushed to do homework. She had plenty of friends with whom she got along well, and she enjoyed outdoor activities, such as soccer and skiing. Family history was significant for ADHD in her father and uncle, as well as 2 cousins. There was also a fairly strong family history for reading disabilities on her mother's side of the family. Physical examination was unremarkable except that her rapid finger movements were slow and awkward and neurologic examination showed some difficulty with fine motor movements.

Her mother brought in psychoeducational testing results from school. Her overall IQ was in the average range, but reading scores were in the 70s on standard reading achievement tests. Math scores were also in the normal range. To help clarify whether her attention problems were related to reading difficulties or attention problems, a continuous performance test was administered. There are many varieties of these, but essentially these are tests that are designed to be very boring, but are simple otherwise and don't require any high level of reading skills. On this test, she exhibited no evidence of impulsivity, but attention scores were in the 60s to 70s. There was also no hyperactivity evident during this test. Behavioral questionnaires were completed by her parents and teacher and all were consistent in showing difficulties with attention but not with hyperactivity, and scores in all other areas were in the normal range.

She was diagnosed with specific learning disorder in the area of reading, and ADHD-inattentive type. Based on these results she was started on Concerta, which helped with focusing at school but caused her to be very irritable, especially when the medication wore off in the early evening. The medication was changed to Adderall XR and she had good results with that with much less side effects. She remains in resource at school but is making significant progress academically, and seems to be much less frustrated with school.

Middle school also can be a tremendously challenging time for students for many reasons. From the students' perspective, they are expected to go to school 8 hours a day and do what 8 different teachers tell them to do, and then to go home at the end of the day and spend more time on their own doing homework. Their reward for doing all this day after day is that at the end of the term they are given grades that basically say "you did a great job, a pretty good job, or a lousy job". For many students, especially those who experience good success and grades, they are motivated to continue to work hard. However, most students are under the impression that high school grades are important, but middle school grades are not so much. So the motivation for those who struggle to get decent grades and all the effort that entails may not be very high, and they may give up easily. For adults, we may be able to tolerate a job that may not be ideal, because we know at the end of the month we're going to get a nice paycheck for our efforts. Not many of us would tolerate a job that is as big of a struggle as some of our middle school students are having, with no paycheck at the end. Oftentimes, success is its own reward. Students who are starting to see success from their labors will become more motivated and there can be an upward spiral in the right direction, to where they are starting to enjoy school more and the learning process. So sometimes, with some helpful interventions, students can show huge improvement.

Jacob was 14 years old and was being evaluated for academic struggles. He was in eighth grade and had done pretty well during elementary school. However starting in sixth grade, school became much more difficult for

him, and grades declined. His mother reported that he had a school evaluation to see if he had learning disabilities, but she was told that the results
were normal and that he just needed to work a bit harder. He spent hours
doing homework, which generally required parental supervision, but in
spite of all of his work, he was barely passing most subjects. He was frustrated, and frequently angry about his school experience. When asked what
was so difficult about school for him, he said he didn't know exactly, but he
felt there was too much work, and he just couldn't keep up. He said he had
so many different teachers and he was having a hard time keeping track of
all of the assignments. Homework assignments seemed overwhelming, and
he often didn't get them done. He said the hardest class for him was science
because he seemed to have a hard time understanding the material and
quickly got lost. When pressed for details, Jacob stated that he liked his
teacher and thought he was very interesting, but would get lost during his
lectures. He described how his teacher would pace back and forth, lecturing
the whole time and would draw diagrams and pictures on the board. He
said he could listen for a bit and keep up, but the students were also
expected to take notes. Jacob stated he had a hard time knowing what
material was important, and by the time he had written down what he was
supposed to, the teacher had moved on and Jacob was now lost. His medical history was unremarkable, and his physical exam was normal, as was his
hearing and vision.

To further evaluate these difficulties, behavioral questionnaires were sent
home to be filled out by Jacob, his parents and a few of his teachers to get a
better sense of his difficulties. In addition, we requested a copy of the school
testing results, and planned on seeing him back in a few weeks. Several
weeks later he was back with his parents, having completed their assignments. Behavioral questionnaires from all of the respondents were consistent
in the results and showed an adolescent whose behavior was exemplary and
who seemed to be working very hard, and who seemed smart, but was
floundering with staying organized, getting homework turned in, and
seemed overwhelmed. His scores were significant primarily for attention
problems and anxiety. Behavioral scores were otherwise all in the normal
range. We reviewed the results of the psychoeducational testing and they
were insightful. Standard scores for most of the psychoeducational testing
that was done are 100, with a standard deviation of 15, meaning that scores
between 85 and 115 are considered to be in the normal range. His IQ score
was 106, just a bit above average. His reading scores were in the normal
range, but somewhat low, averaging in the high 80s to low 90s. Strikingly
his written language scores were in the 70s. Language testing was also done,
and although expressive language scores were normal, his receptive language
scores were again in the high 80s. When asked what they were told about
the results, his parents indicated that school personnel had reviewed these
results with them and felt that Jacob did not exhibit any specific learning
disabilities and that most of the scores were in the normal range except for

his writing. They said he was a little bit behind in reading, but they attributed much of his difficulties to his evident distractibility and disorganization. They recommended a study skills class to help with keeping up with assignments and to help him stay organized.

In light of these test results, his difficulty in the science class became explicable. Based on our testing he met criteria for having ADHD-inattentive type, causing him to have a hard time staying focused on difficult tasks. Additionally he had significant writing problems, and he confirmed that taking notes was a very slow and laborious task for him. Additionally he had mildly low scores in reading and in receptive language. In that classroom setting he was being asked to stay focused, to listen and understand what his teacher was lecturing about, to read the notes on the board and take notes. Each of these tasks he could have done if they were isolated tasks, but he was being asked to do all four of them at the same time, and he quickly became overwhelmed. Multi-tasking is generally a myth. People are able to perform one task well at a time, while any additional tasks typically are put on auto pilot. This is the problem with texting and driving for example.

As we reviewed the difficulties that he had and the reasons for them, it became clearer why he was having struggles when he got to middle school. In elementary school tasks were meant to be mastered one at a time, and he was able to keep up. Behavior was not a problem. When he got to sixth grade, he now had many teachers instead of one, and his ability to keep up with the level of organization expected was stretched. Additionally the types of tasks that he was asked to do were now more complex, and he no longer had a single teacher who knew him well and could communicate with his parents when he was having struggles. Based on school testing, he indeed did not qualify for any special help, such as resource help, but based on his ADHD diagnosis he now qualified for 504 plan interventions.

We discussed some possible options that might be helpful for him. He and his parents agreed to a trial on stimulant medication to help with the focusing component. They met with his school counselor and some of the teachers. They had already arranged to help by having him in an extra study class that was designed to help him get his homework done and stay organized. Additionally, during times where he was being asked to multi-task, several of his teachers agreed to provide him with lecture notes so that he just had to listen and pay attention. They set up a tracking program for him so that he, his teachers and parents all knew what was expected and when assignments were due and to be sure they were completed and turned in on time. A number of additional accommodations were made.

He was seen back in a month, to follow up on the medication trial and recommendations. He seemed a bit more positive and stated he felt like he could concentrate a little bit better and felt hopeful that the accommodations would make school less stressful. By the end of the year he was passing all of his classes, and was looking forward to high school. His anger and anxiousness were much diminished.

Variations on this scenario are commonly seen in this age group. Children with ADHD inattentive type who don't have behavioral problems often don't come to attention until their struggles become more profound in middle school. In elementary school students have only one or very few teachers, who are quick to communicate with parents when there are struggles. During those years, parents will often help their children with homework and elementary students are supervised fairly closely. The system changes drastically in middle school and often children go from receiving a lot of support from parents and teachers to almost a college-level environment and expectations. They now have multiple classes and teachers, with schedule changes each term, and they do not have the close supervision in school they had in elementary school. Also, adolescents may become resentful of their parents' attempts to assist in homework, and enforce good grades. Often the consequences are failing grades, increasing frustration and sometimes eventually increasing anxiety, depression and oppositional behavior. Behavior may be chalked up to adolescence or hormones, and perhaps that plays a role, but the environmental expectations are very different between elementary and middle school, and can lead to a lot of frustrations for students who struggle to make the transition.

A classic example of this in our school district has been the big projects that are done in different grades. In the past, in fifth grade, all of the children were expected to do a social studies project on a state, where they were expected to learn all about the state, and summarize it in a poster presentation. They worked on this project for months. To accomplish the end results, the teachers would break the project into different sections. Initially, the students would just choose the state they were interested in. Then they would learn how to find out about different resources. The teachers would then help them find books and reading materials on their particular topic, and each day a new component of the project was learned. Each day there was a new task related to the overall project, and when many weeks went by, there was an end product that each of the students could be proud of, and they were all now experts on their chosen state.

Contrast this to the sixth or seventh grade science projects. At the beginning of the year, each student was told they were expected to do a science project on an area of their choice. These would be presented at the end of the year in the science fair, and there would be a competition and awards. Although there was some help during the year on making sure the projects were chosen and some help, the stepwise approach from elementary school was absent. It was almost universal that all students and their parents stayed up all night the night before the science fair completing the project at the last minute, and there was often a lot of pain and anguish in completing this assignment. Imagine the difficulties for those students who had ADHD and/or learning difficulties.

Clinical Conditions

There are several categories that we need to define. These may be defined differently depending on whether it is from a clinical assessment such as from a physician, psychologist, speech or occupational therapist, or from an educational assessment such as would be done in school. Clinical diagnoses are based on the most recent criteria as defined in the DSM 5. First is *intellectual disability* or *intellectual developmental disorder*. This term replaces the old mental retardation category, and describes individuals with "intellectual and adaptive functioning deficits in conceptual, social, and practical domains." This would be diagnosed based on scores on a standard IQ test and also a measure of adaptive functioning, which assesses how well an individual is able to function in their environment compared with others of the same age and socio-cultural background. The term global developmental delay is used for individuals who are under the age of 5 when testing cannot be reliably done, but there is evidence of delays in several areas of intellectual functioning.

Second is *specific learning disorder*. This refers to having difficulties learning and using academic skills in a particular area, especially effecting learning in reading, writing or math. These areas include reading out loud, reading comprehension, spelling difficulties, difficulties with written expression, difficulties with math facts and calculation and difficulties with mathematical problem solving. A diagnosis is made if the area of difficulty is significantly below what is expected for age and educational opportunity. Formerly, learning disorders were diagnosed based on a discrepancy between IQ scores and achievement scores, but this is no longer necessarily the case. However, diagnosing a learning disorder assumes average intelligence, or that the area of learning is significantly below what is expected if intellectual disability is present. Learning disorders are a developmental condition and not due to specific neurologic problems such as injuries, hearing or vision problems or other neurologic conditions. Technically one could have difficulties in any area of learning including such things as mechanical skills, athletic skills and so on, but these are not so important for academic success. The term developmental coordination disorder is used for individuals whose acquisition of motor skills is significantly below expected age, and not due to intellectual disability or sensory or neurologic conditions.

Third are *communication disorders* that include difficulties in language, speech and communication. Speech refers to the production of sounds and articulation, language refers to using words to communicate, and communication includes not just language but also nonverbal communication such as body language, facial expressions, and gestures. One can have a language disorder in expressive and/or receptive language, and again is defined as language abilities that are significantly below what is expected for age. Speech and language disorders are often diagnosed at an early age, because of speech delays or articulation problems.

Educational Terms and IDEA

Clinical diagnoses made by clinicians are not necessarily the same as educational terms and diagnoses. Schools are given the task of identifying conditions that adversely affect a child's ability to learn in the regular school classroom to determine whether they are eligible for special education services. Clinical diagnoses are made based on meeting criteria for a particular condition, regardless of whether they affect school performance. A little background will help. Prior to 1975, schools were not required to admit those they felt were not educable, and a large percentage of children with disabilities did not receive an adequate appropriate education. Many were in institutional settings. This changed with the passage of PL 94–142, the Education for All Handicapped Children Act, in 1975. In 1990 the act was reauthorized by Congress and the name changed to the Individuals with Disabilities Education Act (IDEA). The last revision of IDEA was in 2004. In 1975, nearly 1.8 million children with disabilities were excluded from public schools, and now through IDEA legislation 6.9 million children with disabilities receive special education services specific to their needs. It is hard to believe that so much has changed in educational opportunities in so short of a time, but these legislative and policy changes over the last 43 years have hugely changed the face of education for millions of those with disabilities. We are all astounded with the remarkable developments in technology with computers and the internet, but this seems no less remarkable a development in the area of public policy.

The stated purpose of the IDEA is:

- to ensure that all children with disabilities have available to them a free appropriate public education that emphasizes special education and related services designed to meet their unique needs and prepare them for further education, employment, and independent living;
- to ensure that the rights of children with disabilities and parents of such children are protected;
- to assist States, localities, educational service agencies, and Federal agencies to provide for the education of all children with disabilities;
- to assist States in the implementation of a statewide, comprehensive, coordinated, multidisciplinary, interagency system of early intervention services for infants and toddlers with disabilities and their families;
- to ensure that educators and parents have the necessary tools to improve educational results for children with disabilities by supporting system improvement activities; coordinated research and personnel preparation; coordinated technical assistance, dissemination, and support; and technology development and media services;
- to assess, and ensure the effectiveness of, efforts to educate children with disabilities.

Source: Education for All Handicapped Children's Act of 1975[1]

Essential components of IDEA include the right to a free and appropriate public education in the least restrictive environment (meaning mainstream classes as much as feasible and reasonable), appropriate evaluation, development of an individual educational program specific to the needs of the child (IEP) after appropriate assessment and evaluation, with parent and teacher participation, as well as rules governing procedural safeguards. There are 13 categories under which students may be eligible, including specific learning disabilities, autism, hearing and vision impairments, intellectual disability, speech or language disabilities, post traumatic brain injuries, orthopedic disabilities, emotional disturbance, and other health impairment, which includes conditions such as ADHD, seizure disorders, severe cardiac conditions and others, which must be of a degree that they adversely affect the child's educational performance. As of 2014, 6.6 million children ages 3–21 in the United States were receiving special education services, 13 percent of all public school students. Of these 35% had specific learning disabilities, 20% had speech or language impairment, 13% other health impairment, 9% autism and 6% intellectual disability.[2]

So what is the process for helping a student who is having significant school challenges? If a child is struggling in school, there are a number of steps that may occur. Prior to 2004, the discrepancy model was used to determine eligibility for special education services based on having a specific learning disability. This meant there had to be a significant difference between the IQ score and academic performance based on achievement test scores. The problem with this model was that if tested too early, the discrepancy may not have been enough to qualify for services, and required the student to fall well behind classroom peers before a learning disorder classification could be determined. In other words, the school had to wait long enough for the child to fail before being able to intervene. This is no longer required. As part of IDEA, children can now receive initial services before formal evaluation for learning disabilities. Initially they may receive early intervening services which are meant to be extra help for students who are falling behind for any reason, in the regular classroom. This may include small group instruction, small reading groups, remedial reading and other help. If these are effective, no further intervention is needed.

A more formal next step is the response to intervention (RTI) model. Children found to be at risk for educational delay based on school screening tests receive supplemental instruction such as small group instruction, and progress is monitored closely through curriculum based assessments. If there is still inadequate progress, they will then receive more intensive interventions, and eventually interventions that are individualized, intensive and target the specific skills deficit. Failure to progress with these interventions would then warrant a formal psychoeducational evaluation. The advantage of this approach is that students are targeted earlier, before they fall seriously behind, and before undergoing a formal evaluation. If these methods are helpful, no additional investigation or interventions are required. They are monitored closely with brief frequent curriculum based testing, and if significant improvement is not seen, then they move on to the next tier. The lack of progress with response to intervention is one of the variables taken into account to determine whether a student qualifies for special education services.

Another similar model is MTSS or multi-tier system of supports. This includes universal screening for all students each year, and attempts to identify early any students who are struggling. It includes not only academic concerns but social, emotional and behavioral concerns. It may include the RTI model, but also may incorporate behavior intervention plans. Increasing support is provided as the need is demonstrated, ultimately leading to a formal special education evaluation and specific testing if necessary.

ADHD and Learning Disabilities

Because of the high prevalence of learning disabilities in children with ADHD, there should be a very low threshold for testing for learning disabilities in children who are suspected of having ADHD. Testing is generally fairly straightforward and often is done through the school district. Generally this testing is done by school psychologists or other special educators designated who are trained in psychoeducational testing. The actual testing varies depending on the protocols of the school district and the state in which they reside, but generally entails doing a standardized measure of intelligence and also achievement tests in any areas of concern, typically reading, math and writing. Language testing is also often important to do, as language difficulties are also very common. Language difficulties may include having trouble understanding spoken language (receptive language), being able to use language to speak (expressive language), and using language and higher level communication skills to communicate (pragmatic language). This testing is typically done by a speech therapist.

Measures that are commonly used for IQ testing include the Wechsler Intelligence Scale for Children (WISC-V, now the fifth edition), the Stanford–Binet–V, and the Woodcock Johnson III Tests of Cognitive Abilities. There are likewise a number of different achievement tests that may be used, including the Wechsler Individual Achievement Test (WIAT-III), the Woodcock Johnson IV Tests of Achievement or the Kaufman Test of Educational Achievement (KTEA-3). There are also many different tests used to assess all aspects of speech and language. These are all heavily researched and normed based on testing children of all ages and have a high degree of validity and reliability. Behavioral questionnaires screening for autism, ADHD and other neurodevelopmental conditions may also be included.

After testing, the examiner and other appropriate personnel will meet with the family and review results. Sometimes this meeting can be overwhelming for parents, with the presentation of a large amount of bewildering material and results, often accompanied by a lot of statements delineating legal rights and requirements. Understanding the test results is not difficult, but interpreting the meaning of the results can be a challenge. Each of the previously mentioned tests and most others are based on a standard score of 100, meaning at any given age the average score in the area being tested is 100. If you remember the bell curve that shows normal population distributions of any given trait, this applies to psychoeducational testing as well. The standard deviation on these measures is usually 15, which would give an average range of normal scores of 85–115. So typically any child scoring within that range will be considered to have scored in the normal range on that particular test. A child is expected to have achievement scores that are similar to the IQ score.

One of the challenges with interpreting results is the assumption that the results are valid. There are obviously many factors that may impact the child's scores on these tests. These tests are intensive and exhausting, and are usually done in a one-on-one setting with the examiner. Ideally the test results reflect the individual's true abilities based on the student's best effort, but for many reasons this may not be the case. If the child is ill or sleep

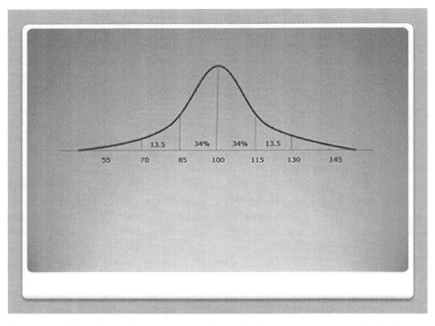

Figure 5.1 The figure shows a normal distribution pattern of standard IQ and achievement tests, with standard deviation of 15. Some 68% of the population will score between 85 and 115, 95% between 70 and 130. A similar pattern would be seen if the average were 500 and standard deviation 100. Likewise, T-scores that are commonly used in behavior questionnaires have a mean of 50 and standard deviation of 10.

deprived this will impact the results. Likewise if the child has difficulty focusing because of ADHD, he or she may not perform as well on these measures. Years ago we published a study from our clinic comparing psychoeducational testing results in children who were diagnosed with ADHD before and after treatment. Generally IQ scores were considerably higher in children who were being treated with medication, than in those who had ADHD and did not take medication.[3] This does not mean that the medication made them smarter, but that the results were likely a better representation of the student's true abilities because they were now able to focus better. Likely the same thing applies to achievement tests. It is certainly true that scores can vary over time and so testing results must always be interpreted carefully.

Individualized Educational Program

After testing, an IEP (individualized education program) will be developed for each student meeting qualification requirements. The IEP plan and goals are formulated by the IEP team which is made of the child's parents, teachers, special education representative, and an administrative representative who knows the availability of resources in the school district, and any others who are deemed appropriate, including at times the student. The intent is to provide the means to an appropriate education that fits the needs of the child and in the least restrictive environment. The IEP includes a statement about the student's current level of functioning and academic level. It will also include goals that are being targeted and services and interventions to be put in place to meet those goals. This may include resource help for the particular area of difficulty, accommodations to be put in place, such as special testing environments, accommodations in the classroom setting, and so on. IEP's are reviewed yearly with the IEP team, and updated as needed. Reevaluations are generally done every 3 years to determine if the student still needs services.

504 plan

Students who have medical conditions or disabilities that are impacting their ability to learn in the regular school environment but don't qualify for IEP services, can also get help through a 504 plan. The name comes from section 504 of the Rehabilitation Act of 1973, which prohibits discrimination of individuals with disabilities in any federally funded program, including schools. A 504 plan is different from an IEP in that it doesn't provide individualized instruction, but is a means of establishing accommodations that can be helpful.

Examples of accommodations might include dividing work tasks into smaller segments that are to be completed before the next set, so as to seem less overwhelming, such as in the 5th grade social studies project above. Or, working in small groups or peer tutoring so each student can help each other to accomplish the task. Students with ADHD will often do better sitting near the front of the room if possible, as opposed to the back of the room next to open doors and windows and other distractions. One creative teacher in our district allowed the student to be out of his seat, but had to be within reach of his seat at all times, and had to agree to not disrupt the other students. He thrived in that environment. Handwriting is often laborious and illegible in students with ADHD, and accommodations might include being allowed to keyboard or even dictate homework assignments. Frequently parents will report that homework takes hours of time and is a frustrating and painful process. Sometimes it can help to have teachers require an amount of time of productive homework as opposed to amount of work accomplished. Work completed is frequently not turned in (once the student's parents are no longer supervising, it is out of sight and out of mind), so developing a tracking plan so teachers, parents and the student all know what is required, when it is due, and if it has been turned in. There are many accommodations that could potentially be made, and which ones are ultimately implemented is determined by the team setting up the 504 program, where problems and potential solutions are agreed upon. The 504 plan is not as formal as an IEP, and the rules are less stringent, but it is an avenue to provide extra help for some struggling students.

Sometimes a student will have significant academic struggles, but not qualify for any specific school interventions. At times resources outside school may need to be utilized, such as tutoring, occupational therapy and counselling. But the greatest resource for helping the child with learning challenges is the school, and having a good relationship with school personnel, and understanding how different school services can help is essential for assuring school success.

Bibliography

1. S. 6–94th Congress: Education For All Handicapped Children Act. www.govtrack.us. 1975. February 11, 2019. https://Www.Govtrack.Us/Congress/Bills/94/S6
2. National Center for Education Statistics. Fast Facts, Students with Disabilities. https://nces.ed.gov/fastfacts/display.asp?id=64.
3. Gimpel GA, Collett BR, Veeder MA, et al. Effects of stimulant medication on cognitive performance of children with ADHD. *Clin Pediatr (Phila).* 2005;44 (5):405–411. doi:10.1177/000992280504400504.

6 Disruptive Behavior Disorders

J. Dennis Odell

Mitch was 8 when he first came to our office for evaluation. He was accompanied by his parents, who stated they were having trouble managing his behavior. He became angry very easily, and would argue about everything. It didn't seem to matter whether he agreed or not, whatever his parents said, he would argue with them. He frequently got into trouble at school for aggressive behavior towards peers, and for being defiant with teachers. Whenever he got in trouble, he always had a story about how it was the other person's fault, and lately had taken to lying and stealing. Even when confronted by adult witnesses, he would stand by his story. He had few friends because of his volatile behavior. Although he was well aware of the rules at home, he frequently ignored them; seemingly thinking they did not apply to him. He fought often with his 2 younger siblings, and the home was not a happy place because of his frequent disruptive behavior. His mother gave an example, where getting into the car, he wanted to sit in the seat his sister was already occupying. She refused to move, and he smacked her in the head and started shoving. When told to sit in the other seat, he screamed that she always got that seat, and he hated her. This was a many times a day occurrence. He responded to what he perceived as unreasonable requests with anger and aggression, kicking and hitting, and tantruming. Classmates and siblings had learned to avoid him as his temper was unpredictable, and he often lashed out at anyone who got in his way. He pushed, tripped and hit schoolmates, and the school threatened to expel him on more than one occasion. In discussion with Mitch, he stated that he enjoyed outdoor activities, and watching TV and playing video games. He liked building with Legos. He stated he hated school, and especially homework. When asked about friendships, he stated he had many friends, but often they annoyed him. He agreed he didn't get along with his siblings, as they often bothered him. He felt that since he was the oldest, he should have first choice in everything at home, and didn't seem to understand the concept of sharing or being a good example for his younger siblings.

Academically he seemed to be bright, and was keeping up, but he often didn't complete assigned work. His teacher reported that there was no evidence of learning problems, and he understood the material well. In reviewing past medical history, he was generally very healthy and there were no obvious medical causes for his behavior. Family history was positive for ADHD in cousins and uncles, as well as several family members who had been incarcerated and others who had gotten in trouble for drug abuse. Evaluation included behavioral questionnaires from caregivers and his teacher, as well as review of school information, and he was diagnosed with Oppositional Defiant Disorder (ODD). His assessment was also positive for ADHD, with a significant impulsive component.

He was treated with stimulant medication and also with a strong recommendation to see a child psychologist for behavioral therapy. At follow-up one month later, he was doing better as far as academics, and seemed a bit less aggressive, but would still have frequent oppositional episodes, and the arguing did not abate. He also had some significant rebound effects from the medication, and so behavior in the evening remained problematic. They had not accessed behavioral therapy. The medication was continued, with some dosage adjustment, but again recommended getting help from a behavioral therapist, which they did. Over time, behaviors gradually improved, and his parents agreed many of the behavioral interventions that were recommended helped a lot to minimize behavioral problems. Irritable mood improved, he seemed generally happier, and school performance improved. He also took more interest in group activities, including baseball and soccer.

Oppositional Defiant Disorder

This case scenario demonstrates a classic presentation for a child with both ADHD and oppositional defiant disorder. Of all the associated conditions, ODD is the one most commonly associated with ADHD, with estimates of co-occurrence of about 40%.[1] Oftentimes non-compliant behavior is attributed to ADHD. But oppositional behavior is not part of the core symptoms of ADHD. If a parent asks a child to go upstairs to clean their room, there will be different explanations for lack of compliance 2 hours later. The child with ADHD will have started to go his room to clean it as asked, but along the way noticed a sibling playing a video game or watching TV. Attention was then diverted to that activity, and when later asked why the room wasn't cleaned as requested, will innocently reply "I forgot". On the other hand, the oppositional child had no intention of cleaning his room, because he was doing something else, and didn't want to. When pushed to do as asked, he will argue and tantrum and do anything to get out of doing something he doesn't want to do. Oppositional defiant behavior might be described as behavior that is typical for a 2 year old, with willful defiance of authority, regardless of whether that authority is a parent, teacher, or other adult. Behavior is often angry and aggressive.

In the DSM-5 definition, symptoms include angry and irritable mood, manifesting as often losing temper, is touchy or easily annoyed, and often angry and resentful. Additionally there is argumentative and defiant behavior, manifesting as often arguing with authority figures, often actively defiant or refusing to comply with requests from authority figures, deliberately annoying others and often blaming others for mistakes or misbehavior. Finally there may be a component of vindictiveness. By definition symptoms should have been present for at least 6 months, and be at developmentally inappropriate levels. As in all of the conditions that we have discussed, symptoms should be enough to significantly impact life functioning of the individual.[2] Symptoms of ODD may be present in 2-year old children, but may be hard to distinguish from typical 2-year old behaviour (terrible twos). However in those with ODD, symptoms do not improve as expected with age and normal disciplinary practices.

As with ADHD, ODD appears to be more common in boys, but may be underreported in girls, and most outcome studies looking at long term complications have looked more at males than females. Girls may show less physical aggression, and symptoms may be manifested as verbal attacks, lying, excluding others, maliciousness, refusal to talk and noncompliance.[3] Social media and cyber bullying have made more available opportunities for aggressive behavior towards peers. As with boys with ADHD, about 40% of girls with ADHD also have oppositional defiant disorder.[4] For both genders, as with ADHD, there may be a strong genetic component, but there also is a higher likelihood of family social difficulties and mental health problems. Parental depression is common, and may improve as the child's oppositional behavior improves.[5] Factors such as poverty, disrupted family life, abuse and neglect, and ineffective disciplinary practices increase the risk of oppositional defiant behavior. Likewise parental mental health and substance abuse disorders increase the risk.

Oppositional behavior may begin at an early age. Young children may respond to unwanted requests, demands or frustration by tantruming or being defiant. If that leads to withdrawal of the request, or if they then get what they want, then they have learned that having a tantrum brings about the desired effect, meaning the child gets what s/he wants (negative reinforcement). Some parents may respond by giving the child more attention, trying to reason with the child or bargaining, again reinforcing the behavior (positive reinforcement). And some may respond by yelling or escalating demands, and if done consistently, the child learns that s/he doesn't need to respond until the parental demands are very significant and repeated. Parents and their oppositional child may be in a cycle of behaviors and responses that are counterproductive. It is these non-productive behavioral responses that are targeted in behavioral therapy, and that if addressed early, can lead to good results with more appropriate behavioral responses to frustration.

A good percentage of young children with oppositional defiant disorder improve with age and especially with treatment. But there is a significant long term risk for the development of conduct disorder, antisocial personality disorder and substance abuse, so early and appropriate intervention is indicated for prevention of later complications. In our general pediatric clinic, we have instituted a preventive mental health program that is geared for all parents of 2 year olds. The program provides behavior management strategies for the oppositional behaviors that are typical of 2 year olds, with the intent that early appropriate parental interventions of problematic behaviors in 2 year olds will lessen the likelihood of sustained behavior problems later in life.

Although oppositional defiant disorder is strongly associated with ADHD, it appears the hyperactivity and impulsivity component carry the biggest risk, and strictly inattentive type of ADHD carries a lower risk of associated ODD. As in the above case scenario, the primary intervention that is helpful is behavioral therapy, including parent training to help parents learn effective strategies to manage the child's behavior, social skills training to help the child learn how to interact more positively with peers, and cognitive behavioral therapy to learn positive more socially acceptable ways to respond when frustrated. Because there is such a high rate of concomitant family mental health and environmental issues, treatment may not be effective without considering a whole family approach. Medication has a place, especially if there are associated ADHD or mental health disorders such as anxiety, depression and bipolar disorder. Medications that are shown to be helpful include stimulant medications, atomoxetine and guanfacine. [6] Additionally risperidone is shown to be helpful, at least on a short-term basis, but also comes with a lot of side effects.[7],[8] For those with ADHD, it appears that the combination of ADHD and disruptive behavior problems carries the highest risk for long-term complications, and is probably the most difficult to treat of the ADHD comorbidities.

It is important in treating oppositional behavior to develop a good understanding of where the behavior is coming from. As with any behavior, there may be hidden triggers for the behaviors that are being displayed. Some children just have oppositional behavior that stems from an attitude of "I'm not going to do it and you can't make me". However some may appear to have oppositional behavior, but it may be manifest for a different reason. For example individuals with autism or Asperger syndrome may have extreme sensory issues, such as extreme fear of loud noises. If that individual is required to go to school where there may be fire alarms or loud chaotic lunchroom environments, the ensuing physical discomfort may be overwhelming, resulting in refusal to go to school. This is not oppositional behavior per se, but self-preservation. This may be seen in those with extreme anxiety, obsessive-compulsive disorder and depression as well. Interventions will vary depending on the cause of the behavior.

Conduct Disorder

Conduct disorder is frequently associated with oppositional defiant disorder, and children with ODD may develop conduct disorder as they age, especially into adolescence. It is defined as behavior that violates the basic rights of others, or societal norms or rules. This includes aggression to people and animals, including bullying, threatening, initiating physical fights or use of a weapon that can cause physical harm. It includes physical cruelty to people or animals, stealing or forced sexual activities. It includes destruction of property, theft, and serious violation of rules such as truancy, running away from home or breaking firmly set curfew rules. These may be associated with lack of remorse, lack of empathy, no concern about school or work performance and emotionally flat or insincere. Symptoms should have been present for at least 12 months.[2] Symptoms may be present in young children, but more often are seen in older children and adolescents who have previously been diagnosed with oppositional defiant disorder. Symptoms may improve by young adulthood, but risk for adult antisocial personality, drug abuse and criminal behavior is significant.

Bibliography

1. Brown RT, Freeman WS, Perrin JM, et al. Prevalence and assessment of attention-deficit / hyperactivity disorder in primary care settings. *Pediatrics*. 2001;107 (3):e43. doi: https://doi.org/10.1542/peds.107.3.e43.
2. American Psychiatric Association. Taskforce on DSM-5. *Diagnostic and Statistical Manual of Mental Disorders*, 5th ed. 2013. doi:10.1176/appi. books.9780890425596.744053.
3. Trepat E, Ezpeleta L. Sex differences in oppositional defiant disorder. *Psichothema*. 2011;23:666–671.
4. Tung I, Li JJ, Meza JI, et al. Patterns of comorbidity among girls with ADHD : A meta-analysis. *Pediatrics*. 2016;138(4):e20160430. doi:10.1542/peds.2016-0430.
5. Katzmann J, Dopfner M, Gortz-Dorten A. Child-based treatment of oppositional defiant disorder: mediating effects on parental depression, anxiety and stress. *Eur Child Adolesc Psychiatry*. June2018. doi:10.1007/s00787-018-1181-5.
6. Pringsheim T, Hirsch L, Gardner D, Gorman DA. The pharmacological management of oppositional behaviour, conduct problems, and aggression in children and adolescents with attention-deficit hyperactivity disorder, oppositional defiant disorder, and conduct disorder: A systematic review and meta-analysis. *Can J Psychiatry*. 2015;60(2):42–51. doi:10.1177/070674371506000202.
7. Pringsheim T, Hirsch L, Gardner D, Gorman DA. The pharmacological management of oppositional behaviour, conduct problems, and aggression in children and adolescents with attention-deficit hyperactivity disorder, oppositional defiant disorder, and conduct disorder: a systematic review and meta-analysis. *Can J Psychiatry*. 2015;60(2):52–61. doi:10.1177/070674371506000203.
8. Loy JH, Merry SN, Hetrick SE, Stasiak K. Atypical antipsychotics for disruptive behaviour disorders in children and youths. *Cochrane Database Syst Rev*. 2017;8: CD008559. doi:10.1002/14651858.CD008559.pub3.

7 Anxiety, Mood Disorders and ADHD

J. Dennis Odell

Anxiety Disorders and ADHD

Samuel was 8 years old when he was first seen in the pediatric clinic with concerns about nausea, abdominal pain, and headaches. These symptoms had been present for several years. Sometimes, they were severe enough that he was missing school. They were less prevalent on weekends and did not seem to be a problem over the summer. He had no fever associated with this, no change in bowel habits, no unusual travel history, no known toxic exposure, and no weight loss, although weight gain had slowed. He struggled academically in school, and both he and his mother reported that he was bullied at times. He reported that he did not like going to school because it was hard. He usually had to stay in at recess to catch up on work, and often spent hours doing homework. Physical examination was unremarkable, except that his weight was low compared to his height. Basic labs were ordered and were unremarkable. Behavioral questionnaires were sent home and Samuel completed an anxiety questionnaire. Parents and his teacher reported that behavior was generally good but he could be defiant at times. He had friends, but tended to be shy. Academically, he was performing somewhat below grade level, and seemed lost at times. Profiles on the questionnaires were consistent in showing that he struggled with attention problems, a little bit with behavior, and significantly with anxiety. He was diagnosed with ADHD inattentive type, with associated learning difficulties, and anxiety. Treatment was directed at each of these, and over time, his abdominal pain, and headaches resolved.

Anxiety disorders are extremely common in children with an estimated prevalence of 12–25% of children and adolescents experiencing an anxiety disorder at some time.[1] They very commonly co-occur with ADHD with 25–60% of children with ADHD suffering from at least one anxiety disorder.[2] The DSM-5 categorizes a number of different anxiety disorders, listed in order of typical developmental onset. These include separation anxiety, selective mutism, specific phobia, social anxiety disorder, panic disorder, agoraphobia, and generalized anxiety disorder. Each of these disorders shares features of excessive fear (emotional response to real or perceived imminent threat), anxiety (anticipation of future threat), and related behavioral disturbances.[3] We all experience anxiety as part of life, but those with anxiety disorders have symptoms that far exceed what is expected given developmental level, and enough that they are seriously impacting the life of the individual. Somatic symptoms, such as nausea, headaches, diarrhea and abdominal pain are extremely common.

Separation anxiety refers to the fearfulness, associated with separation from specific caregivers, to a degree that is developmentally inappropriate. This is very common in preschoolers and in kindergarten, but should be less of an issue as the child gets older. Selective mutism refers to limited or no speech in certain environments. These children may not speak at all or very softly at school and other locations outside of the home, but speak very well in the home environment. Specific phobias refer to excessive fears in a specific situation, such as fear of dogs or flying or heights. Social anxiety refers to difficulties in social situations such as groups or at school. There is often a fear of being embarrassed or judged, and individuals will often consciously avoid uncomfortable situations. Panic attacks occur when there is overwhelming fear in a specific situation that leads to loss of emotional control. Agoraphobia refers to anxiety surrounding situations such as being in crowded or enclosed places, or other similar situations. Lastly, generalized anxiety disorder refers to a general overall sense of worry that is pervasive and in many different situations. And of course, those who have been severely traumatized in any way may suffer from post-traumatic stress disorder with associated anxiety.[3]

Symptoms of ADHD and anxiety often overlap. Children with anxiety disorders may appear to have attention problems, because they are thinking about whatever it is they are worried about instead of what they are supposed to be attending to. They may have behavior outbursts and oppositional behavior when they are forced into situations that aggravate their anxiety. Sometimes anxiety is a secondary symptom of ADHD due to challenges and frustrations that come about with struggles associated with school, behavioral and social difficulties consequent to the ADHD. And, frequently ADHD and anxiety coexist as two separate disorders. Usually, there is a very strong family history for others in the family with similar difficulties. In all of these situations behavioral disturbances, sleep problems, physical/somatic symptoms and school failure are common occurrences. Those that have autism as a comorbidity will have an even higher likelihood of also having anxiety.

Anxiety symptoms may not be obvious. Individuals may experience anxious thoughts and fears without expressing them or manifesting any outward symptoms. Symptoms that are manifest may be unrecognized as stemming primarily from anxiety, such as physical symptoms such as abdominal pain, sleep problem or headaches, or behavioral problems including irritability and oppositional behavior, or even restlessness and inattention. Significant anxiety may persist for years before being recognized. In addition to ADHD, those with a specific anxiety disorder also may experience other anxiety disorders, and co-occurrence with depression is very common.

A certain amount of worry is healthy. If we are preparing a talk or lecture and are fearful of not performing well, we will prepare or practice, and that is a good thing. If we do not worry about danger (as is frequently the case in those with ADHD), we face physical harm. But perseverating on a fear can be incapacitating. If we worry so much about embarrassment when giving a lecture, we may just avoid it entirely, and growth stops. Excessive worry comes from perseverating about a fear and being unable to get it out of our minds. At an extreme, fear may be appropriate for those who have experienced traumatic life events, such as being physically, sexually or emotionally abused or physical trauma such as being in a motor vehicle accident, natural disaster or others. When Elizabeth Smart was in the news so much after being kidnapped, there was a clear spike in the numbers of young children (and parents) seeking help for anxiety and fears about personal safety. Our ready access to everything happening in the world today through electronic media with such emphasis on sensational events has made the world seem out of control, and it is an issue we all must deal with. Additionally ready access to social media and its associated challenges increases the opportunities for experiencing anxiety. Perhaps the current trend towards uncivility and lack of discussion stems from our collective sense of anxiety and need to preserve what we think of as our values, and an attempt to maintain our comfort zones.

In treating the combination of ADHD and anxiety, it is appropriate to try to identify which is the principal disorder, or at least the one leading to the most distress, and targeting that first. Often, if ADHD symptoms can be reduced, with resultant decrease in stress and frustration, anxiety symptoms may naturally diminish. Likewise, for those with primary anxiety, decreasing anxiety symptoms may result in less physical symptoms, less stress, better sleep and improved attention. Often however both need to be treated. It is appropriate to consider medicines for both, but as important is including therapy, especially cognitive behavior therapy (CBT) and other forms of psychotherapy that have a proven track record in ameliorating the symptoms of anxiety. The combination of cognitive behavior therapy and medication is very affective for treating all varieties of anxiety, and for those who also have ADHD, adding CBT leads to much higher rates of improvement in long term outcomes.

Depression and ADHD

Lara was 9 years old when she was first evaluated at our clinic. She was struggling academically, and lately was having anger outbursts that were uncharacteristic of her, and symptoms were worsening. She was in fourth grade and had struggled in school since first grade. Homework took hours, and, in spite of all the effort, she was barely getting by in school. She had friends and normally got along well with them, but lately she was withdrawing and not participating in activities with her friends. There had been a question of learning disabilities because of her school struggles, but scores on psychoeducational testing were all in the normal range. She and her parents were told she just needed to work harder and be more organized, as she did good work when she put in the effort. Because she wasn't getting all her work completed, she had to complete it at home, and in fact she started losing privileges until she could get caught up on homework, including her favorite activity, which was spending an hour each day working with her father in his shop. Past medical history was unremarkable for any significant health issues. Family history was positive for depression and anxiety. Physical exam was unremarkable, although she was very withdrawn and hard to engage in discussion. She warmed up eventually and said she was very frustrated in school. She felt she tried hard to keep up, and didn't know why it took so long to get her work done. In class she didn't always understand the instructions or material, and then would get behind, and seemingly never caught up. When asked what she did for fun, she said she didn't have time for fun anymore because she spent all her time doing schoolwork. She said she felt like giving up because nothing she did seemed to work and she must just be stupid. She had expressed to her parents during one of her crying episodes that she felt she would be better off dead.

School testing was reviewed, and showed no evidence of intellectual or learning problems. There were frequent reports of off task behavior, daydreaming, not working up to potential, missed assignments, and lately, school absences. She was reportedly well behaved in school, and seemed to be well liked and got along with peers well. Lately she seemed sad and disengaged. Behavioral questionnaires were completed by parents, teachers and Lara, and results were consistently high for inattention, but also for depression. Scores were high for sluggish cognitive tempo as well. Initially it was felt the depression was secondary to the frustrations related to school and demands exceeding her capacity to accomplish. She was started on stimulant medication, and also started working with a counselor. The counselor recommended ensuring that she had at least 1–2 hours per day, time that was not tied into school or homework and wasn't something that was taken away as punishment, but that was just her time to do whatever she wanted. She also was able to have accommodations at school based on her ADHD and depression diagnoses that provided her with help in school to keep up on her work, and volume of homework expected was decreased. With these measures she improved significantly, but there remained some sadness and depression symptoms that didn't resolve, and she was ultimately started on antidepressant medication as well. It took some time, but over the next 6–12 months symptoms gradually improved, and although school struggles remained, her mood, irritability and overall attitude improved remarkably. She continued to receive counselling help, continued with 504 accommodations, and remained on both stimulant and antidepressant medications.

As with anxiety, a high proportion of those diagnosed with ADHD also have depression, and as with anxiety, symptoms may be secondary to the stresses and frustrations associated with ADHD, or there may be primary depression independent of the ADHD. A significant percentage of adolescents with depression endorse many symptoms of ADHD as well.[4] Actual prevalence is difficult to determine because of overlapping symptoms, failure to recognize internalizing symptoms of anxiety or depression and changes with age, but the overall risk is sizeable. With the increased risk of depression, and with impulsivity as a core feature of ADHD, the risk for suicidal ideation and suicide attempts is increased for those with both disorders. Additional increased risk factors associated with suicide in ADHD are risks for substance abuse and conduct disorders.[5]

Two major categories of depression are major depressive disorder (MDD) and persistent depressive disorder (dysthymia). MDD is characterized by at least several weeks of symptoms that are a change from previous functioning that includes persistent sadness, emptiness and feelings of hopelessness. In children this may be manifest as excessive irritability. There is decreased interest, pleasure and participation in usual activities. Additional symptoms may include weight loss, sleep disturbances, feelings of agitation or decreased energy, fatigue, feelings of worthlessness, attention difficulties, indecisiveness and suicidal thoughts.[3] These are more than the common fluctuations in mood that most people experience, and are to a degree that they are significantly impacting daily function. Symptoms may be severe enough to be incapacitating. Whereas those with MDD have a distinct period or periods of severe depressive symptoms, those with dysthymia have chronic persistent lower level of depressive symptoms that may last for years. Individuals with dysthymia, because symptoms are so persistent, may not even be aware that their symptoms are abnormal.

As with all associated disorders with ADHD, a high index of suspicion is helpful to not miss associated depression, and screening for depression and carefully reviewing family history to assess for genetic predisposition is important in any ADHD evaluation. Treating the ADHD symptoms may make a significant impact in depression symptoms, but it is not uncommon to have both disorders independently, and both need to be addressed and treated. ADHD medication and antidepressants may be necessary, as well as counselling. Medications of all varieties including stimulants for ADHD may contribute to mood symptoms and irritability, so it is important to consider medication side effects as a possible cause of depression symptoms.

ADHD and Bipolar Disorder

Bipolar disorder is one of the conditions that commonly co-occurs with ADHD, and is particularly confusing because symptoms often overlap. One of the reasons for adverse reactions to medications used to treat ADHD is the presence of unrecognized bipolar disorder. Bipolar disorder has been described even in ancient times, and has been a known entity for centuries, but it has until relatively recently been felt to be very rare in childhood. There is much controversy and uncertainty about how to diagnose bipolar disorder in pediatric patients, in part because symptoms change over time, and are affected by the developmental level of the child. And, because so often children and adolescents with bipolar disorder also have ADHD, oppositional defiant disorder, conduct disorder, and other mood disorders, these are often diagnosed and treated without recognizing that bipolar disorder is also present, which dramatically effects treatment efficacy. Accurate diagnosis of bipolar disorder, with or without ADHD is very important, as treatment is often complicated, and misdiagnoses can lead to significant complications in treatment of other conditions.

Bipolar disorder in children is currently defined in the DSM-5 using essentially the same criteria used for diagnosis in adults, with some exceptions. A manic episode is characterized by a distinct period of being abnormally energized, with persistent elevation of mood or irritable mood and increased goal directed behavior, lasting at least a week. Symptoms include hugely inflated self-esteem and grandiose thoughts, decreased need for sleep (not difficulty sleeping as in insomnia), overly talkative or pressured speech, racing thoughts, easily distractible, agitated, excessive involvement in pleasurable and risky behaviors associated with poor judgement. Hypomania refers to similar symptoms but less severe and disabling as mania.

Bipolar disorder is subdivided into 3 main subtypes. Bipolar 1 disorder (formerly manic-depressive disorder) requires the occurrence of at least one manic episode that is sufficiently severe to result in marked impairment in functioning or even hospitalization. Usually, but not always there are major depressive episodes as well. Bipolar II Disorder requires the presence of episodes of hypomania persisting at least 4 days, and other distinct periods of depression lasting at least 2 weeks. It is characterized by longer duration of symptoms than Bipolar I, and more of a depression component. Individuals with Bipolar II often present with concerns about depression, and the hypomania may be unrecognized. Depression and hypomania may occur at the same time. Cyclothymic Disorder refers to extended periods (at least a year in children and 2 years in adults) with numerous periods of hypomania and depressive symptoms that are present most of the time, but are not severe enough to warrant a diagnosis of hypomania or major depressive episode.[3]

The prevalence of bipolar disorder is estimated to be about 1% of the general population, but the risk is increased significantly if there is a family history of bipolar disorder. There is a strong genetic component for acquiring bipolar disorder. If a parent has bipolar disorder, the risk to each child is 15–30% and in identical twins the concordance rate is estimated to be 70%.[6] Although bipolar disorder is most often diagnosed in adulthood, many experience first symptoms in adolescence or early childhood, and the diagnosis is often not made for many years, with delayed diagnosis increasing the risk for worse outcome.[7] It is not uncommon for those afflicted with bipolar disorder to experience auditory and visual hallucinations, which can lead to misdiagnosis of schizophrenia. Children may have symptoms that are less obvious than in adults, and may have some associated symptoms long before overt bipolar symptoms appear. They may present with depression, and prepubertal depression is a risk for bipolar disorder. Rather than prolonged episodes of change in mood, children may experience severe mood changes many times a day. Manic symptoms may present as irritability rather than elevated mood. Children may exhibit hypersexual behavior in speech or action without a history of abuse. Children with bipolar disorder may react far out of proportion to even trivial slights with aggression and prolonged rages. As with adults, bipolar disorder carries a very high risk for suicidal thoughts and suicide. When ADHD with associated impulsivity is present, the risk is increased.

Those with bipolar disorder may have symptoms that appear very similar to those with ADHD who also have oppositional defiant disorder. Hyperactivity, aggressive and defiant behaviors, tantrums, inattention, ability to focus on an interest to the exclusion of all else, irritability and sleep problems are frequent in both groups. The distinguishing feature of bipolar disorder is distinct periods of mood changes that are very different than the usual behaviors. Psychotic symptoms such as hallucinations are not part of ADHD/ODD. Hypersexual behavior and very grandiose thinking are not normally part of ADHD/ODD either. Family history is especially helpful, and a strong family history for close family members with bipolar disorder should raise concern about possible bipolar disorder. Having a manic episode or bipolar condition in childhood carries a high risk of recurrence, and many with a bipolar subtype will convert to other subtypes.[8]

Screening for bipolar disorder can be done utilizing behavior questionnaires such as the Young Mania Rating Scale, or more general screening questionnaires such as the Achenbach Child Behavior Questionnaires. Bipolar disorder with associated ADHD or other disorders is often treated with medications, and with psychotherapy such as cognitive behavior therapy. Because of its complexity, and difficulty in diagnosis, it is recommended that bipolar disorder be treated by psychiatrists as opposed to general practitioners or pediatricians.[9] Treatment normally entails getting bipolar symptoms under control first with mood stabilizers or atypical antipsychotics, and then targeting remaining symptoms such as ADHD symptoms.

Disruptive Mood Dysregulation Disorder

Disruptive mood dysregulation disorder (DMDD) presents as chronic and severe irritability, with frequent temper tantrums, anger and irritability.

Temper outbursts are far more than what is expected in the situation, more than just a moody child, and more than appropriate for developmental age. In between temper outbursts, mood is usually angry and irritable. Symptoms are typically present most of the time and should be present prior to 10 years of age, last at least a year, and result in significant impairment.[3] This is a newly classified diagnosis that was not in previous editions of the DSM, and research into best treatment practices is limited. In the past it has been considered by some to be a manifestation of childhood bipolar disorder, and labelling those who have symptoms of DMDD with bipolar disorder is part of the explanation for the rising rates of bipolar diagnoses in children. Unlike bipolar disorder however, there are no distinct periods of mania or hypomania. Rarely does it evolve into adult bipolar disorder, but there is a significant risk of evolving into depression and anxiety.[3] Treatment options include stimulants, especially if there is co-occurring ADHD, antidepressants and atypical antipsychotics, such as are used for bipolar disorder. Behavior therapy and parent training interventions may also be helpful.

OCD, Tics and Tourette Syndrome

It is generally thought that ADHD carries an increased risk for obsessive-compulsive disorder (OCD), although the research evidence on this is contradictory. By definition, OCD seems to be almost the opposite of ADHD. Those with OCD tend to be overly concerned with consequences of their actions, avoid risky behaviors and may be hypervigilant in social situations, whereas those with ADHD will often have the opposite behaviors. Obsessions refer to intrusive unwanted involuntary thoughts that are present much of the time, and that others might consider silly or unnecessary. Compulsions are acts or responses to the obsessive thoughts. So for example, a common obsession is a fear of germs or contamination, and the associated compulsion might be frequent washing of hands, fear of touching other people or being in environments felt to be germ laden, such as doctors' offices or public restrooms. Oftentimes behaviors may become ritualistic, such as not stepping on cracks, lining things up in a particular order, checking to see if doors are locked, and doing so in a particular order or multiple times. These symptoms are common in everyone, and only would be considered a disorder if they lead to significant functional impairment. Obsessions are not the same as addictions, which are behaviors initiated as pleasurable, but that the individual becomes dependent on. So a teenager who spends a huge amount of time playing video games or watching YouTube may obsess about their activities, but it is only an OCD behavior if there is a ritualistic or compulsive component to it. Superstitious behavior may have an OCD component to it. Witness the rituals and routines that many professional athletes perform, especially baseball batters and tennis players, before each activity. Another form of OCD is scrupulosity, where the individual experiences excessive guilt associated with feeling they have broken a religious commandment, moral doctrine or law. They may then do compulsive cleaning rituals, excessively seek forgiveness, repetitive praying, constant self-checking and analyzing. This is not uncommon in those with high functioning autism or Asperger Syndrome with the tendency toward concrete thinking and rule oriented behavior. OCD usually coexists with anxiety. If an individual obsesses about germs, and compulsively washes their hands, limiting handwashing can lead to anxiety because the fears are still present, but now they can't do anything about them because activities to mediate them have been limited.

Estimated rates of co-occurrence of ADHD and OCD vary widely, ranging from 0–60% with lower rates in adults than in children.[10] Part of the difficulty with estimating comorbidity is the overlap in symptoms and possibility of misdiagnosis. An individual who appears to be inattentive in a classroom setting, may be not paying attention because of perseverative obsessive thoughts or anxiousness that override their ability to attend to something that may not seem as important at the time. Because symptoms are internalized, they may be more difficult to recognize than externalizing ADHD symptoms, especially in children who may not be able to communicate their thoughts or may not be as insightful in recognizing causes of inattentiveness.

A condition that usually includes ADHD and OCD symptoms is Tourette syndrome. By definition, Tourette syndrome refers to the presence of both vocal and motor tics for at least a year, with onset before age 18. Tics are sudden repetitive rapid movements that serve no purpose and are under partial control, and can be either motor/movement tics or vocal noises. Examples would be eye scrunching, neck jerking, shoulder shrugs, sniffing, throat clearing and coprolalia (sudden uncontrollable swearing). If individuals having tics are asked to stop, they usually can, but when they are no longer trying to suppress them, the tics recur. An example of how to understand what it is like to have tics is the experience of blinking that we all do. If requested to not blink for a few minutes, we can do this, but the longer we go without blinking, the stronger the urge to blink, until when the time is up there is great relief, and an excess of blinking for a time. Tic disorders range from simple tics that are very common in children, to chronic motor or vocal tics, to Tourette syndrome.

Tourette syndrome symptoms usually start in early childhood. Tics are usually not a big concern, except in cases where they draw undue attention to the individual, or rarely can cause physical discomfort. Tics can be treated by medication or cognitive behavior therapy or habit reversal therapy. However having a teacher or parent explain to classmates or peers the nature of tics, and the inability of the individual to control them is often sufficient to decrease the unwanted teasing and negative attention tics can cause. For those with Tourette syndrome, often the ADHD and OCD symptoms that frequently accompany it lead to greater difficulties. Tics are aggravated by some medications, especially stimulants used to treat ADHD, so the decision to treat someone with Tourette syndrome with stimulants has to be made with the realization the tics may worsen.

Like ADHD, OCD symptoms have a strong genetic component, as does Tourette syndrome. Taking a good family history and determining the presence of OCD and tic disorders in family members can help in determining whether an individual is at risk for these disorders, and can help sometimes in clarifying confusing symptoms. In some cases OCD, tics and Tourette syndrome can be triggered in those who are genetically predisposed by strep infections, the so called PANDAS (Pediatric Autoimmune Neuropsychiatric Disorders Associated with Streptococcal infections). The mechanism of this is felt to be similar to rheumatic fever which is a condition triggered by strep infections and causes heart, joint, skin and chorea (abnormal movements), and which may be associated with behavioral symptoms as well.

OCD and tics can be treated with specific therapies such as cognitive behavior therapy, and treatment can be quite successful. OCD symptoms are thought to be mediated by the neurotransmitter serotonin (and possibly glutamate), and medicines that increase serotonin levels (SSRIs, SNRIs) can be helpful in decreasing OCD symptoms. Tics are also treatable with a number of medications, including alpha agonists such as clonidine or guanfacine (which also may benefit ADHD symptoms) or the more potent antipsychotics such as risperidone or haloperidol. However, the side effects of the antipsychotics may be worse than the tics that are being treated, so should be used cautiously in treating tic disorders.

Bibliography

1. Connor MG. Anxiety in children. 2008;(192). http://www.crisiscounseling.com/Articles/AnxietyinChildren.htm.
2. Sciberras AE, Lycett K. Anxiety in children with attention-deficit/hyperactivity disorder. *Pediatrics*. 2014;133(5):801–808. doi:10.1542/peds.2013-3686.
3. American Psychiatric Association. Taskforce on DSM-5. *Diagnostic and Statistical Manual of Mental Disorders*, 5th ed. 2013. doi:10.1176/appi.books.9780890425596.744053.
4. Lundervold AJ, Hinshaw SP, Sørensen L, Posserud M-B. Co-occurring symptoms of attention deficit hyperactivity disorder (ADHD) in a population-based sample of adolescents screened for depression. *BMC Psychiatry*. 2016;16. doi:10.1186/s12888-016-0739-3.
5. Balazs J, Kereszteny A. Attention-deficit/hyperactivity disorder and suicide: A systematic review. *World J Psychiatry*. 2017;7(1):44–59. doi:10.5498/wjp.v7.i1.44.
6. Singh T. Pediatric bipolar disorder: Diagnostic challenges in identifying symptoms and course of illness. *Psychiatry (Edgmont)*. 2008;5(6):34–42.
7. Leverich GS, Post RM, Keck PE, et al. The poor prognosis of childhood-onset bipolar disorder. *J Pediatr*. 2007;150(5):485–490. doi:10.1016/j.jpeds.2006.10.070.
8. Birmaher B, Axelson D, Goldstein B, et al. Four-year longitudinal course of children and adolescents with bipolar spectrum disorders: The course and outcome of bipolar youth (COBY) study. *Am J Psychiatry*. 2009;166:795–804.

9. Shain BN. Collaborative role of the pediatrician in the diagnosis and management of bipolar disorder in adolescents. *Pediatrics*. 2012;130(6):e1725–e1742.

10. Abramovitch A, Dar R, Mittelman A, Wilhelm S. Comorbidity between attention deficit/hyperactivity disorder and obsessive-compulsive disorder across the lifespan: A systematic and critical review. *Harv Rev Psychiatry*. 2015;23(4):245–262. doi:10.1097/HRP.0000000000000050.

8 Autism and ADHD

J. Dennis Odell

Autism is a complex condition and it is beyond the scope of this book to include a thorough discussion of all aspects of autism. Nevertheless, it is now a very common condition, and some degree of autism symptoms frequently are found in individuals who have ADHD. Sometimes, these symptoms can be masked by more overt ADHD symptoms, and not recognized. Therefore to understand the spectrum of conditions associated with ADHD, it is necessary to have an understanding of autism.

Autism used to be considered a very distinct condition from ADHD. In the DSM-IV, those two diagnoses were mutually exclusive. Many years ago in our medical laboratory at Utah State University, we were working on basic research on potential different genetic and immunologic causes for autism. At that time, we were also doing separate studies on children who had ADHD. In order to determine if a particular immunologic or genetic finding was specific for autism, we would always do the same studies on control groups. Generally, we would have a control group consisting of children who had no identifiable developmental conditions, but we also naïvely included another control group of children who did not have autism, but had ADHD. To our bewilderment, we oftentimes found the same abnormal findings in children with ADHD as we saw in the group with autism. Additionally, years ago, in reviewing symptoms of ADHD, it was often stated that many children with attention deficit/hyperactivity disorder had difficulties with social interactions and often didn't understand how their behaviors were perceived by other people. It is now clear that many of those children probably had some features of autism. It has now been widely reported and recognized that there is a lot of overlap between ADHD and autism.[1] Many children with autism have features of ADHD and vice versa. This does not mean that they are the same condition.

What is Autism?

The definition of autism and our conception of what it actually is have evolved over time. Autism as currently defined in the DSM-5 requires two main categories of difficulties, difficulties with social communication and social interactions, and presence of repetitive and restricted patterns of behavior. Like ADHD, it is best conceptualized as a condition on a continuum, thus the term autism spectrum disorders. Furthermore, autism should not be thought of as a specific disease or disorder, but as a syndrome, with many different causes or diseases that lead to the symptoms that we recognize as autism.[2]

Social skills deficits: The first required category for autism is social skills deficits. There are 3 components considered to be part of the social skills deficits seen in individuals with autism. First is at some level there are deficits in social–emotional reciprocity. This refers to back and forth social interactions. As early as 2 months of age, infants will exhibit eye contact and will smile responsively at their caregivers. A 1-year-old who has injured himself will go to a parent for comfort. Older children will seek out peers to play and interact with, and will try to engage caregivers in their activities. These are interactions that may not be present in young children with autism. Older children and adolescents may struggle with such areas as back-and-forth conversation, sharing interests and responding to social interactions. Second, there are deficits in nonverbal communication, such as lack of eye contact, facial expressions, abnormal body language and difficulty understanding and using gestures. Third, there are deficits in developing, maintaining, and understanding relationships at an age-appropriate level. This would include difficulties understanding how to act in a particular social context, difficulties in sharing imaginative play or in making friends, and absence of interest in peers.[3]

The communication component of autism can probably best be conceptualized at some level as having a learning disability in the ability to read and understand how other people think. Normally when we are conversing with another person or persons, we assess their interest in the conversation based on social cues such as eye contact, facial expressions, tone of voice, gestures, and we generally have an understanding when someone is being sarcastic or teasing. These aspects of reading other people do not come easily for individuals with autism. They often will have difficulty understanding another person's perspective, thinking that others think as they do. Temple Grandin has helped clarify what it is like to have autism through her own experiences. In her book *Thinking in Pictures*, she eloquently describes difficulties she had in understanding that others were often not able to visualize or conceptualize problems in the same way that she did, and she often got herself in trouble for complaining about their lack of understanding.[4] In a similar fashion, individuals with ADHD may struggle with understanding how their behaviors are perceived by other people, and not understand why others may be avoiding them or may not want to interact with them. They may often misread others' intents and become easily offended when no offense was intended. Although most individuals with ADHD do not meet criteria for a diagnosis of autism, it is very common to have some autism symptoms, particularly the difficulties with social interactions. This often leads to difficulties making and keeping friends, and struggling with relationships.

Restricted, repetitive patterns of behavior: The second required category for autism is what is called restricted and repetitive patterns of behavior. There are four components that may be included. First are persistent repetitive motor movements, use of objects, or speech for no obvious purpose. This might include hand flapping, repetitive sounds, spinning, rocking, sniffing others, lining up objects in a particular order or color repetitively, turning cars upside down and spinning the wheels.

Second are difficulties with change in routine. In the DSM-5 this is described as insistence on sameness, inflexible adherence to routines, or ritualized patterns of behavior. Examples include extreme distress at small changes such as unexpected changes in routine. Children with autism often have to be prepared ahead of time for any new activity or significant distress may occur. They may be very focused on an activity they are doing and again become distressed when expected to transition to a new activity. There may be rigid thinking patterns or rituals related to eating, dressing or going to sleep. Memory is often excellent, and a child with autism may correct a parent who is not driving to school the correct way.

Third are highly restricted, fixated interests that are abnormal in intensity or focus. Individuals with autism often become experts at whatever area grabs their attention. They may know everything there is to know about trains, dinosaurs or Pokémon. They may be experts at certain video games and computer technology. Because of this ability to hyperfocus on an area of interest, they can become extremely knowledgeable. One of the characteristics of Asperger syndrome (an autism spectrum condition) as originally described was coming across as a "little professor", and being able to lecture about a topic way beyond a degree that would be expected for age.

Fourth is over or under reactivity to sensory input or unusual interests in sensory aspects of the environment. Often, individuals with autism will be extremely sensitive to stimuli that don't normally bother most people. Most of us will feel extremely uncomfortable in the presence of someone scratching their fingernails on a chalkboard or squeaking balloons or Styrofoam. Autism may lead to this level of discomfort or worse from any number of other triggers. This can be loud noises such as vacuum cleaners or flushing toilets or the general din of the school lunchroom, or it can be discomfort from the texture of certain clothes. It can lead to extremely picky eating because of discomfort from different food textures. There may be indifference to pain or temperature. At times this may manifest as excessively smelling or touching of objects or people, or visual fascination with lights or movement.

Individuals in the autism spectrum may have extremely high or low IQs, may have virtually no speech or may be able to speak eloquently, may have very poor coordination or the opposite. Children are often first suspected of having autism based on symptoms such as poor eye contact, not responding when their name is called, profound speech delays and not being able to point to indicate wants or needs. The more severe the symptoms, the earlier the diagnosis can be made, but for those with very high functioning autism, the diagnosis may be delayed for many years, and there are surely many people with autism who have never been diagnosed.

What Happened to Asperger Syndrome?

Asperger's syndrome was originally defined by an Austrian pediatrician named Hans Asperger. Asperger syndrome described often highly intelligent individuals who struggled with social awkwardness, having difficulty understanding social cues, reading facial expressions, understanding gestures, teasing and sarcasm. Usually language tended to be very concrete and nuances and subtleties of language were often not understood. Many had extreme difficulties with motor coordination. Individuals with Asperger syndrome often were very rule oriented, having a very strong internalized sense of right and wrong, with a tendency to become extremely upset when anyone went against those rules. This, coupled with the difficulty in understanding others' intents made for difficult social interactions and could often be a setup for bullying. Because of so much vagueness in how the condition was defined and conceptualized, in the latest version of the DSM, Asperger syndrome has been taken out of the diagnostic categories. People who had a previous diagnosis of Asperger syndrome would now be diagnosed either with high functioning autism if all of the above criteria are met, or social communication disorder if there are only primarily the social skills difficulties. Another category that used to be considered part of autism spectrum disorders was a condition called pervasive developmental disorder. This diagnosis was often used in young children where it was not yet clear if they met criteria for a full diagnosis of autism, but who clearly had some features of autism.

How Does Autism Present?

It may be helpful to share a few examples of how autism has presented in our clinic. One is a 3-year-old preschool student, who was severely developmentally delayed, with very little intelligible speech. This child seemed to be developing normally up until about age 18 months, when, for no apparent reason, as the parents described, the lights went out. Previous skills were lost, and behavior became difficult. There were frequent severe behavioral meltdowns that seemed to occur randomly and could last for a prolonged period of time, and that could end suddenly with behavior back to baseline. This child loved to line his toy cars up in particular order of colors, and became very upset if his siblings tried to play with his cars or change the order. He cried whenever he was around loud noises such as the garbage disposal or vacuum cleaner, but on the other hand loved fireworks.

He chose to play by himself, and if approached by siblings or peers would either ignore them or push them away.

Another child with autism presented as an 8-year-old who was in third grade. This child had a slightly below average IQ but had some significant speech difficulties as well as reading disabilities. She received resource help and also speech therapy but was above grade level in mathematics. She was frequently argumentative with teachers and she resisted help from them or her parents. She was easily frustrated, and tended to be a perfectionist. She refused to turn work in that she deemed imperfect. She was socially awkward, had no friends, and was frequently teased. She was a very picky eater and was extremely underweight. She had significant anxiety and often missed school. Her parents reported that she often had severe abdominal pain and a lot of sleep problems.

Another presentation was a seventh grade student who was being seen because of poor school performance. He was felt to be very bright, and IQ scores were quite high. He had difficulty focusing on tasks that he deemed to be tedious or a waste of his time, and was very defiant when teachers or parents pushed him to complete his work. He loved playing video games and watching YouTube. He often got in fights at school and teachers felt he was aggressive and lashed out at anyone who teased him or crossed him. He did not pay much attention to personal hygiene. He hated sports, and felt he was a victim of a lot of bullying. Ultimately his parents pulled him out of public school and he is now participating in an online home school.

Lastly, was a junior in high school who excelled in math and science. He had a 4.0 grade point average, and excelled in all areas academically. He was on the varsity swim team. He was respected by classmates and teachers, but reported that he had only a few close friends who had similar interests. He stated that he seemed to offend people easily and didn't understand why. He had some behaviors that others described as quirky, and he had rare episodes where he lost control of his temper. In spite of his high achievement and many accomplishments, he suffered from anxiety and depression.

Each of these individuals met criteria for autism, demonstrating how widely different the presentation can be. The first child described above showed a characteristic that is seen in approximately 20% of children with autism where they seem to regress during the toddler years. Autism is a relatively recently described disorder, with the first description reported in a publication by Dr. Leo Kanner, a psychiatrist at Johns Hopkins University, in 1943.[5] About the same time, Dr. Hans Asperger described a group of children with characteristics of the syndrome that would later be named after him.[6] The conceptualization and treatment approaches have been quite rocky over the years. Initially autism was felt to be a condition stemming from parents who were emotionally distant, the so-called refrigerator parents. Early treatments included removing the children from the home and putting them in an environment that was felt to be more loving and more emotionally connected. Many children were institutionalized. By the

1960s it became evident that autism was a neurologically based condition, not based on parental psychopathology. Researchers started finding evidence of a strong genetic predisposition to developing autism. In the 1970s twin studies demonstrated a clear genetic link to autism.

Up until relatively recently autism was felt to be a distinct disorder, and much research effort was dedicated to trying to find the single cause of autism. It was also felt to be exceedingly rare. When I trained as a pediatric resident in the early 1980s, we admitted one child to our behavior unit who was diagnosed with autism. Everyone in the program had to see and visit this child, because we were told we needed to recognize the symptoms, but it was so rare that we were likely to see but a few cases in our entire pediatric careers. In the 1980s the prevalence of autism was determined to be only about 4 per 10,000 individuals in the population. These were children who were very severely affected. Since that time, it has become clear that autism can manifest with much milder and subtler symptoms. It is now recognized that the spectrum of symptoms is extremely broad, and severity of symptoms varies widely. As genetic studies have become more sophisticated, it has been found that there are many different conditions that can lead to autism. The number of individuals being diagnosed with autism has risen alarmingly. It appears however that much of these diagnoses are made in individuals who would not previously have been diagnosed with autism, because of symptoms that are either not as straightforward or milder. Additionally up until relatively recently there were very few professionals who could even recognize the symptoms of autism, and that has now changed. However, it is not clear that there is not a real rise in the incidence of autism, and the reasons for the significant increase have not been determined. Recent statistics from parent reported autism diagnoses have found that now one in 40 children ages 3–17 has a diagnosis of autism spectrum disorder, with the prevalence in boys almost 4 times that of girls.[7]

Associated Conditions

Like ADHD, there are very common associated conditions in people who have autism. For those with severe autism, intellectual disability and seizures are not uncommon. In part because many of those with autism eat a very restricted diet, gastrointestinal disturbances are common as are feeding problems. Anxiety is nearly universal and mood disorders generally are frequent. Learning disabilities and ADHD are also very common. Sleep disorders are also frequently seen. For those with specific genetic conditions contributing to the autism symptoms there will be other health issues as part of the genetic syndrome. For example it has been estimated that 5–39% of children who have Down syndrome also have autism,[8] and with Down syndrome comes intellectual disability, short stature, specific physical characteristics, and a high-risk for cardiac disease, vision and hearing problems, Alzheimer's disease and even conditions such as intestinal blockage and leukemia. Each genetic condition comes with a spectrum of problems. This emphasizes the importance of identifying an underlying genetic condition if it is there, so as to be able to identify potential other problems that need monitoring and intervention.

How is Autism Diagnosed?

Like ADHD, the evaluation for an individual with autism can be very complicated, and the presentation may be less straightforward than for those who have ADHD as the primary concern. Partly the extent of the evaluation is determined based on the severity. Initial concerns are often raised by parents, by health care providers during well checks, or by preschool teachers. Parents may present to their pediatrician or school with concerns about possible autism. There are a number of autism screeners that are designed for use in a primary health care setting. The American Academy of Pediatrics has made a recommendation that all children ages 18 months and 2 years of age be screened for autism using a tool called the M-CHAT-R. This is a brief questionnaire that is completed by the parents that is designed to detect early signs of autism. Additionally there are screening questionnaires that are used in preschools and elementary schools that can be used to determine if the child is at risk for autism. Generally, if the concerns are significant enough based on symptoms and results of preliminary screening, children will be referred to a specific autism testing center.

Testing that is done during a formal autism assessment typically will include speech and language testing, evaluation for sensory processing difficulties, medical evaluation, psychoeducational testing, and specific autism measures. Two that are commonly used are the autism diagnostic inventory (ADI), which is a very in-depth and lengthy interview reviewing symptoms of autism, and the autism diagnostic observation scales (ADOS), which is a battery of programmed play and interactive activities appropriate to the age and communication level of the individual being tested, that is designed to bring out symptoms of autism, and gives a score that helps determine severity. Although these assessments will accurately determine specific diagnoses and recommendations, they are labor-intensive, take a long time and can be prohibitively expensive. They also are not readily available in all communities, and sometimes the wait list for evaluation can be very long.

School districts may render an educational diagnosis of autism based on psychoeducational testing and autism measures done at school that can allow a student to receive services and an IEP. Just as in learning disabilities, a school diagnosis is not the same as a medical diagnosis however. Because there is such a high degree of potential medical conditions that co-occur with autism, it is essential that anyone diagnosed with autism be seen by a medical professional. The extent of the medical evaluation for an individual with autism is somewhat controversial, but most important is a thorough medical history, family history and physical exam. Because there are so many genetic conditions that are associated with autism it is now recommended that genetic testing be undertaken.[9] This is now done with a test called a chromosomal micro-array that is able to identify many of the common genetic disorders that have been associated with autism. Technology in genetic diagnoses is evolving rapidly and there are other more sophisticated tests that are available or soon will be. The problem of course is that these tests are very expensive, and insurance may not cover the cost. Additional testing may include specific lab tests and imaging studies such as MRI scan, if there are concerns based on history and physical exam. Hearing and vision testing is also essential.

What Kinds of Treatments are used for Autism?

Any treatment regimen for an individual with autism has to be personalized to the specific difficulties and conditions being treated. But in general there are several treatment categories likely to be helpful for most people with autism. First, because a big part of the difficulties has to do with communication difficulties, working on speech and language problems is a priority. This may be speech therapy for those with significant language delays, or on a higher level, social skills and/or pragmatic language therapy. Although the core difficulty in autism is difficulty understanding social cues and social communication, these can be learned. Most of us take social cues for granted and rarely as parents do we train our children how to recognize facial expressions or what differences in tone of voice mean. For people with autism however this may be necessary, and can certainly be taught. There are many different approaches that may be used for this, and it can be done on an individual basis or in a group. For example one of the approaches in a group setting is to do role-playing, having one individual play out a certain scenario, and having each member of the group try to understand what that

Table 8.1 Some genetic conditions associated with autism

15q duplications (Prader Willi/Angelman region)

Tuberous sclerosis

22q11.2 deletion syndrome (DiGeorge/Shprintzen/velocardiofacial)

16p11.2 microdeletions and duplications

Turner syndrome

Williams syndrome (7q11.23)

Fragile X

PTEN macrocephaly syndrome

Rett syndrome (X-linked MECP2)

Mitochondrial disorders

person is thinking and how they should respond in that setting. This helps the individual try to understand what someone else is thinking, and in a group setting presents the realization that not everybody sees the situation in the same way. Most of us would probably benefit from this type of therapy, and the sessions are often very enjoyable. Participating in drama or acting classes for the same reason can be helpful.

Occupational therapy can be very helpful for individuals with autism. Children with autism may have difficulties with fine and gross motor coordination, handwriting, activities of daily living, and occupational therapy can be helpful for these difficulties. They may be able to help with social communication and interaction and with being able to deal with transitions. Additionally, sensory processing difficulties are often extreme, and can lead to significant behavioral problems. If the child has an aversion to loud noises or crowds, attending school can be very challenging, and occupational therapy techniques can help desensitize a child to the sensory issues that are causing distress. A type of occupational therapy is sensory integration therapy which is designed to help individuals with sensory processing difficulties. Sometimes measures such as being brushed, massage, swinging or spinning, or using weighted blankets can be soothing for people with autism, and can be helpful in calming an agitated child.

For behavioral problems such as oppositional behavior, and mood disorders and anxiety, working with a child psychologist can be beneficial. Students with autism may present with very oppositional behavior for a variety of reasons. The child may resist going to school because of sensory issues that overwhelm him, and he resists going in order to avoid significant physical discomfort. For example sometimes children may have a panic attack when the fire alarm goes off, and so may avoid school because of the fear of the alarm, and never knowing when it might go off. This may appear to be just oppositional behavior but in fact is driven by the child's fear of being exposed to physical pain, and is really more driven by his desire for self-preservation. Or there may be significant bullying at school, or discomfort with social interactions, and the child may resist school because of anxiety surrounding the school day. Treating challenging behaviors starts with understanding the root of the behaviors, and then treatment strategies can be developed. In order to achieve the best results for children with these challenges, it is essential to work with a therapist who has expertise in working with children and who has a good understanding of autism. In adults with autism, intervention may be even more challenging, because getting at the root of the behaviors can be obscured by coping and defensive strategies that the individual has developed over the years.

For children with more severe autism symptoms, more intensive therapy is recommended. The most common and well-known of these is ABA or applied behavior analysis. This therapy may be provided at autism treatment centers or in the home and is often very intensive, as much as 20 or more hours per week. ABA therapy is becoming more widely available and may be covered by insurance. There are a number of different teaching strategies employed as part of ABA therapy, and different providers may use widely different techniques. The essence of treatment though is to analyze specific behaviors in a way that they can be defined and measured, and then working towards improving behavior through specific interventions. When done properly, ABA therapy can be incredibly beneficial. It is very time-consuming and very expensive, and because ABA providers have widely different levels of expertise and treatment approaches, it is important to work with an ABA provider that provides the closest fit for the individual child. Many children with autism do not have symptoms severe enough to warrant that level of intervention, so it is not recommended for everyone.

It is certainly true that early intervention makes a huge difference, thus the push to identify children who have autism as early as possible. All states provide early intervention services to some degree to young children who are identified as having developmental delays or specific medical conditions such as Down syndrome that lead to developmental delays. These services are free of charge and are an excellent resource for any family with a child where there are developmental concerns. An initial assessment is done, and if the child is eligible based on the degree of developmental problems, services are provided, usually up until age 3. Programs vary from state to state, but services are available in every state. After age 3 if there are still concerns, children may be enrolled in developmental preschool. Also there are many autism treatment centers throughout the country where more intensive intervention can be obtained, such as ABA therapy.

There are medication options for treating autism as well. There is no specific autism medication; rather medications are used to target specific symptoms. For example if a child with autism is extremely hyperactive, impulsive and inattentive, the usual medications used to treat ADHD may be employed. Likewise for those who have severe anxiety, the typical medications used to treat anxiety may be prescribed. Although controversial, there are a number of medications that may be beneficial for tempering extreme aggressive, irritable or angry behavior. These medications are reviewed in detail in the chapters on medication management. Sleep problems are very common and can be severe and unsettling, and sometimes specific medications for sleep are utilized. For the small percentage that also have seizures, specific anticonvulsant medications are employed. It should be mentioned, that just as individuals with autism can be overly sensitive to environmental stimuli, they also may be particularly sensitive to medication effects and side effects. For any new medication intervention, it is therefore often best to start at a low dose, and carefully monitor effects and side effects before increasing the dose.

Gastrointestinal disturbances are very common. Sometimes special diets are used, probably the most common being the gluten-free/casein free diet. This is quite controversial and very challenging, but in selected children may make a difference with behaviors. Because of restricted diet, constipation can be an ongoing challenge and may require dietary changes or the chronic use of medications such as MiraLax or GlycoLax. Certain conditions such as gastroesophageal reflux disease, celiac disease, eosinophilic gastroenteritis and irritable bowel syndrome are common, and each has its specific medical intervention.

Autism Controversies

Before leaving this discussion on autism it is worth mentioning some of the controversies surrounding the etiology and treatment of autism. I know of no area in medicine that has engendered more controversy than the field of autism, to a degree that has at times been extreme and even volatile. The early theories blaming parents for causing autism in their children, and misguided treatment attempts led to a lot of mistrust of the medical establishment and government agencies. Also, before effective treatment strategies became available, families with children diagnosed with autism were given very little hope for any intervention that would help them. And, because autism is behaviorally defined, diagnostic boundaries are fuzzy, and there are no reliable biomedical markers that can aid in diagnosis. We are used to medical conditions such as diabetes, that if there are symptoms suggesting the possibility of the disorder, a simple laboratory test, in this case a blood glucose level, will make the diagnosis definitively. There are no such tests, because there are no biomedical markers that define autism. Lastly, the striking apparent increase in prevalence of autism has suggested an epidemic that is getting out of control. This has made the field ripe for speculation about possible causes and best treatment approaches.

The list of potential etiologies is long, and each one can have defenders that are almost militant. Suggested contributing factors include faulty diets, excessive use of antibiotics and yeast infections, various mineral toxicities such as mercury or lead poisoning, toxins in our environments, such as chemicals in foods, or pesticides and food allergies. Interventions touted to be effective have included special diets, such as casein free/gluten free diets, chelation therapy designed to eliminate toxic heavy metals from the body, antifungal treatments, vitamin therapies and hyperbaric oxygen chambers. Perhaps most harmful has been the controversy surrounding vaccines and their possible role in causing autism. Original concerns were related to the MMR vaccine and to thimerosal, the mercury containing preservative used in many vaccines (but was not in the MMR vaccine), touting it as a likely cause. In spite of the lack of evidence indicating thimerosal use caused autism, thimerosal was removed from most vaccines, but this did not make any difference in the rising incidence of autism. Even though their role in autism has been refuted[10] there remains a mistrust of vaccines amongst many in our society. And part of the difficulty is that since autism apparently has so many causes and is such a broad spectrum, interventions that seem to work anecdotally for one may show no benefit in others.

Conclusion

Our understanding of autism has evolved quite a bit over the past 75 years. Autism used to be a dreaded diagnosis, with a dire prognosis and very little hope for any effective interventions. We now know that there are many effective treatments for autism, and as with most people, individuals with autism come with a unique set of strengths and weaknesses, some of which can be profound. There are reputed to be many famous historical figures who some suspect may have had autism based on historical reports, including Isaac Newton, Albert Einstein, Charles Darwin and even Thomas Jefferson. In a lecture by Temple Grandin, she advocated always having someone with autism as part of any problem solving group because of their ability to often think outside of the box and come up with unique solutions. Having both ADHD and autism comes with extra challenges. For example a student with both diagnoses who is observed to not be attending well, may be inattentive because of hyperfocus on an area of intense interest with an inability to shift that focus to the next expected task, or may be inattentive because of easy distractibility. The treatment approach is different depending on the cause. There are some with autism with extremely severe symptoms, who need lifelong help and interventions, but there are also many with milder symptoms who can benefit from less intense and focused interventions, directed at understanding the basis for behaviors of concern.

Bibliography

1. Zablotsky B, Bramlett MD, Blumberg SJ. The co-occurrence of autism spectrum disorder in children with ADHD. *J Atten Disord*. June 2017. doi:10.1177/1087054717713638.
2. Gillberg C, Coleman M. *The Biology of the Autistic Syndromes*. 3rd ed. Mac Keith Press; 2000.
3. American Psychiatric Association. Taskforce on DSM-5. *Diagnostic and Statistical Manual of Mental Disorders*, 5th ed.; 2013. doi:10.1176/appi.books.9780890425559 6.744053.
4. Grandin T. *Thinking in Pictures*. Doubleday; 1995.
5. Kanner L. Autistic disturbances of affective contact. *Nerv Child*. 1943.
6. Asperger H. Die 'Autistischen Psychopathen' im Kindesalter. *Arch Psych Nervenkrankh*. 1944;117:76–136.
7. Kogan MD, Vladutiu CJ, Schieve LA, et al. The prevalence of parent-reported autism spectrum disorder among US children. *Pediatrics*. 2018;142(6):e20174161. doi:10.1542/peds.2017-4161.
8. Channell MM, Phillips BA, Loveall SJ, Conners FA, Bussanich PM, Klinger LG. Patterns of autism spectrum symptomatology in individuals with Down syndrome without comorbid autism spectrum disorder. *J Neurodev Disord*. 2015;7(1):5. doi:10.1186/1866-1955-7-5.

9. Shen Y, Dies KA, Holm IA, et al. Clinical genetic testing for patients with autism spectrum disorders. *Pediatrics*. 2010;125(4):e727 LP–e735. doi:10.1542/peds.2009-1684.

10. Destefano F, Price CS, Weintraub ES. Increasing exposure to antibody-stimulating proteins and polysaccharides in vaccines is not associated with risk of autism. *Pediatr Pol*. 2014;89(5):T31–T38. doi:10.1016/j.pepo.2014.07.003.

9 Other Symptoms and Conditions Associated with ADHD

J. Dennis Odell

Sleep Disorders

While research studies vary widely in reported rates of sleep disorders in those with ADHD, individuals with ADHD and family members consistently report that sleep problems are a frequent and challenging problem, and symptoms of sleep deprivation may mimic or aggravate ADHD symptoms. This appears to be an even greater problem in adults with ADHD compared to children. Additionally the many conditions associated with ADHD also carry a high risk of sleep problems, including anxiety, depression, bipolar disorders and autism. Sleep problems, including difficulty falling asleep, frequent awakening, and waking early are often reported. Often these are behavioral, with difficulty settling down to go to sleep, defiance of parental ordered bedtime routines, disruptive family sleep problems and hyperactivity. Overuse of electronic devices adds to the likelihood of sleep difficulties. Additionally, sleep disorders such as obstructive sleep apnea (sleep disordered breathing),[1] restless leg syndrome and periodic limb movements[2] are also reported to be more common in those with ADHD. And of course, stimulant medication and other medications used to treat ADHD and associated conditions may aggravate sleep problems that are already present. Because it is so commonly an issue with ADHD, it is always worth asking details about adequacy of sleep during the initial assessment, and monitoring throughout the treatment period. Oftentimes, treatment for sleep disorders needs to be done in addition to treating ADHD symptoms.

At least as far back as the ancient Greeks and Aristotle, people have wondered about the phenomenon of sleep, its purpose and meaning. The science of understanding sleep took a leap forward with the invention of the EEG by the German psychiatrist Hans Berger in 1924, which enabled the recording of the electrical activity in the brain. Much has been learned since then. The 2017 Nobel Prize in medicine was awarded to three scientists who identified the underlying biologic mechanisms that control circadian rhythm, the biologic clock that enables us to adapt to the environmental fluctuations of the day, especially light and dark, and influences our sleep cycles. It appears our modern society, especially with the introduction of artificial lighting, and increasingly our obsession with electronics and screens, has led to major changes in sleep habits compared to the past. The average American sleeps 2 hours less than a century ago. It turns out sleep is more than just passive resting. There are many important functions and activities that occur while sleeping, and chronic sleep deprivation can increase the risk of a number of diseases.

Our brains are not less active when we sleep, but the type of brain activity is distinctly different. While awake, our brain is stimulated by our activities, and the brain collects and registers external stimuli. When we are asleep, the brain makes connections that help us to retain and solidify that information. Memory is enhanced by the processing that occurs while we sleep.

When we sleep, we go through a number of sleep cycles throughout the sleeping period, stages 1–4 and the REM (rapid eye movements) phase. Stage 1 is light sleep, the transition between wakefulness and deeper sleep. It lasts usually only a few minutes, and can be easily disrupted by external stimuli. Stage 2 is also light sleep, but characterized by the presence on EEGs of spindles, ½ second electrical bursts that are thought to stimulate the cerebral cortex to preserve memory. This may also help us make sense of information or problems that may become more apparent after "sleeping on it". About ½ of our sleep time is spent in stage 2, up to 50 minutes of the first cycle, but relatively less in ensuing cycles. Eventually, heart rate and breathing slow, core temperature decreases, and awareness of external stimuli fades. Stage 3 and 4 are characterized by deep sleep with characteristically slower brain wave patterns. We are much less responsive to outside stimuli when in deep sleep. This is the time when the body is undergoing muscle and tissue repair, and the highest level of growth hormone is produced. Brain cells transiently shrink in size allowing excretion of cellular toxins. Stage 4 is the deepest stage of sleep, and puts us in an almost comatose state. It is during this stage that bedwetting and sleepwalking usually occur. The last stage is REM sleep, when the most intense dreaming occurs. During this stage our muscles are at rest or even paralyzed (presumably so we don't act out our dreams). During a typical night, most will go through 4–6 sleep cycles, although not necessarily in order. REM duration increases with successive cycles. REM sleep is felt to be important in regulating mood and consolidating memories.

Many bodily functions and hormone levels vary at different times of the day and are influenced by sleep habits and the circadian rhythm, and can be disrupted by poor sleep habits as well as medications. Sleep is as important to our brains as food is to our bodies. Adequate quality and quantity of sleep is considered essential to high performance levels. All animals need to sleep, and animals will die of sleep deprivation before starving. Our cells produce proteins that accumulate during the day that promote sleep. Our sleep/

wake clock is affected by light. The release of melatonin, a hormone often used to treat sleep difficulties, occurs with darkness. Light, especially blue light such as in electronic screens, suppresses melatonin release, and may delay our sleep cycle.[3]

How much sleep is enough? The recommended amount of sleep for pediatric populations is for infants 12–16 hours, 1–2 year olds 11–14 hours, 3–5 year olds 10–13 hours, 6–12 years 9–12 hours and teenagers 13–18 years old 8–10 hours. Adults should get 7–8 hours. Sleeping the recommended hours is associated with better health outcomes in improved attention, behavior, learning, memory, emotional regulation and mental and physical health. Problems such as depression, obesity, attention and behavioral problems and even suicidal thoughts and attempts are increased with sleep deprivation.[4]

Interventions for sleep problems should start with behavioral approaches before relying on medications. Sleep hygiene, the use of helpful sleep promoting behaviors and consistency is often helpful. This includes being consistent with bedtime and time of awakening, even on weekends, as much as possible. Highly stimulating activities should be avoided before bedtime, including exercise, TV and videogames, and even electronic readers because of the effects of screens on sleeping. Napping during the day should be avoided, and stimulating foods, such as caffeinated beverages and chocolate should be avoided, especially later in the day. Caffeine has a long ½ life, taking at least 8 hours for its effects to wear off, and caffeine suppresses melatonin release. Keeping TVs out of the bedroom, and having reading material and dim lighting in the bedroom can help with sleep induction. Physical activity during the day is also important. Behavioral interventions including cognitive behavior therapy can be instituted in more difficult sleep situations. Keeping a sleep diary can be helpful to get a good sense of sleeping habits and patterns and can help target interventions. A good sleep diary can be downloaded from the National Sleep Foundation website (www.sleepfoundation.org) or from the sleep education website (www.sleepeducation.org) sponsored by the American Academy of Sleep Medicine. Weighted blankets can be helpful for some, and have been used effectively especially in those with autism.

Specific medical sleep disorders need to be ruled out. Sleep apnea, especially obstructive sleep apnea caused by upper airway narrowing is not uncommon. In children it is often due to enlarged tonsils and allergies, in adolescents and adults it may be due to obesity. Symptoms suggestive of obstructive sleep apnea include excessive snoring, labored breathing during sleep, and irregular breathing with gasping, snorting and prolonged pauses between breathing. The presence of any of these should lead to a medical evaluation and possibly sleep study.[5] Restless leg syndrome is a disorder characterized by an irresistible urge to move the legs, usually associated with discomfort. The restlessness is more prevalent while resting, and the discomfort is relieved by movement. Symptoms are the worst at night. As these symptoms may be aggravated by iron deficiency, running a lab test for anemia and low iron is recommended. Sometimes antidepressant medications can aggravate these disorders.

There have been many medications used to enhance sleep, but few have been well studied in the pediatric population, and there are currently no medications that are approved by the FDA for treating insomnia in pediatrics.[6] Over the counter antihistamines, such as diphenhydramine (Benadryl) are often used, but sometimes can cause paradoxical worsening of sleep problems, and children will often quickly develop tolerance to their effects, limiting long term usefulness.

Melatonin is widely used. It is available as an over the counter dietary supplement and preparations of melatonin vary, as melatonin is not regulated by the FDA like prescription drugs are. Melatonin has been shown to help with time to sleep onset and total sleep time, but may not help with frequency of night-time awakenings. It is generally felt to be safe for short term use, but long term effects in children have not been studied, and because it is a hormone, it has other effects on the body.[6] Best dosage has also not been rigorously studied. Low doses of 0.5mg may be effective for many, and doses above 5–6 mg are not recommended, nor is there evidence that higher doses or extended release melatonin are useful. Low dose melatonin (0.5–3mg) may be most effective when taken 2–3 hours before bedtime, as that mimics the natural melatonin cycle. However, it also has mild sedating properties, and so may be helpful when taken ½ hour before bedtime. Side effects include headaches, daytime sleepiness, irritability, stomach pain and dizziness, and possibly depression. Even though it is a nonprescription drug, it can interact with a number of other drugs.

Those with ADHD for whom behavioral approaches and melatonin are ineffective may benefit from low doses of clonidine. It is a medicine with some beneficial effects in treating ADHD itself, so for those who can't settle down before bedtime it can be helpful. But its main side effect is sedation, so it can directly help with falling asleep as well. Dosage is usually 0.1mg, ½ to 1 tablet before bed. Because its effects last only 4 hours, it doesn't help as much with night-time awakenings. But also its effects are well worn off by morning, so doesn't lead to daytime drowsiness when taken at night. More details about clonidine and related medications can be found in the chapter on ADHD medications.

For those with associated depression and anxiety, treating those disorders can be helpful. Antidepressants often aggravate sleep problems, so sometimes sedating antidepressants such as trazadone or mirtazapine in low doses are added. Their use in children and adolescents is not well studied. If atypical antipsychotics such as risperidone or quetiapine are already being used for severe behavior problems such as can occur in autism, dosing at night before bedtime may help insomnia, but because of significant side effect profile, are not recommended as primary sleep aids. L-theanine (one of the ingredients in green tea) has been touted as helpful for children with ADHD with sleep problems, in part because of its relaxation properties, and is non-sedating.[7] Herbal teas such as chamomile or passionflower teas are also touted to help for those preferring nonprescription options. For those with documented iron or vitamin D deficiency, normalizing those levels with vitamin D or iron supplements may provide improvement in sleep quality.[6]

Enuresis

Enuresis can be either daytime urinary incontinence or night-time bed-wetting, and both are more common in children with ADHD. Although both are very common in childhood, the risk for enuresis is doubled in those with ADHD.[8] There is much speculation on why this may be, from associated neurodevelopmental delay to genetically linked predisposition to inattentiveness. Nocturnal enuresis (bedwetting) is quite common in children and prevalence decreases naturally as children age. It is possible that the nocturnal enuresis seen in ADHD is part of the neurodevelopmental lag that is seen in MRI imaging studies. Nonetheless, bedwetting is seen most prominently in children who sleep very deeply, and during the deepest stages of sleep those with bedwetting are sleeping nearly to unconsciousness, and then lose whatever is in the bladder at that time. This is not associated however with loss of bowel control.

Most often parents will try to treat bedwetting by restricting fluids before bed, and randomly waking the child during the night to void. This rarely is effective. The enuresis incidents occur typically during the deepest stages of sleep, stages 3 and 4 as described above. At that point, they lose whatever is in the bladder, and the kidneys are constantly making urine, even if fluids are restricted before bedtime. And there is no practical way to predict when children are in their deepest stage of sleep, so randomly waking them in hopes that it will help usually fails.

Nocturnal enuresis is most effectively treated with an enuresis alarm, which is basically a moisture detector (pad with sensor) that is placed in the underwear before bed, and sets off a very loud alarm at the first sign of moisture/ wetting. Like any alarm that we use regularly, over time we become accustomed to when the alarm is going to sound, and become aware of the need to awaken, and so eventually no longer need the alarm. The enuresis alarm trains the child to recognize the cues to wake up, and for most will cure the bedwetting after a few months. Sometimes it helps to use star charts or similar techniques to monitor progress and keep the child motivated to use the alarm. To use the star chart, a reachable goal is agreed on, such as using the alarm regularly for a week, then trying to go at least one night dry during the next week, and so on, with achievement of each goal resulting in a tangible and meaningful reward. Stars are placed on a calendar to mark progress. The point is to make the goal very reachable, but to be gradually heading towards improvement each week and eventual resolution. When used in conjunction with an enuresis alarm, cure rates are quite high.

Occasionally medications are prescribed for nocturnal enuresis. DDAVP is a synthetically produced version of vasopressin, a natural hormone that regulates urine output. It can be very effective for treating bedwetting, but doesn't often result in a cure. Also with dehydration there can be a risk of electrolyte imbalances. Imipramine is another medication that when used at low doses can help with bedwetting, but also comes with side effects. Nocturnal enuresis naturally improves with age, and even without treatment will eventually resolve for the great majority of people.

Daytime enuresis in children with ADHD is often the result of inattentiveness and being more interested in a current activity and ignoring the need to void. Constipation may also aggravate the condition. Sometimes there may be medical conditions such as small bladder capacity, urinary tract infections, or neurologic problems such as seen in those with cerebral palsy that can cause urinary incontinence. Some medications may aggravate the problem. High dose vitamin C for example acidifies the urine and can cause bladder irritation. Carbonated beverages and caffeine or chocolate also may increase urinary urgency.

For inattentiveness to voiding cues, a simple timer set at frequent intervals, usually every 2 hours, or less if needed, can take away the need for parental nagging, with the understanding that when the timer goes off, the child needs to go to the bathroom, whether they feel the need or not. Again, star charts can help if needed. Treating any co-occurring constipation is also important. If problems persist, a medical evaluation is indicated to rule out any medical causes. Medications such as Ditropan can be used if there is poor bladder control and biofeedback if available can be helpful.

Constipation and Encopresis

Encopresis refers to bowel accidents and soiling of the underwear. Constipation and encopresis are also almost twice as common in children with ADHD.[8] Constipation is frequent in children in general, and especially in children with ADHD. It may come about because of limited diets consisting of highly refined foods and minimal fruits and vegetables, leading to hard stools. Also, as in enuresis, the child may ignore cues to use the bathroom when they are busy. As constipation worsens, and bowel movements become larger and more infrequent, passing stool becomes painful. This may start a vicious cycle where they further resist having bowel movements, and withhold defecation for longer periods of time. There are nerves in the lining of the large bowel that when stretched from the presence of stool signals the brain to empty the bowel. Over time though, if the cues are ignored, and the nerves get over stretched, they cease to work, and the child will lose the urge to pass a bowel movement. Then they may feel that signal only when there is a large impending stool, resulting in great urgency, and need to have a bowel movement immediately. Also, looser stool from behind the large stool bolus will leak around the stool, and the child will be unable to control its passage, leading to soiling and bowel accidents. So it may appear the child has diarrhea, but in fact it is caused by chronic constipation. The clue is that every several weeks there is passage of very large stool, with intermittent loose stools in the interim and very little control or great urgency to use the toilet for bowel movements. A plain x-ray of the abdomen will often make the diagnosis obvious if there is uncertainty.

Treatment is fairly straightforward in most cases. Evaluation by a physician initially is necessary to rule out any of the rare medical causes of these conditions. These include underlying neurologic problems, dietary problems, primary mental health conditions and bowel problems such as Hirschprung's disease. Understanding the underlying causes of constipation and encopresis helps towards intervention. For resolution, it is important to do whatever it takes to ensure normal sized daily bowel movements. Most parents do not have a clue what their child's bowel habits are like, so it is important that stools be observed and monitored by parents, as embarrassing as that might be. It takes a long time for the overstretched colon to get back to normal caliber and for the nerves to recover, often weeks to months depending on how long the condition has been present. So a pattern of normal daily bowel movements is essential for recovery. Limiting constipating foods such as highly refined foods, like white rice, noodles, and white bread, and most fried or fast foods, and encouraging fiber, fruits and vegetables is important. For some milk and cheese is very constipating. The easiest medication to use is miralax or glycolax, which is a powder to be mixed in water or juice. Contrary to popular belief, long term use of laxatives is both necessary and not unsafe. The usual dose is about a tablespoon in 8 ounces of fluid given daily, but at times higher doses are needed. Although enemas or suppositories may be helpful for initial bowel evacuation, they may be traumatic for the child, and are usually not necessary.

To begin treatment of severe constipation and encopresis it often helps to have a contract with the child. Their responsibility is to take the medication, work on whatever dietary changes are needed, and attempt to have regular bowel habits by sitting on the toilet once or twice per day to try to have a bowel movement. The parents' responsibility is to administer the medication, provide the appropriate diet and to monitor stools. That's it. There is no need for any punitive measures, just mutual support, and with a bit of patience and simple interventions, the great majority of time the problem will resolve. Often there has been a cycle of punishment and frustration on the parents' part and compensatory resistance or seeming indifference on the child's part, thus the point of the contract. If these measures are not helpful, referral to an encopresis clinic (usually staffed by pediatric gastroenterology specialists and dieticians) may be indicated.

Eating Disorders

It is usually assumed that those with ADHD have relatively low weight compared with those who don't have ADHD, especially those who are hyperactive. High activity level, irregular eating habits and especially stimulant medications used to treat ADHD are all associated with lower weight, and it is important to monitor adequacy of weight gain in anyone with ADHD treated with medication. Paradoxically however, the risk for obesity is actually quite high in those with ADHD, in children and adults. [9] There are many potential reasons for this. Impulsive eating habits and relative lack of self-control in regards to eating may play a role. Although stimulant medication suppresses appetite, some taking medication will miss meals during the day, and then binge eat when the medication wears off in the evening. It is not uncommon for children on longer acting stimulant preparations to skip lunch and sometimes dinner, but to eat ravenously in the late evening. Again, paradoxically, some with ADHD may have sedentary lifestyles, eschewing sports and outdoor activities for television and videogames. Also other conditions often co-occurring with ADHD may increase the risk of obesity, including depression and anxiety with emotional overeating, and conduct disorder.[10] Sleep disorders that are common in those with ADHD can also increase the risk of obesity. And, genetic and familial factors play a role. Maternal obesity increases the risk of ADHD in their children.[11] This may be from increased genetic risk and/or from shared familial and environmental factors.

The actual cause of increased obesity in those with ADHD is a matter of debate, but it is clear that ADHD carries a significant risk of developing obesity, in spite of high activity levels and the frequent use of medications that would be expected to lower weight.[12] As part of the assessment and management of ADHD, it is important to monitor weight and growth, with increased risk of both malnourishment and obesity. Treatment of ADHD may help lower the risk, not necessarily because of the decreased appetite with stimulant medications, but more from the resulting better self-control and better life style habits.

Internet Use, Gaming, Gambling

Many have speculated on the association between modern electronics and technology and their effects on developing brains and risk of behavioral problems including ADHD. Indeed even shows like Sesame Street with its high level of educational programming may contribute to development of short attention spans with its fast pace and rapid transitions between topics. This is designed to keep viewers interested, and is certainly effective, but how do kindergarten and grade school teachers compete with that? One can argue the merits of our increasingly technological society and how we are evolving, but there is little question that our reliance on electronics for babysitting, entertainment and education of even our youngest children is altering the developing brain compared to pre high technology eras.

One early study published in the journal *Pediatrics* in 2004 reported a direct association with TV viewing time in children ages 1–3 with the presence of attention problems at age 7.[13] The researchers cautioned that association was not necessarily causation, and that it was possible ADHD children are more likely to watch television, or because of behavioral challenges in their children, parents with children with ADHD may be more likely to control behavioral problems with increased television viewing. Content of television viewing may make a difference as well, with viewing of more violent and fast paced shows increasing the risk, as opposed to educational programming.

There is concern about media use in young children blunting normal developmental skills. Infants and toddlers are developmentally not able to learn as well from media as from the physical presence and interaction with their caregivers. The most important learning tool for toddlers exposed to media is to have caregivers watch with them and then reteach the content. [14] The use of touchscreens with educational media can also be helpful. Certain media with educational content can enhance children's' learning and preparation for grade school, when viewed in moderation.

Electronic media use is almost universal amongst adolescents. Some 75% of teenagers use at least one social media site, and most use multiple sites; 88% of teens have access to mobile phones, the great majority smartphones. Teenagers average 30 texts per day. Most have access to desktops, laptops and tablets as well as videogame consoles with only 1% of teenagers owning no such devices.[15] Known risks of excessive media use include obesity with a significant increased likelihood of becoming obese with increased screen time. Having a TV in the bedroom also increases the risk of obesity. As detailed previously, there are significant sleep problems associated with media use as well. Risks of internet addiction and internet gaming disorder, with concomitant difficulties and lack of interest in offline social interactions, are particularly increased among those with ADHD. And of course media content influences behavioral choices such as diet, alcohol and tobacco use, sexual behaviors and body image. Cyberbullying is rampant, especially with the ability to express oneself anonymously on the internet. Given the pervasiveness of media in our lives, controlling media use in children, adolescents and adults is extremely challenging, but given the widespread potential consequences, having guidelines and monitoring appropriate use is a critical component of modern day parenting.[16]

Current guidelines from the American Academy of Pediatrics recommend no media prior to age 18 months except for video-chatting, and for toddlers recommend parents watch high quality media with their child to help children understand what they are seeing. For ages 2–5, it is recommended that screen time be limited to 1 hour per day of high quality programs. Balancing media use with other healthy behaviors in school-aged children and adolescents is recommended, and having media-free zones, such as the bedroom, and family time such as meals, free of media. Avoiding media use for an hour before bedtime is recommended in all ages, as is keeping televisions out of the bedroom. Children will mimic parental viewing habits, so having healthy family media use is critical. A media tool calculator is available on the AAP website (AAP.org) that can facilitate budgeting time including media use for children and adolescents.[14]

Substance Abuse and Risky Behaviors

As discussed in chapter 3, ADHD carries an increased risk for substance abuse and addictive behaviors that are not attributed to stimulant medication prescription use. The risk is particularly high for those who also have conduct disorder. This is a major challenge when considering stimulant medication use in high risk individuals, and emphasizes the importance of including non-medicine therapeutic interventions in the treatment process. Increased risky sexual behaviors is also seen in those with ADHD, including earlier initiation of sexual activity, more sexual partners, more casual sex and more risk of pregnancies.[17] Suicidal ideation and suicide attempts are also an increase risk, in part because of impulsive behavior and challenges that come with ADHD, but also with the other associated conditions such as conduct disorders and mood disorders. Bipolar disorder especially carries a risk of suicidality.

As would be expected in those with hyperactive and impulsive behaviors, the likelihood of experiencing a myriad of physical injuries, accidents and accidental poisoning is much higher in those with ADHD. Add the inattentive component and easy distractibility, and for some motor coordination problems, and the risk becomes higher, estimated to be about double compared to those without ADHD.[18] This applies to driving risk and motor vehicle accidents as well, especially with distractibility, decreased inhibitory control, and with the executive function deficits associated with ADHD.[19] Enhanced driver education and simulator training may be warranted in some with ADHD, especially those who have previously demonstrated high risk behaviors.

Conclusion

Some of the more common problems and conditions associated with ADHD have been reviewed, but the list is incomplete. Having a diagnosis of ADHD carries a significant risk for other health issues listed here and in previous chapters. It is vital to include evaluation for all of the discussed conditions as part of an assessment for ADHD, and to understand the different problems that may present at different stages of life. This discussion is not meant to paint a dour picture or to predict bad outcomes in those with ADHD, but to raise awareness that ADHD is not just a collection of a few behavioral symptoms, but comes with a myriad of potential problems that can affect the success of the individual with ADHD. Each of the conditions discussed comes with treatment measures that are effective, and so awareness and monitoring for problems as they arise can greatly improve outcomes.

Bibliography

1. Sedky K, Bennett DS, Carvalho KS. Attention deficit hyperactivity disorder and sleep disordered breathing in pediatric populations: A meta-analysis. *Sleep Med Rev.* 2014. doi:10.1016/j.smrv.2013.12.003.
2. Cortese S, Konofal E, Lecendreux M, et al. Restless legs syndrome and attention-deficit/hyperactivity disorder: A review of the literature. *Sleep.* 2005. doi:10.1093/sleep/28.8.1007.
3. Finkel M. The science of sleep. *Natl Geogr Mag.* 2018;(August):40–77.
4. Paruthi S, Brooks LJ, D'Ambrosio C, et al. Recommended amount of sleep for pediatric populations: A consensus statement of the American Academy of Sleep Medicine. *J Clin Sleep Med.* 2016. doi:10.5664/jcsm.5866.
5. Moturi S, Avis K. Assessment and treatment of common pediatric sleep disorders. *Psychiatry (Edgmont).* 2010;7(6):24–37. http://www.ncbi.nlm.nih.gov/pmc/articles/PMC2898839/.
6. Bruni O, Angriman M, Calisti F, Comandini A, Esposito G, Cortese S, Ferri R. Practitioner review: Treatment of chronic insomnia in children and adolescents with neurodevelopmental disabilities. *J Child Psychol Psychiatry.* 2017;59(5):489–508. doi:10.1111/jcpp.12812.
7. Lyon MR, Kapoor MP, Juneja LR. The effects of L-theanine (Suntheanine(R)) on objective sleep quality in boys with attention deficit hyperactivity disorder (ADHD): A randomized, double-blind, placebo-controlled clinical trial. *Altern Med Rev.* 2011;16(4):348–354.
8. Mellon MW, Natchev BE, Katusic SK, et al. Incidence of enuresis and encopresis among children with attention deficit hyperactivity disorder in a population-based birth cohort. *Acad Pediatr.* 2013;13(4). doi:10.1016/j.acap.2013.02.008.
9. Güngör S, Celiloğlu ÖS, Raif SG, Özcan ÖÖ, Selimoğlu MA. Malnutrition and obesity in children with ADHD. *J Atten Disord.* 2016;20(8):647–652. doi:10.1177/1087054713478465.
10. Han T. ADHD as a risk factor for obesity. *Current state of research.* 2018;52 (2):309–322.
11. Rivera HM, Christiansen KJ, Sullivan EL. The role of maternal obesity in the risk of neuropsychiatric disorders. *Front Neurosci.* 2015;9(May):1–16. doi:10.3389/fnins.2015.00194.
12. Cortese S, Tessari L. Attention-Deficit/Hyperactivity Disorder (ADHD) and obesity: Update. 2016. *Curr Psychiatry Rep.* 2017;19(1). doi:10.1007/s11920-017-0754-1.
13. Christakis DA, Zimmerman FJ, DiGiuseppe DL, McCarty CA. Early television exposure and subsequent attentional problems in children. *Pediatrics.* 2004;113 (4):708–713. doi:10.1542/peds.113.4.708.
14. Patton GC, Sawyer SM. Media and young minds. *Med J Aust.* 2000;173(11–12):570–571. doi:10.1542/peds.2016-2591.

15. Lenhart A. Teens, social media and technology overview 2015: Smartphones facilitate shifts in communication landscape for teens. *Pew Res Cent.* 2015; (April):1–47. doi:10.1016/j.chb.2015.08.026.
16. Swanson. Media use in school-aged children and adolescents. *Pediatrics.* 2016;138 (5):e20162592–e20162592. doi:10.1542/peds.2016-2592.
17. Flory K, Molina BSG, Pelham WE, Gnagy EM, Smith BH. Childhood ADHD predicts risky sexual behavior in young adulthood. *J Clin Child Adolesc Psychol.* 2006;35(4):571–577. doi:10.1207/s15374424jccp3504_8.
18. Nigg JT. Attention-deficit/hyperactivity disorder and adverse health outcomes. *Clin Psychol Rev.* 2013;33(2):215–228. doi:10.1016/j.cpr.2012.11.005.
19. Walshe EA, McIntosh CW, Romer D, Winston FK. Executive function capacities, negative driving behavior and crashes in young drivers. *Int J Environ Res Public Health.* 2017;14(11). doi:10.3390/ijerph14111314.

Part III
Assessment and Treatment

10 Assessment

J. Dennis Odell and Martin Toohill

After the preceding discussions, it should hopefully be evident that an evaluation for an individual suspected of having ADHD needs to be thorough, to assess all of the possible contributing factors that might be leading to the symptoms of concern. Frequent presenting symptoms are behavioral concerns with a child who is off task, distractible, oppositional, overactive and disruptive. Or there may be concerns about significant academic struggles related to inattentive behaviors. There may be concerns about difficulty socializing appropriately with peers, or serious acting-out behaviors. As we have seen, these symptoms may be from ADHD, but there are many other potential causes and frequently other conditions to consider, as well as the possibility that the symptoms of concern are compensatory symptoms from some other underlying condition. And while ADHD is very common, the other associated conditions are also very common, and need to be considered in any ADHD evaluation.

Children and adolescents will often first present for assessment either through the school district related to school academic and behavioral concerns, or to their primary health care provider. Adults may present to their family physician, or to psychologists, psychiatrists or counselors. Schools may do a preliminary assessment, and often do testing for learning problems and disabilities. They will not usually make a diagnosis of ADHD however, because ADHD is considered a medical condition. If concerns about ADHD are raised by the school, the child may be referred to medical providers for assessment, especially if there is the possibility that medical intervention may be needed.

An assessment for possible ADHD begins with a good history. What are the specific symptoms of concern, how long have they been present, how are the symptoms impacting the individual, the family, the classroom? Also important to know is what previous assessments have been done, and what interventions have been tried, including interventions by the parents. Background information on potential mediating causes is also very important, and includes factors such as health problems, developmental history, stressors in the home or school, parenting style, past medical history of adverse health such as prematurity, significant illnesses, surgery or infections, exposure to toxins or drugs, abuse, any medications being taken and allergies. The list of medical conditions alone that can cause ADHD symptoms is very long, and includes almost any chronic illness, genetic conditions, and of course mental health conditions.

Another important part of the assessment is a detailed family history. It is helpful to know if there are others in the family, including siblings, parents, aunts, uncles, cousins and grandparents, and beyond if known, with ADHD and related conditions, as well as any other health condition that runs in the family such as autoimmune disorders, endocrine, gastrointestinal and mental health disorders. It is also helpful to know what treatments were used for those individuals that helped, and any interventions that resulted in negative reactions.

The physical exam focuses on determining if there are any medical conditions that might be contributing to symptoms. This probably seems obvious, but ensuring that hearing and vision are normal is important. We have seen more than a few children whose symptoms were brought about by giant tonsils and resulting sleep apnea and sleep deprivation, whose symptoms resolved with tonsillectomy. Sleep problems are important to identify, as sleeplessness can affect attention and concentration. Sleeplessness can result from conditions like sleep apnea, but depression and anxiety also can be primary causes. Parents may not always be fully aware of sleep problems, or may minimize them. Seizure disorders that are unrecognized, gastrointestinal disturbances such as celiac disease, genetic conditions such as Turner syndrome and fragile X syndrome, thyroid disturbances, undertreated asthma and allergies are all examples of medical conditions that can mimic ADHD. Also, accurate measurement of blood pressure, pulse, height, weight and sometimes head circumference are essential for initial assessment and monitoring over time. Besides the general exam, a thorough cardiac exam is essential, not only to detect any underlying cardiac problems, but also because medication can affect cardiac status and can potentially worsen underlying conditions. Thorough neurologic exam is important as part of the evaluation for any underlying developmental or contributing neurologic conditions, including seizures, tic disorders, cerebral palsy and neurologic soft signs.

Part of the history should also include a review of systems, a body wide system review of any health issues. This includes any history of hearing, vision, heart and lung problems, gastrointestinal disturbances, orthopedic and neurologic problems, immune problems, frequent infections such as ear and respiratory infections, sleep difficulties, eating problems, allergies, any potential stressors such as recent moves, job changes, and family stressors such as new siblings, divorce, legal or financial problems. This is a long list of items to review, and can be made easier by having the family complete a health history form before the evaluation. Our medical background information packet is 17 pages long, and seems cumbersome, but does not take a long time to complete, and having it completed in advance helps immensely in guiding the medical part of the evaluation. Lab tests are not routinely recommended in the ADHD assessment, unless there are concerns in the history and physical exam of underlying medical conditions. These might include dietary insufficiencies, concerns about genetic conditions, endocrine conditions and others that would lead the examiner to order specific lab tests or imaging studies. Common potential tests might include testing for iron deficiency, vitamin D, magnesium, zinc, lead poisoning, thyroid disorders, electrocardiograms, EEGs with seizure concerns, genetic testing and others depending on the medical evaluation.

Keeping in mind the many potential areas that need to be assessed, the initial interview and history should provide the examiner with a good sense of what areas need further exploration. Accordingly, the evaluation proceeds with additional tools to assess ADHD and all of the potential associated conditions. Although the history of concerns is critical, additional information can be obtained with the use of appropriate evidence based questionnaires. There are many behavioral questionnaires that not only help determine what symptoms are present, but also the severity of those symptoms. It is useful to obtain information from multiple sources, different people who know the individual being assessed, at the least parents and teachers, or spouse/family members if appropriate. Questionnaires are an efficient way to obtain this collateral information, and in the case of children, help determine if the symptoms of concern are out of the range of what is expected for age. Many of the questionnaires also include items that address potential associated problems such as anxiety, depression, oppositional behavior, and sleep problems.

Behavior and ADHD Rating Scales

There are many questionnaires available now that are used for assessing ADHD. Questionnaires may be either broad band that screen for multiple different conditions including ADHD, or narrow band questionnaires that focus on a particular diagnosis. In assessing ADHD symptoms it is often worthwhile to include both a broad-band questionnaire to screen for associated problems, and a specific ADHD narrow-band questionnaire. Additionally, if concerns are picked up for other associated conditions such as anxiety or bipolar disorder, specific narrow-band questionnaires for those disorders can be helpful. There are so many questionnaires available that it is difficult to review all of them. Many questionnaires are regularly updated to include expanded normative data, or changes in our understanding of ADHD. Most practitioners will use a few questionnaires with which they are familiar and comfortable. Some questionnaires are public domain, free for anyone to use; others are copyrighted and can only be used if purchased. Some are included in ADHD assessment manuals that allow photocopying of the questionnaires for use in clinical practice.

Broad Band Scales

A commonly used broad band group of questionnaires are the Achenbach (ASEBA-Achenbach System of Empirically Based Assessment) child behavior checklist, youth self-report and teacher report form (www.aseba.org). These are heavily researched and have a long track record of reliability, and there is research information available on use in multiple cultures. These are somewhat lengthy 4-page questionnaires, taking about 15 minutes to complete, and include sections that also ask about interests, hobbies, social interactions and very useful sections for personal comments and observations. There are versions available for use from ages 1 1/2 to 18 and are normed for age and gender. There is also an adult version for use in ages up to 60 and another for ages 60 and beyond. Computer scoring is available, and the scoring provides a graphic profile of both symptoms as well as DSM-5 oriented conditions, including ADHD, anxiety and depression, ODD and conduct disorders. In addition, the results from multiple informants can be combined into an integrated report. The Achenbach checklists are designed to assess for a wide range of emotional and behavioral problems, not just ADHD. There are fees and costs associated with their use, and all forms are copyrighted.

Another broad band group of assessment instruments is the Behavior Assessment System for Children, third edition (BASC-3)[1] that assesses for ADHD and multiple associated conditions, similar to the Achenbach questionnaires. The third version of the BASC rating scales is rather complete and includes parent and teacher versions, a self-report questionnaire, a student observation system to record direct observations in the classroom and structured developmental history that reviews background information on the individual. Questionnaires come in preschool, child and adolescent versions, and can be used for those from ages 2–22. The BASC-3 is used widely in school districts as part of school psychoeducational assessments. Like the ASEBA series of questionnaires, there is computer scoring, and results are displayed in graphic form. The BASC-3 is also copyrighted, and requires a fee for use. Like the Achenbach scales, the BASC-3 provides standardized behavior data on a range of clinical conditions that often co-exist with ADHD.

Narrow Band Scales

Questionnaires specific to ADHD assessment include the NICHQ Vanderbilt Assessment Scales. The Vanderbilt Scales come in a version for parents and for teachers, and there is also a follow up version to monitor symptoms and side effects over time for those treated with medication. These are short and easy to complete and basically review DSM-5 criteria for ADHD, oppositional defiant disorder, conduct disorder and anxiety/depression, and also have a section to rate the degree of severity of symptoms in different environments. These are scored based on DSM criteria for presence of specific symptoms in each category.

The original or first edition NICHQ (2002) was for children aged 6–12 and is still available for free download, English version only. The second edition was released in 2011 as part of the *American Academy of Pediatrics Caring for Children with ADHD: A Resource Toolkit for Clinicians.*[2] The age range was extended from age 4 to 18 years, and additional resources have been added for identification, diagnosis, and management of ADHD and various comorbid conditions. The second edition also is available in Spanish. The entire Resource Toolkit is available from the on-line American Academy of Pediatrics (AAP) Bookstore.

The SNAP-IV (Swanson, Nolan and Pelham Questionnaire) is a 90-item rating scale for parents and teachers, also in the public domain and uses DSM-5 criteria for ADHD. There are versions in English and Spanish. It was originally developed for ADHD assessment based on DSM-III criteria, but has been updated as the DSM has been updated. It also has brief screening questions for a variety of other disorders that may mimic ADHD.[3]

Beginning in the 1990s, Russell Barkley, George DePaul, and their colleagues have created a number of behavior rating scales for children, adolescents, and adults that have been centered on ADHD criteria as specified in the *American Psychiatric Association's Diagnostic and Statistical Manual of Mental Disorders*, fourth edition (DSM-IV) and the fifth edition (DSM-5). Ratings for the related disorders of Oppositional Defiant Disorder and Conduct Disorder are also included. These behavior rating scales have been published in commercially available manuals and workbooks, and allow the individual purchaser to reproduce the checklists for use with their patients. In addition, normative data based on frequency and severity of ADHD symptoms, age, gender, and the informant (parent or teacher) have been provided and updated over the years. These behavior rating scales are usually quickly completed and scored.

- The *ADHD Rating Scale for Children and Adolescents: Checklists, Norms, and Clinical Interpretation* is used for Children and adolescents ages 5–17. [4] It was updated to the DSM-5, with extensive reliability and validity data based on a nationwide 2014 sample. There are separate home and school versions that incorporate measures of severity of functional impairment. There are both English and Spanish versions which take less than 10 minutes to complete.
- The *Barkley Adult ADHD Rating Scale-IV* is used for adults ages 18–89. It utilizes rating scales of both current behaviors and childhood behaviors completed by the client and by significant others.[5] While the scales were based on the DSM-IV criteria for ADHD, which are similar to the current DSM-5 criteria, reliability and validity data were sound, based on a demographically representative nationwide sample of over 1,300 adults completed in 2010. Symptoms of inattention known as

slow cognitive tempo are examined. Like the child/adolescent ADHD rating scale, the adult scales can be completed in minutes. There is only an English language version.

Dr. C. Keith Conners has been a leading researcher in the field of ADHD and has published rating scales that have been widely used by clinicians. The Conners third edition (Conners 3) is the most recent version, intended for children from age 6 to 18, and includes parent, teacher, and self-report forms, and takes about 15–20 minutes to complete.[6] The Conners questionnaires are a bit more specific for ADHD than the Achenbach questionnaires, and at least the parent versions are probably similar in their sensitivity and specificity in detecting ADHD.[7] The scoring sheet also provides a graphic view of results. It is copyrighted and there is a cost to use it. There is a DSM-5 supplement that updates the scoring in line with DSM-5 changes. It also addresses the common comorbid conditions of oppositional defiant disorder and conduct disorder. A Spanish language version is available, and computer scoring is available.

For assessment of details of attentional problems and executive function, the Brown Attention-Deficit Disorder Scales (Brown ADD Scales) is a helpful tool.[8] There are versions available for use in ages 3 through adulthood, and results break down difficulties into 6 clusters of behavior including organization skills, focusing and sustained attention, regulating alertness, managing frustration, utilizing working memory, and monitoring and self-regulating action. This is particularly helpful in sorting out specific aspects of attentional difficulties, and can be a helpful adjunct in assessing an individual with concerns about ADHD, especially the inattentive component. For younger children, teachers and parents complete a questionnaire. For children 8 and above, The Brown ADD Scale utilizes an interview format for obtaining both self-report and collateral ratings. A newer version that focuses more on executive function deficits, the Brown Executive Function/Attention Scales was recently released, with versions available for ages 3 through adulthood.

Another helpful tool for assessing executive function as part of an ADHD assessment is the BRIEF (Behavior Rating Inventory of Executive Function) and the more recent BRIEF-2.[9] It is helpful in elucidating details of difficulties related to executive function in a variety of disorders, including ADHD. This measure includes parent and teacher questionnaires designed for use in ages 5–18, along with an adolescent self-report form (11–18). There are screening forms for parents, teachers, and adolescents designed to determine if more comprehensive executive function evaluation is necessary. A preschool version (ages 2 to 6) is also available. For adults, there is an adult version (ages 18–90) with both self-report and informant (significant other) formats. The BRIEF2 is available in Spanish. In addition, both online scoring and administration is available for some of the BRIEF versions.

Many rating scales and assessment measures can be downloaded from CADDRA (Canadian ADHD Resource Alliance). CHADD (Children and Adults with Attention-Deficit/Hyperactivity Disorder) is another site that provides information on rating scales.

Rating Scales for Specific Associated Disorders

Additional rating scales are available that target other specific areas of concern. These include anxiety disorders, depression, bipolar disorder and autism. There is a plethora of rating scales available and only a few selected scales are reviewed here. One source for many self-reported measures that are meant to be part of healthcare monitoring is the PROMIS (Patient Reported Outcomes Measurement Information System) Health Organization. PROMIS measures are publicly available, and can be accessed at their website (www.promishealth.com).

Depression: There are multiple rating scales used to assess depression symptoms and severity, and can be used both for diagnosis and monitoring interventions.

- The Patient Health Questionnaire is widely used as a screening tool in medical offices as a basis for the need for further assessment for depression.[10] The PHQ-2 is a 2 question tool that asks about depressed mood and lack of interest or pleasurable activities over the past 2 weeks. If either question is answered as a concern, further evaluation for depression and suicidal ideation using the PHQ-9 (a 9-item depression scale), other diagnostic instruments, or direct interview are recommended. The PHQ-2 and PHQ-9 are public domain with details available on the internet, and are very easy to administer.
- The Children's Depression Inventory 2 (CDI 2) is used for ages 7–17. [11] It is a 28 item self-report measure with scales that include emotional problems, functional problems, negative mood/physical symptoms, and negative self-esteem. It gives a measure of depression severity.
- Another is the Beck Depression Inventory-II (BDI-II) which is a 21 item self-assessment questionnaire that provides an overall score enabling measurement of severity of depression symptoms, and is useful for monitoring treatment effects. It is designed for use in ages 13 and above, and is copyrighted.[12]
- The third edition of the Piers-Harris Self-Concept Scale (Piers-Harris 3) is for use in ages 6–22 and is a self-assessment measure using a simple yes/no format.[13] It is particularly useful for use in pediatrics to analyze symptoms based on the individual's own perceptions rather than observations of caregivers and teachers. The various scales provide information on behavior, anxiety, happiness, school status, physical appearance and social acceptance.

- Finally, the Hamilton Rating Scale for Depression (HRSD or HAM-D) has been in use since the 1960s.[14] It is designed for adults and assesses various symptoms of depression and is designed for use as part of a clinical interview and not to be used as a diagnostic instrument. It has been criticized for its emphasis on somatic symptoms of depression such as sleep difficulties and less so on negative thoughts, feelings of worthlessness, and suicidal actions.

It should be emphasized that results of these depression questionnaires will not render a diagnosis, but are useful for getting a sense of the presence and severity of specific symptoms and can guide the clinical interview. It is important to examine responses to individual items and when needed ask the client to elaborate further. Some specific depressive symptoms which need careful scrutiny include those reporting thoughts of self-harm or harm to others.

Anxiety Rating Scales: There are a number of scales and questionnaires used to assess anxiety and related disorders in children.

- The RCMAS-2 (Revised Children's Manifest Anxiety Scale) is a widely used tool that is useful as an assessment of overall anxiety in children and adolescents from ages 6–19.[15] It is a 49 item measure of the level and nature of anxiety, and answers are in a yes/no format. Subscales include physiological anxiety, worry, social anxiety, defensiveness, performance anxiety and an index to measure inconsistent responding. It takes 10–15 minutes to complete and paper-pencil and online versions are available. The items are short and fairly easy to read for children with reading skills at the 2nd/3rd grade level or better. An audio version of the test items also is provided. The RCMAS-2 is copyrighted and there is a cost for use.
- The STAI (State-Trait Anxiety Inventory) is a 40-item self-report questionnaire that measures the intensity of current symptoms (state) and more chronic and enduring anxiety symptoms in general (trait). There are versions for both adolescents over 15 to adult[16] and children (ages 9–12) but can be verbally read to younger children.[17] The STAI has been adapted for use by children in medical settings.
- The MASC-2 (Multidimensional Anxiety Scale for Children) is a 50 item rating scale that captures both the range in severity of anxiety symptoms.[18] It is used in those aged 8–19, with a parent version and child self-report version (requires 3rd grade reading skills). Both online and paper-and-pencil versions are available. It is also copyrighted.
- Spence Children's Anxiety Scale consists of 44 items with six categories, social phobia, separation anxiety, panic, OCD, generalized anxiety and fear of physical injury, so is helpful for specifying anxiety subtypes based on DSM-IV criteria for children and adolescents (ages 8–15). It was originally intended for children, can be completed by the

child or the parent/caregiver, and although copyrighted, is freely accessible with some restrictions (www.scaswebsitecom). It has been psychometrically evaluated in numerous countries. A shorter preschool edition (ages 2.5–6) has been developed.

- Another similar questionnaire is the SCARED (Screen for Child Anxiety Related Disorders), which is a 41 item self-report or parent report questionnaire, yielding a total score for anxiety and also scores for panic disorder or somatic symptoms, generalized anxiety disorder, social anxiety and school avoidance.[19] It is free of charge and information is accessible online (www.pediatricbipolar.pitt.edu under resources/instruments).

Bipolar Disorder: Diagnosing bipolar disorder can be challenging, especially in children. While the lifetime prevalence of Bipolar I disorder is low (1%), bipolar spectrum disorders (bipolar I and II, cyclothymia) are more common in those with ADHD, especially among those displaying symptoms of depression. Misdiagnosis can have profound consequences. Rating scales for bipolar disorder in pediatrics have a high false positive rate, but still can be helpful in assessing risk and presence of bipolar symptoms. Specific mania rating scales are available and most are in the public domain. While the scales listed below focus on symptoms of mania, it is imperative that any assessment of bipolar disorder also include careful evaluation of depressive symptoms (using one of the above measures and clinical interview) to identify any suicidal or other potentially lethal/risky behaviors being displayed or experienced by the individual.

- The Child Mania Rating Scale (CMRS) is a 21-item screening/initial evaluation tool for assessing symptoms characteristic of a manic episode (using DSM-IV criteria) in children 5–17. It can be used to assist in diagnosis. The parent version (CMRS-P) has been found to have excellent sensitivity and specificity and children with mania from control children and those with ADHD.[20] A teacher and brief version are available, and all can be used for monitoring treatment progress. These are in the public domain and available online.
- The Young Mania Rating Scale (YMRS) is an 11 item inventory for individuals 18 years or older who display symptoms of a manic episode. [21] It reviews the client's subjective report of symptoms experienced over the last 48 hours, and is completed by the clinician based upon the interview and clinical observations. It is meant to evaluate symptoms at baseline and to monitor symptoms over time. This is normally used by psychiatrists, or others who have specific experience in evaluation for bipolar disorder. For children ages 5–17, parent and teacher versions were adapted from the original YMRS and are used for assessing Bipolar Disorders, Type I and II.

- The Mood Disorder Questionnaire is a brief self-report measure that screens for lifetime histories of manic or hypomanic symptoms.[22] It originally was developed for adults, but has been studied in adolescents 11 years and older. A parent-report version was created in 2006 allowing for assessment of bipolar symptoms in children and adolescents from a caregiver perspective, with some research using it for children as young as five years of age. It takes only 5 to 10 minutes to complete. It is free and available online.

Additional Measures

At times developmental assessment is indicated and is usually part of general well child medical visits with measures such as the Ages and Stages Questionnaires, screening for early intervention programs, and school assessments. Psychoeducational testing is often part of the ADHD evaluation, and is reviewed in the chapter on learning disabilities. Likewise autism screening and evaluation may be indicated, with screening instruments such as the M-CHAT-R for young children, and the Social Communication Questionnaire, Autism Spectrum Disorder Evaluation Scale, and the Gilliam Autism Rating Scale-3 which are screening instruments for older children and adolescents. A useful screening instrument for substance abuse in adolescents is the CRAFFT.[23] It is a very brief measure meant to elicit risk of substance abuse and is either completed as a self-report measure or as a brief clinical interview. It is available for free online.

Generally, unless neurologic problems are suspected based on history and physical examination, imaging studies such as MRI or CT scans, and EEGs are not indicated. That being said there are some clinics around the country that utilize more specialized imaging techniques to aid in diagnoses and management of those with ADHD and other mental health and developmental concerns. SPECT scans (Single Photon Emission Computed Tomography) are CT scans done of the brain after injection of a radioactive isotope that allows assessment of blood flow in different parts of the brain and is therefore a measure of brain activity. Those who advocate for these claim they can more accurately characterize the root of ADHD symptoms and therefore more optimize treatments. Radiation exposure is not high, but is an issue nonetheless, and is a bigger concern in children. The costs of the procedure are high, and use of SPECT scanning in assessment of ADHD is very controversial, and neither the American Academy of Pediatrics nor the American Academy of Child and Adolescent Psychiatry recommend routine neuroimaging as part of the ADHD evaluation.

Another controversial procedure for assessment of the brain in ADHD is EEGs (electroencephalography), and especially quantitative EEGs. These purportedly reveal distinct brain patterns that can be helpful in clarification of the cause of ADHD symptoms. One device was U.S. Food and Drug Administration (FDA) approved for use in ADHD assessment in 2013

(NEBA-Neuropsychiatric EEG-Based Assessment Aid), and reportedly helps in clarifying the ADHD diagnosis and ruling out other disorders that may mimic the ADHD symptoms. It is also costly, but comes with no radiation risk. Again quantitative EEGs are not currently recommended as part of the routine assessment, but there appears to be some promise as technology improves in the use of these modalities for fine tuning the ADHD diagnosis.

Simpler and far less expensive measures of ADHD include the continuous performance tests that have been used for years to measure ADHD symptoms in a clinical setting. These are computer measures that are based on performance of very tedious vigilance tasks, and the ability of the individual to stay focused and on task is measured. The reliability is somewhat questionable in accurately diagnosing ADHD, but can be a helpful adjunct. Types of continuous performance tests available include the Integrated Visual and Auditory Continuous Performance Test (IVA), Gordon diagnostic system and Conners Continuous Performance Test (CPT).

It is important to emphasize that diagnoses are not made based on scores of behavioral questionnaires alone. The questionnaires yield information about specific symptoms and the degree to which these symptoms are causing impairment in various settings (for example home and school), and if they are out of the typical range of behavior. This information obtained from multiple informants is used in addition to the history, background information, specific testing and clinical impression to render a formal diagnosis. For all available data, it is important to recognize the variability across cultures, and the need to take into consideration cultural differences in behavioral expectations.

Bibliography

1. Reynolds, Cecil R and Kamphaus RW. *Behavior Assessment System for Children, Third Edition* (BASC-3). Pearson.
2. *Caring for Children with ADHD: A Resource Toolkit for Clinicians, 2nd Edition.* 2011. American Academy of Pediatrics.
3. Bussing R, Fernandez M, Harwood M, et al. Parent and teacher SNAP-IV ratings of attention deficit hyperactivity disorder symptoms: Psychometric properties and normative ratings from a school district sample. *Assessment.* 2008;15(3):317–328. doi:10.1177/1073191107313888.
4. Dupaul GJ, Power TJ, Anastopoulos AD, Reid R. *ADHD Rating Scale-5 for Children and Adolescents Checklists, Norms, and Clinical Interpretation.* Guildford. 2016.
5. Barkley RA. *Barkley Adult ADHD Rating Scale-IV (BAARS-IV).* Guildford. 2011.
6. Conners CK. *Conners 3rd Edition.* WPS. 2008.
7. Chang L-Y, Wang M-Y, Tsai P-S.Diagnostic accuracy of rating scales for attention-deficit/hyperactivity disorder: A meta-analysis. *Pediatrics.* 2016;137(3): e20152749–e20152749. doi:10.1542/peds.2015-2749.
8. Brown TE. *Brown Attention-Deficit Disorder Scales® (BrownADDScales).* Pearson.

9. Gioia GA, Isquith PK, Guy SC, Kenworthy L.Behavior rating inventory of executive function®, second edition (BRIEF®2). *Child Neuropsychol (Neuropsychology, Dev Cogn Sect C)*. 2015. doi:10.1076/chin.6.3.235.3152.

10. Kroenke K, Spitzer RL, Williams JB. The PHQ-9: validity of a brief depression severity measure. *J Gen Intern Med*. 2001;16(9):606–613. doi:10.1046/j.1525-1497.2001.016009606.x.

11. Kovacs M. *Children's Depression Inventory 2 (CDI 2)*. WPS. 2010.

12. Beck AT. *Beck Depression Inventory-II (BDI-II)*. Pearson. 1996.

13. Piers E V., Shemmassian SK, Herzberg D. *Piers-Harris Self-Concept Scale, Third Edition*. WPS. 2018.

14. Hamilton M. A rating scale for depression. *J Neurol Neurosurg Psychiatry*. 1960;23:56–62.

15. Reynolds CR, Richmond BO. *Revised Children's Manifest Anxiety Scale, Second Edition (RCMAS-2)*. WPS. 2008.

16. Spielberger CD. *State-Trait Anxiety Inventory for Adults*. Mind Garden. 1977.

17. Spielberger CD, Edwards CD, Montuori J, Lushene R. *State-Trait Anxiety Inventory for Children*. Mind Garden. 1970.

18. March JS. *Multidimensional Anxiety Scale for Children, 2nd Edition* (MASC 2). Pearson. 2012.

19. Birmaher B, Brent DA, Chiappetta L, Bridge J, Monga S, Baugher M. Psychometric properties of the screen for child anxiety related emotional disorders (SCARED): A replication study. *J Am Acad Child Adolesc Psychiatry*. 1999;38 (10):1230–1236. doi:10.1097/00004583-199910000-00011.

20. Pavuluri MN, Henry DB, Devineni B, Carbray JA, Birmaher B. Child mania rating scale: development, reliability, and validity. *J Am Acad Child Adolesc Psychiatry*. 2006;45(5):550–560. doi:10.1097/01.chi.0000205700.40700.50.

21. Young RC, Biggs JT, Ziegler VE, Meyer DA. A rating scale for mania: reliability, validity and sensitivity. *Br J Psychiatry*. 1978;133:429–435.

22. Hirschfeld RMA, Williams JBW, Spitzer RL, et al. Development and validation of a screening instrument for bipolar spectrum disorder: The mood disorder questionnaire. *Am J Psychiatry*. 2000;157(11):1873–1875. doi:10.1176/appi.ajp.157.11.1873.

23. Knight JR, Shrier LA, Bravender TD, Farrell M, Vander Bilt J, Shaffer HJ. A new brief screen for adolescent substance abuse. *Arch Pediatr Adolesc Med*. 1999;153(6):591–596.

11 Medication Management

J. Dennis Odell

Introduction

The following is a discussion of medications currently used to treat ADHD and related conditions. General principles and guidelines are outlined, but specific recommendations for any of the conditions discussed need to be carried out under the direction of the prescribing provider. Before going over specific medications it is worthwhile reviewing a few basic principles regarding medication use in general, and especially in children. Although most of the conditions described in this work are behaviorally defined, and have behaviorally driven therapeutic interventions, many of the symptoms of each of these conditions can be at least partly ameliorated by medications. All medications, and side effects, and any decision regarding instituting medication requires an understanding of benefits as well as side effects and a decision as to whether the benefits are worth the risks. In children there are additional considerations. Children are not just little adults when it comes to medications. Responses to medications vary with age, based in part on metabolic rate. Often children require relatively higher doses per weight than adults, and side effects may be more prevalent and severe. There are also potential unknown side effects related to effects on growth and neurodevelopment.

There are additional factors to consider, as we do not all metabolize medicines the same way. Oftentimes we simplistically assume that one dose fits all. For example, for a headache, for adults and older children, the dose of ibuprofen is two 200mg tablets, and it does not matter whether you are 15 or 80 years old, male or female, 80 pounds or 500 pounds. Obviously, if we want to be accurate, dosage needs to be fine-tuned more than this. Additionally there are significant variations genetically in how individuals metabolize medications. This can actually be measured with new DNA technology, so it is possible to determine what one's metabolic profile is by doing a specific genetic test for that purpose. Although these tests are available, they are not done widely because of the cost, and are often not necessary. Additionally there are variations that have to do with time of day, other medications or foods on board, body habitus, age and gender. All of these factors play a part in dosing and have to be considered in determining the best dose and regimen for an individual.

A word about medication costs in general. Medication costs have sky-rocketed, and costs are widely different depending on the preparation and whether it is generic or brand name. Choices of which medications are going to be prescribed have to take into consideration the costs, which can be prohibitive. Insurance companies vary widely on what medications they will cover, and costs are different at different pharmacies. Given the costs that may be involved, doing a little bit of homework can often save quite a bit of money. Additionally there are often coupons that are provided to physician's offices or pharmacies, or they can be obtained on line, that can provide significant discounts. For example, generic Adderall XR 10mg capsules are listed as anywhere from US$136 to $177 for a month's supply at pharmacies in our area. This same prescription with a discount coupon from GoodRX can be obtained from $67 to $104 depending on the pharmacy. Websites like GoodRx and others can also provide information on medication costs at different pharmacies in an area, helping to find the least expensive options. And, some pharmacies will match prices if a medication can be found for a lower price at another pharmacy. Some medications come as tablet forms that are scored and can be cut in half. The cost for the medication may be the same, regardless of strength, so for example ½ of a sertraline 50mg tablet will cost about ½ of the price of 25mg tablets. It would be nice not to have to worry about expense when deciding on the best choice of medication, but unfortunately, for many medications used to treat ADHD and related problems, costs can be huge.

Off-label Use of Medications

Medications are approved for use by the US Food and Drug Administration (FDA) based on studies and trials that demonstrate evidence of efficacy and safety for a specific indication and in a specific age group. The approval is made only for those studied indications, and any other use is considered "off label". Any additional indications for that drug would require additional studies at additional costs to the sponsor (usually pharmaceutical company), and so often no additional studies are done, and medications are officially approved only for the initial studied indications. This is especially a problem in pediatrics because often the drug trials are only done in adults. Obtaining clearance to do studies in children is much more difficult and often not done. Off label use means a drug is being prescribed for an indication that is not in the FDA approved labeling for that drug. It does not mean it is being used illegally or improperly, or that its use is not supported by clinical research and experience, only that evidence for safety and efficacy for that indication was not submitted to the FDA for review or met standards demonstrating evidence for that indication. Off-label use of a medication is up to the judgment of the prescriber. Post marketing surveillance is done by the FDA to monitor for unexpected side effects after marketing of a new drug, and if adverse events are reported, the FDA will request further studies, add warnings to the drug labelling, or if needed withdraw FDA approval.[1]

Many medications that are used for children may be being used off label. In a review of the *Physicians' Desk Reference* catalog of medications 2009, less than ½ had some information on pediatric use in the labelling.[2] This means that the physician has the prerogative to use the medication, but the original studies, allowing approval by the FDA have not been done on the particular age or diagnosis being treated. So for example, Ritalin and methylphenidate are not FDA approved under age 6, in spite of stimulant guidelines recommending their use in children under age 6 if symptoms warrant it.[3] So it is not uncommon for young children to be treated for ADHD with methylphenidate or Ritalin based on those studies. However, this would still be considered off-label use.

Generic vs Brand Name Drugs

Usually, but not always, generic medications are less expensive than brand name drugs, and insurance companies usually will cover the costs of generics at a lower price than brand name. Usually this is not a problem, but there have been occasions where generic medications are not equivalent to what they are supposed to be replacing. Years ago, when Dilantin was often used to treat individuals with seizure disorders, there were problems with Dilantin generics. Patients who had been doing well started having seizures again when they were switched to what were supposed to be generic equivalents. Part of this had to do with the unique characteristics of the medicine itself, as Dilantin is unusual in the way it is metabolized. But it clearly emphasizes the point that generics are not "identical" to the brand name drugs they are supposed to replace.

Another more recent example was with the stimulant drug Concerta. When the patent ran out, three different manufacturers started making a generic version. The original Concerta had a unique delivery system that was designed to provide about 12 hours of methylphenidate activity, the active ingredient. It has been widely used for treating ADHD. The generic versions were touted as being the same as Concerta, but soon after they hit the market, patients reported less efficacy of the new generics. The FDA reviewed the products again, and determined that the new generic versions from 2 drug manufacturers were in fact not delivering the medication at the same rate as the Concerta, so were not bioequivalent. The designation was changed to a statement that data are insufficient to determine therapeutic equivalence for 2 of the manufacturers, but also a third manufacturer (the one that made the original brand name version) was felt to be bioequivalent to Concerta.[4] The products are still on the market, but should not be considered the same as brand name Concerta. Concerta used to be very straightforward and consistent in its results, but now with several different manufacturers that are providing less than bioequivalent generics, the results are much less consistent. And, equivalence between generics is also not demonstrated, so switching from one generic to another will not necessarily give equal results. Part of this has to do with the uniqueness of the Concerta delivery system that is not exactly replicated in the generic versions.

There are standards that generics must meet that they are shown to be essentially the same as the brand name medicine as far as effects, side effects, stability of the product, and quality. The active ingredients have to be the same. For the most part, comparisons between generics and brand name products show them usually to be very close.

Monitoring Effects and Side Effects

All medications come with side effects. Most of the side effects that are seen are common and predictable, but occasionally there are rare side effects that are unique to the individual being treated. There are certain medical conditions, including heart disease, seizure disorders, liver and kidney diseases that require special precautions when using most medications. In the case of most of the medicines we will review, it is appropriate and recommended that periodic follow up in the prescribers office be done to ensure symptoms are being adequately treated and side effects are minimal. This normally entails reviewing the treatment effects and adverse effects since the last office contact, but also performing a physical exam that includes growth parameters, blood pressure and pulse rate, as well as careful cardiac and neurologic exam.

It is important to be clear what symptoms are being treated, what the expected effects of the medication are, and what side effects are to be anticipated. There are symptom rating scales and side effect monitoring tools that can be used for medicines used to treat ADHD. It is often helpful when initiating medication for the family to start a medication diary where they can notate symptoms being treated, and can record observations at home, school, work and social interactions on the beneficial effects and any side effects that are seen. This is especially useful over the long term, as results of different medication trials may not be recalled otherwise. Use of multiple medications, which can be very common, raises the concerns of potentially more side effects, as additional medications may affect the metabolism of concurrently used medicines.

Medications for ADHD

Having a diagnosis of ADHD does not mean that medication is required for treatment. However, if symptoms are severe enough to warrant it, medication management can be very beneficial, and there is a long history of effective treatments of ADHD that include the use of medications.

Stimulants

There are multiple medications on the market now that are used for treating ADHD, and it may seem overwhelming to decide which one is best. However, they can be divided into broad categories that help make sense of the options. Stimulant medications are generally the first choice for treating ADHD symptoms. Stimulant medications have been in use for treating behavior problems in children since 1937, but came into more widespread use starting in the 1960s. They are by far the most widely used medications for ADHD in the United States. There are now at least 30 different stimulant medications currently on the market in the United States for treating ADHD, but they can be divided into 2 main classes, either methylphenidate (Ritalin) preparations or amphetamine derivatives. Generally, the effects and side effects of all of the stimulant medications are similar, and the main differences amongst all of the different types of stimulants available have to do with how they are delivered (pills, liquid, chewable, capsules, tablets, patches), how long they last (4–16 hours), and cost. They are very similar but not identical in their mechanism of action. Technically, methylphenidate increases the levels of the neurotransmitters dopamine and norepinephrine in nerve synapses in the brain by inhibiting their reuptake after they have been released in the synapse, while amphetamine does the same plus increases the rate of release of those 2 neurotransmitters, and both do this primarily in the prefrontal cortex and related structures.[5]

Stimulants are prescribed widely because their efficacy can be striking, and they are generally very straightforward as far as effects and side effects. Stimulants work quickly, with onset usually ½ to 1 hour after administration, depending on the preparation. They do not have to build up over time to be effective, unlike medicines typically used for depression and anxiety. They are used to suppress the symptoms and enhance self-control and cognition, but do not cure ADHD. Their effect is analogous to pain medicines such as acetaminophen or ibuprofen, where onset is fairly quick, they last a number of hours, and then wear off. Stimulants are generally very effective, regardless of which ADHD subtype is being treated.

Stimulant medications are usually well tolerated, but side effects are universal in those taking stimulant medications. Common expected side effects are suppression of appetite with sometimes associated weight loss, and if the medication is still on board, difficulty sleeping. It is very common for children to be moody or irritable with these medications, especially when they are wearing off. There may frequently be rebound moodiness and hyperactivity when the medication is wearing off, and this is more problematic with higher dosages. Stimulant medication may suppress the personality to a degree. The point is to take the edge off of the overactive personality, but not to take away or blunt the personality. If a parent says their child has turned into a zombie on stimulant medication, this suggests the dose was too high or it was the wrong medication. Stimulants can sometimes cause agitation and can cause or worsen tics. Headaches, nausea and dizziness are not uncommon. Sometimes these are manifestations of the decreased appetite, with afternoon headaches occurring because of eating very little breakfast or lunch. Insisting on healthy snacking and adequate fluids, even when not hungry can help. Often side effects become less prominent after the medication has been taken for a few weeks. Rarely there can be more extreme side effects such as extreme irritability, agitation, aggressive behavior, extreme moodiness, restlessness or even psychosis, but these effects are not common. Unusual or uncommon side effects should raise the question of possible other underlying conditions such as bipolar disorder, autism or developmental disabilities.

Long-term Side Effects

Growth: There have been some concerns about long-term stimulant effects on growth. Because of the side effect of appetite suppression, it is not uncommon for individuals to lose weight or to gain weight at a slower rate than expected. There appear to be some mild effects related to height, either in ultimate adult height, or the rate at achieving that height, but effects on height appear to be very minimal.[6],[7] Because of this concern, part of the monitoring of treatment side effects is to monitor height and weight at each office visit, plotting them on standard growth charts to be sure growth rates are appropriate. Drug holidays can help if there is any evidence of growth suppression.

Tics: There have also been questions about stimulant medication in children who have tics or Tourette's syndrome. Stimulants are known to increase tics, and presence of tics used to be a contraindication to the use of stimulants. However, it appears that stimulants do not cause Tourette's syndrome, and although they may make tics worse, tics are no longer considered a contraindication to stimulant use. Methylphenidate appears to be better in those with tics than amphetamine preparations, and sometimes tics may improve with methylphenidate.[8] This is another area that needs to be monitored however.

Drug abuse: Another question that often comes up is whether these medications are addictive or lead to drug abuse, and the answers are complicated. All stimulant medications used for ADHD are schedule II drugs, which are in the same class of medications as narcotics, and means they have a high potential for abuse and addiction. Stimulants are on the list of banned substances for participation in sports, including high school, intercollegiate and Olympics, and can only be taken if there is a medical waiver based on a formal standard ADHD assessment. Because of the abuse potential of these medications, there have been many studies that have tried to address the risk of abuse of stimulants and ADHD. As previously discussed in chapter 3, ADHD itself carries an increased risk of substance abuse, especially when associated with conduct disorder. Long-term follow up in the MTA study demonstrated significantly higher rates in adolescents and adults of cigarette smoking, marijuana use, illicit drugs and alcohol in those diagnosed with ADHD as children, and the earlier the age of substance use, the greater the risk.[9]

To clarify, drug abuse means using the drug in any way other than as prescribed. Using any drug obtained illegally, using someone else's medication, using it at higher doses than prescribed, using it in some other form than prescribed (intravenous, snorting), are examples of drug abuse. Doing this on a long-term or chronic basis, even if intermittent, qualifies as a substance abuse disorder. Substance use disorder is a pathologic pattern of behaviors related to the use of the drug. As defined in the DSM-5, individuals with a stimulant use disorder may have impaired control over the use of the stimulant. This might include taking the substance in larger amounts or for longer periods than originally intended, unsuccessful efforts to discontinue use, large amount of time and effort spent in trying to obtain the drug or recover from its effects and intense cravings to use the drug. They may also exhibit social impairment related to the abuse of stimulants, such as failure to meet work, school or home obligations, persistent use in spite of social or interpersonal problems caused by the use of the drug, and limiting or withdrawing from previous enjoyable activities. Individuals suffering from substance abuse disorder may continue to use the substance in spite of awareness that it is causing significant physical or psychological problems. They may exhibit tolerance to the drug, requiring progressively higher doses to achieve the same effect. They may exhibit withdrawal effects after prolonged heavy use. Because of the vagueness of the definition, the term addiction is not used in the DSM-5 classification, but it is understood that substance abuse disorder covers a wide range of symptoms from mild abuse to a severe disorder of relapsing and compulsive drug use.[10]

As frightening as that sounds, stimulants also have a long track record of safety when prescribed appropriately, and have been taken safely by literally millions of children, adolescents and adults. The question to be answered is does use of stimulant medication increase the risk for substance abuse in those with ADHD. Studies that have looked at this have demonstrated no increased risk of substance abuse, and if anything a decreased risk of later substance abuse in those treated with stimulants. For example, this was demonstrated in a national study in Sweden published in 2014 looking at outcomes for almost 40,000 men and women with ADHD.[11]

In actual practice, the dosage of stimulant medications prescribed is within a rather narrow recommended range. It is not uncommon for an initial low dose to be effective for a few months, but to then lose efficacy, so a higher dose is then needed. This is a one-time, honeymoon effect. After the initial dosage adjustment, the dose does not usually need to be increased for therapeutic effects except as weight increases. As children age into adolescence and adulthood, the dose stabilizes even with increased weight, and often decreases with age. So the need for progressively higher than expected doses is uncommon, and is a red flag for misuse or abuse. With higher doses that are taken daily, tapering the dose to stop the medication is suggested to avoid uncomfortable withdrawal effects, but for low or usual doses it is reasonable and well tolerated to take the medication only on weekdays and not on weekends, holidays or summertime. As expected with anyone with ADHD, remembering to take the medication daily is a challenge, and missing doses is a common occurrence that does not normally cause any adverse effects. Stopping the medication suddenly happens often, either because of running out of medicine and not having a new prescription, or just not wanting to take the medication, and this does not typically cause withdrawal effects. These are not the effects expected for one who is abusing stimulant medication.

In summary, it appears that those with ADHD carry a higher risk for substance abuse disorders, but appropriate treatment with stimulant medications carries no increased risk for substance abuse, and may actually lower the risk. But, stimulants are schedule II drugs, and their prescription and use are tightly regulated and monitored by the FDA. They should only be used as prescribed, and any changes should only be done in consultation with the licensed prescribing provider, and fully documented in the medical record.

Brain development: A potential area of concern is effects of stimulant medications on the developing brain. One of the concerns of any medication used in childhood is that the nervous system in children is still developing well into adolescence, and that medications may adversely and permanently alter the course of that development. This is a concern when mothers take medications during pregnancy, and any medications used at any age in infancy and childhood. This is an appropriate theoretical concern that is difficult to answer, but in fact, there have been studies designed to address this question. As reviewed in chapter 3, there are detectable differences in the developing brain for those with and without ADHD in actual final outcome, and rate of development. Studies looking at structural brain development in ADHD with and without stimulant medication treatment actually demonstrate more normalization of brain structures with medication treatment, suggesting that stimulants may provide some protection against the adverse brain development that may occur with ADHD.[12], [13],[14] Russell Barkley surmises that this makes sense given that stimulants effect the parts of the brain that are known to be under stimulated, and that by normalizing activity in those areas, subsequent structural development may more closely resemble those without ADHD.[15] These are rather astounding observations, and certainly warrant further study.

Cardiac effects: There have been concerns related to cardiac side effects of stimulant medications and especially the risk of sudden cardiac death. It is known that stimulant medications have mild effects on increasing heart rate and systolic and diastolic blood pressure in children[16] and adults.[17] With a growing number of adults taking stimulant medication for attention deficit/hyperactivity disorder, this becomes a growing concern, as they may be more susceptible to cardiac disease, and mild increases in pulse and blood pressure may be more significant in this population. In February 2005, Canada took Adderall XR off the market because of reports from around the world of sudden cardiac death in 20 individuals taking Adderall. Of those individuals 14 were children, most of whom had underlying structural heart problems. After reviewing the information on each of these individuals, in August 2005, Adderall was returned to the Canadian market, with cautions regarding those who had a family history of cardiac death, who had structural heart problems or with strenuous exercise.

Many studies have looked at the potential cardiac effects of stimulant medication, especially since that time. Children without cardiac disease who receive stimulant medication do not appear to be at increased risk for cardiovascular events, including sudden cardiac death, compared to the general population.[18],[19] ADHD is thought to be more common in those with congenital heart disease[20] so the use of stimulants in this population is an important consideration. Adverse events are thought to be rare, with no significant increased risk for serious adverse cardiac complications.[21] Nonetheless, current guidelines recommend that prior to treatment with stimulant medication, there should be an assessment of cardiac risk factors. This includes baseline physical exam, pulse, blood pressure, review of medical history and family history of heart disease. If there are no cardiac risk factors, stimulants are felt to be safe as far as increased risk of cardiac complications. However, if risk factors are identified, a baseline electrocardiogram should be done and consultation with a cardiologist should be considered. Cardiac status, pulse and blood pressure should be monitored as part of ongoing periodic medication monitoring.[22]

Pregnancy and lactation: There is precious little information to guide the use of stimulants during pregnancy and lactation, as little research or observational studies have been done to address this issue. They are considered Class C drugs by the FDA, meaning there is not enough information to know if they are safe or harmful during pregnancy or nursing, and decisions need to be made by the individual and obstetrician/prescriber on the relative merits and potential harmful effects.

Other rare side effects: There have been concerns that stimulants can lower seizure thresholds, meaning for someone who has a seizure disorder, they might be more likely to have breakthrough seizures if they are placed on a stimulant medication. The risk is not high, but should certainly be kept in mind and monitored. Another rare but disconcerting potential side effect is priapism, a painful and prolonged penile erection that requires urgent attention if it occurs. There are reports of developing peripheral blood vessel problems such as Raynaud's phenomenon, which is a painful vascular condition of the hands and feet. This is a side effect that will be seen on occasion, and medication should be discontinued if it occurs. Those who have Raynaud's disease may experience worsening of symptoms on stimulant medication. Stimulants need to be used with extreme caution in the presence of glaucoma, as glaucoma is considered a contraindication for the use of stimulants. If used, it needs to be done with close monitoring by an ophthalmologist.[23] Stimulants may increase the risk of glaucoma. Stimulants should not be used with monoamine oxidase (MAO) inhibitors. These are old antidepressants infrequently used now, but the combination can cause a dangerous hypertensive crisis with associated complications.

Practical Considerations in the Use of Stimulant Medications

So what is the point of all of the different stimulant preparations? Two questions need to be answered in a medication trial. First, does the medication help to make significant improvements in symptoms of concern? At the right dose and preparation, stimulant effects should be fairly dramatic in producing noticeable and significant benefits in ADHD-related symptoms. Any of the stimulants available have the potential to significantly improve symptoms. Second, what preparation has the fewest side effects, the least cost, and is best for the individual's lifestyle and schedule. For most, longer acting preparations that last 8–12 hours are usually preferable, to avoid having to take medicine at school, and often with fewer side effects. Shorter acting preparations however give more flexibility. For those where treatment is only needed for part of the day (kindergarten students, or when a short acting afternoon dose is needed for example), shorter acting preparations may be preferable. Generally the longer acting preparations are far more costly than shorter acting ones. Preference on which specific medication to use has to do with what is tolerated best by the individual, and fits best with their needs and schedule. Also, especially in younger children, swallowing pills or capsules can be problematic, in which case liquid preparations, capsules where the contents can be put into pudding or yoghurt, or the Daytrana patch can be used.

As far as which class of stimulant is best to try first, it is a matter of individual prescriber preference whether to start with a methylphenidate or amphetamine preparation. Somewhat arbitrarily, in our clinic, we will generally use methylphenidate preparations for younger children and amphetamine preparations for older children and teenagers, because they are more potent and may have more side effects. However studies suggest that either option is appropriate for any age over 6. Results vary between studies, but generally, if 100 children diagnosed with straightforward ADHD are put on a methylphenidate preparation, approximately 70% will improve significantly with minimal side effects. If the same 100 children are put on an amphetamine preparation, again 70% will improve, but they are not the same 70%. Of the 30% in either group that did not improve or had significant side effects, another 50–70% will improve significantly on the other medication, so the overall efficacy of some stimulant medication for the child accurately diagnosed with ADHD is about 85–90%.[24],[25] Some children will not respond well to any stimulant medication or may have adverse side effects. This may be because the diagnosis was not accurate in the first place or that there are other mitigating factors, but a small percentage of children with straightforward ADHD do not respond well to stimulant medication.

When first starting a stimulant medication, the general principal is to start low, as some individuals may respond to a low dose. Although there are dosage recommendations for every medication, as stated earlier there are many reasons that the actual effective dose varies amongst individuals. If that dose is ineffective, and there are no significant side effects, then the dose is gradually increased until the expected beneficial effects are seen, or side effects are problematic. The main beneficial effect of stimulant medications that should be seen is improvement in self-control, with less hyperactivity, less impulsivity, and improved ability to focus. If a child is started on stimulant medication, the expectation should be that there is significant improvement in target symptoms with minimal side effects, and if this is not achieved, different medications should be considered. It is important to target and monitor specific symptoms of concern, as there are some differential effects depending on dose.[5] For an individual with ADHD who has been started on a particular stimulant medication, if it is ineffective or there are bothersome side effects, it is appropriate to switch to the other class of stimulants, as not uncommonly there may be a better response to the second medication. A stimulant trial should not be considered a failure at least until a stimulant from the methylphenidate class and from the amphetamine class have been adequately trialed.

It is often stated that medications should be taken before breakfast. Although there are some differences in effects if given before, with or after food, the differences are fairly minor, and it is probably more important to be consistent with medication administration related to food.[26] Especially because stimulants suppress appetite, it has been my practice to recommend giving stimulant medication after meals. With amphetamine products such as Adderall, absorption is impeded by an acidic stomach, so these should not be taken with citrus juices.

Because stimulants are schedule II drugs, there are rules on how they can be prescribed. Prescriptions can only be written for one month at a time, there has to be a prescription in hand, and no refills are allowed, but up to two postdated prescriptions may be allowed. Recently electronic prescriptions have been approved, which decreases the hassle factor for patients, but prescribing restrictions remain. This is not bad necessarily, because it enforces close monitoring of individuals taking these medications. There has to be an office contact on a monthly basis to renew medications, either in the office or by phone. Most physicians will monitor individuals on these medications at least every 3–6 months in the office to monitor for side effects, and to be sure of efficacy.

Use in Children Under Age 6

For reasons that are somewhat obscure, some amphetamine preparations, such as Adderall IR, are FDA approved for children as young as age 3, and methylphenidate is approved for children starting at age 6, this in spite of methylphenidate generally being milder. The AAP policy statement[27] recommends methylphenidate for use in children under age 6 if the symptoms are severe enough to warrant medication, with the understanding that this is off-label use. Most medications used for ADHD in children under age 6 are used off label.[28] For the most part, most physicians are hesitant to treat children under age 6 with stimulant medications unless symptoms are very severe and behavioral interventions have been already tried and are unsuccessful. In our clinical experience, although the medications can have efficacy, side effects tend to be more prominent, and likelihood of efficacy is less than what is seen in older children. This has been borne out in treatment studies of preschool children.[29]

Conclusions

How widely are stimulant medications used in the United States? The statistics are somewhat staggering. From the national survey of children's health by the CDC (Center for Disease Control) done in 2007 and again in 2011, the percentage of children, ages 4–17, taking medication for ADHD, was 4.8% in 2007, and 6.1% in 2011 (3.5 million nationwide), with an average annual increase of 7% per year. Some 8.4% of boys were treated with ADHD medication. There was wide variability between states, with the lowest percentage in southwestern states, Alaska, Hawaii and New Jersey (all <4%), and the highest in certain midwest and southeast states including Louisiana, Kentucky, Arkansas, Indiana, North Carolina and Iowa (>9%).[30]

Stimulant medications have a long track record of efficacy and safety, and there are recommendations in place for close monitoring. There are probably more studies on stimulant medications published than virtually any other medication class on the market. Obviously long-term medication treatment of any child is not to be taken lightly, but for many children with ADHD there is a place for medication treatment. In making a decision about whether to take medication for ADHD, one must consider whether the benefits of the medication are worth the risk of the side effects, known and unknown. This is true of any medication or medical intervention, and it is no different for those with ADHD. One concern is that often medications are so effective, that some of the other recommended and more difficult treatment approaches, such as counseling, classroom and educational accommodations are ignored. Long-term studies have not demonstrated huge benefits from long-term stimulant medication treatment for ADHD when not accompanied by other interventions. When symptoms are mild, or adequately managed with appropriate classroom and home accommodations, and behavioral therapy when needed, medication is probably not warranted. But when there are significant academic, behavioral or social problems that are not adequately addressed by non-medicine approaches, the risk of poor outcomes is high, and medication should be strongly considered. Especially when self-esteem is beginning to suffer, when the child is resisting school, and behavior is declining, medication can help reverse the downward spiral. Physicians can inform families of expected effects and side effects of medications, but whether to start an individual on medication is a personal decision based on the family's expectations and tolerance for side effects.

There is no question that stimulant medications are misused, to add a little bit to the grade-point average or increase the chances of getting into a high level university. Stimulant medications are misused by high school, college and graduate students to improve performance even when ADHD is not present, and frequency of abuse appears to be increasing. Students may fake ADHD symptoms in order to legally obtain stimulant prescriptions. A question often raised is can the diagnosis of ADHD be made based on the response to stimulant medication. The answer is no. Cognitive performance and memory may improve for anyone taking stimulant medication, although the effect is likely more prominent in those with true ADHD, and side effects can be dangerous for those who misuse stimulants.[31] Caffeine, a very legal and widely used stimulant, is used worldwide to improve alertness. Overuse of caffeine has similar problems and can even be mildly addictive if severely overused. This emphasizes some of the moral and ethical issues surrounding the use of stimulant medications in our society, and stimulant medication should only be used for those accurately diagnosed with ADHD who have symptoms of such severity that medication intervention is warranted, and all individuals taking stimulant medications should be closely monitored by medical professionals.

Non-stimulant Medications

Atomoxetine (Strattera)

Because of the issues discussed above there have been attempts at finding other medications that may be helpful for treating ADHD, and over the years there have been many different medications that have also been used. Practically speaking, none approaches the efficacy and safety of stimulant medications. One that is on the market now that is somewhat helpful is atomoxetine (marketed as Strattera). It is a medication that has beneficial effects for many individuals with ADHD, but typically improvement is not as striking as with stimulants. It is classified as a selective norepinephrine reuptake inhibitor, meaning it increases synaptic levels of norepinephrine, but unlike stimulants has little effect on dopamine. However there are some advantages with atomoxetine/Strattera. It has no abuse potential and is not a controlled substance. Oftentimes the personality suppression is much less prominent compared with stimulants. Atomoxetine is a long-lasting medication, meaning it is onboard all day long, so there are not so many of the ups and downs that one can get with stimulants. Atomoxetine has to be taken daily and dosages cannot be skipped. It usually takes up to a month or two before maximal benefits are apparent, so it is more difficult to use than stimulants, and requires patience. The most common side effects from atomoxetine are upset stomach (less so if taken on a full stomach), and tiredness. Headaches, some appetite suppression (but less than with stimulants), irritability, dizziness and moodiness may be seen on occasion. There is a black box warning (meaning potentially serious side effect) of increased risk of suicidal thoughts with atomoxetine, similar to what is listed for antidepressants. The risk is very low, but not zero, and if present, the medicine should be discontinued. There may be beneficial effects on anxiety, and sleep problems are usually not as big of an issue as with stimulants. Atomoxetine can be used in any ADHD condition, but may be particularly useful for those with inattentive ADHD, especially sluggish cognitive tempo, also with ADHD associated with high functioning autism, and ADHD associated with anxiety. It is a good alternative when stimulants are not an option.

Atomoxetine is metabolized primarily by an enzyme system in the liver called CYP2D6. There are 4 functionally different subtypes of this system that affect how atomoxetine is metabolized in different individuals. The majority of individuals (those with 2 normal genes for CYP2D6) metabolize atomoxetine at the expected rate, and usual dosing recommendations are appropriate. Some individuals are missing both genes or have inactive genes and are called poor metabolizers, meaning a normal atomoxetine dose would result in very high blood levels. Because atomoxetine is normally so safe, this is not usually a big problem, but the practical implication is that much lower doses would be effective for these individuals. Statistically, about 2–7% of all people are "slow metabolizers". It is also possible to have one functional gene and one inactive gene (intermediate metabolizers), in which metabolism is mildly affected, and some individuals have more than 2 active genes (ultrarapid metabolizers) who may exhibit decreased efficacy of atomoxetine due to breaking it down too fast. An additional implication of this metabolism system is that many other medications use the same system, and if given concurrently with atomoxetine, may inhibit the metabolism of atomoxetine by competing with the enzyme site. Included in this group are the antidepressants fluoxetine (Prozac) and paroxetine (Paxil). For these reasons, caution must be used when giving additional medications to someone who is taking atomoxetine. Strattera comes as capsules of 10, 18, 25, 40, 60, 80 and 100mg, and typical dose is 1.2mg/kg given once daily and the generic atomoxetine is available.

Alpha-2 Adrenergic Receptor Agonists

An additional group of medicines that is marketed for ADHD are alpha-2 agonists that include clonidine, guanfacine, Intuniv (long acting guanfacine or guanfacine ER) and Kapvay (long-acting clonidine). These medicines have a complicated mechanism of action that includes effects on nor-epinephrine release in certain locations in the brain, indirect effects on serotonin receptors and increased levels of another neurotransmitter, gamma-amino butyric acid (GABA) that can be involved in behavioral disorders. These medications have their place in ADHD treatment, but do not seem to be as effective as stimulants. Clonidine was originally used as a nasal decongestant, and now is used to treat hypertension. It has multiple other uses that may make it beneficial in those with ADHD. It is somewhat helpful in treating ADHD symptoms directly, is one of the most commonly prescribed medications in children for insomnia, is beneficial in reducing tics and for treating Tourette syndrome, is used as an adjunct in procedures requiring anesthesia, can be helpful for anxiety and can be helpful for aggressive behavior.[32] It is a medication that lasts about 4 hours and its main side effects are sleepiness, dizziness, headache, fatigue and it can lower blood pressure, with rare severe cardiac effects. These side effects limit usefulness during the day, but it can be particularly helpful in the evening when stimulants would cause sleep problems, and can also help those who have difficulties falling asleep. Because abrupt discontinuation can cause rebound hypertension, when used long term, the dose should be tapered rather than stopped abruptly. Clonidine comes in tablets of 0.1, 0.2 and 0.3mg, and also patches TTS 1, 2 and 3, equal to 0.1mg, 0.2mg and 0.3mg clonidine per day for one week.

In 2010, the FDA approved extended release clonidine, marketed as Kapvay, for treatment for ADHD, either alone, or in addition to stimulant therapy. It lasts 12 hours, and is meant to be given twice daily, morning and bedtime. Side effects are similar to regular clonidine, and dose needs to be tapered when discontinued to avoid rebound hypertension. Side effects tend to diminish with time.[33] While extended release clonidine may be helpful by itself, it can also be helpful as an adjunct to stimulant medications when improvement in ADHD symptoms is less than optimal with stimulants alone. [34] There are far fewer studies on the use of clonidine in ADHD, and they are mostly short-term studies. Kapvay comes as 0.1 and 0.2mg doses.

Another alpha 2 agonist that can be helpful for some symptoms of ADHD is guanfacine. It is more specific than clonidine in the receptor subtype it binds, which may explain its lower rates of sedation compared to clonidine. Guanfacine will usually last about 8 hours, and side effects are similar, but seemingly less than with clonidine. In 2009, the FDA approved a long acting version of guanfacine called Intuniv for treatment of ADHD. Like clonidine, guanfacine or extended release guanfacine can be used alone or as an adjunct to stimulant medication for treatment of ADHD. It is long enough lasting to be given only once daily. Costs of the extended release versions of clonidine and guanfacine are considerably more expensive than the shorter acting versions. Although alpha-2 agonists are shown to be effective in ameliorating symptoms of ADHD, their efficacy is not usually as strong as is seen with stimulants. Guanfacine comes as 1 and 2mg tablets, and Intuniv (guanfacine ER) comes as tablets of from 1–4mg.

APPENDIX

Methylphenidate Preparations

Methylphenidate is one of two stimulant categories used for treating ADHD, the other being amphetamine derivatives. It was approved initially in the US in 1955. Methylphenidate is thought to block reuptake of norepinephrine and dopamine into the presynaptic neuron, delaying clearance and increasing their effect.[35] Up until the year 2000, the only methylphenidate options were short acting Ritalin or the generic methylphenidate, and a 6–8 hour preparation, Ritalin SR or its generic. Starting with Concerta in 2000, there has been an explosion of different methylphenidate preparations available, providing more long lasting options, as well as different delivery systems. Methylphenidate preparations are now available in short acting versions lasting 4 hours, intermediate 6–8 hour preparations, and longer acting 8–12 hour preparations. They come as tablets, capsules, chewable, liquid, melt in your mouth tablets and a patch. Longer acting preparations are usually far more expensive than shorter acting preparations, as are brand name preparations compared with generics. The following is a brief discussion of each. Information on each medication is obtained from the individual pharmaceutical websites and from the FDA drug label, with additional references as listed. Pharmaceutical companies have been very creative in developing alternative delivery systems, so new preparations are coming on the market frequently, and keeping up with what is available is challenging.

Dosing is quite variable between individuals, and usually dosing is started low, with incremental increases if no effects or side effects are seen. Some will use weight based dosing, which is imprecise, but a general rule of thumb for children is 0.3–0.6mg per kg per 4 hour equivalent, and a maximum daily dose of the lesser of 2mg/kg or 60mg/day. For example, for a 35kg (77 pounds) child, a short acting dose would be approximately 10–20mg, 8 hour preparation 20–40mg, and 12 hour preparation 30–60mg. Generally maximum doses are 20, 40 and 60mg respectively (72mg for Concerta). Focalin and Daytrana would be ½ these dosages (see p.00). Once a steady effective dose is reached, it is increased only with weight increase, and usually stabilizes by early adolescence. Not uncommonly, individuals will respond well to a relatively low dose initially, but the efficacy may wane after a few months. This is a honeymoon period, and the dose may need to be increased at that point. Further dose increases other than for weight gain however should not be necessary. For adolescents and adults, weight based dosages are less useful, and doses are usually started at a low level, and gradually increased until optimal effects are observed, with monitoring for side effects. Maximum daily dose is 60g (72mg for Concerta). Dosage effects are different depending on symptoms being targeted, and benefits have to be weighed against side effects.

Adhansia XR: Produced by Adlon Therapeutics, a subsidiary of Purdue Pharmaceuticals, this is one of the newest methylphenidate preparations on the market. It is designed to last 16 hours, with a multilayer delivery system that releases 20% of the dose immediately, and 80% controlled release throughout the day. It comes in higher doses than other preparations, and the extended length of time may not be appropriate for children, although it is approved for those 6 years and older. It comes in capsules of 25mg, 35mg, 45mg, 55mg, 70mg and 85mg. Capsules may be taken whole, or contents sprinkled onto applesauce or yogurt. Cost is about $350, and the pharmaceutical company does provide discount coupons.

Aptensio XR: Made by Rhodes Pharmaceuticals, it is a methylphenidate extended release capsule, approved for ages 6 and older. It is designed to last 12 hours. The capsules contain multilayered beads with an immediate release layer that delivers 40% of the methylphenidate dose, and a controlled release layer which contains 60% of the methylphenidate dose. It comes as 10mg, 15mg, 20mg, 30mg, 40mg, 50mg, and 60mg capsules. The capsule can be swallowed, or opened up and beads sprinkled onto applesauce or pudding. There is an initial peak in plasma levels 2 hours after ingestion, followed by a slow decline, and then followed by a second peak 8 hours after ingestion. It is meant to mimic methylphenidate immediate-release preparations given 3 times daily, 4 hours apart and to provide effects that last 12 hours. Reportedly when taken with a high fat meal, there was a significant increase in the maximum plasma level, the level of the second peak was decreased and overall concentration of methylphenidate was increased, so effects would be somewhat different when taken with fatty meals than on an empty stomach. It was first released in 2015 in the US, but has been available in Canada since 2006 under the name Biphentin. It is available only as brand name, there is no generic version. Cost is about $250 per month, and it may not be covered by Medicaid/Medicare or insurance. The pharmaceutical company does provide discount cards.

Concerta: Concerta was the first 12-hour-long lasting methylphenidate or Ritalin preparation, and came on the market in 2000. It is now made by Janssen Pharmaceuticals and was approved for adults in 2008. Concerta resembles a tablet, but is comprised of an outer coating containing 20% of the dose that dissolves quickly in the stomach, and gives an initial maximum plasma level peak 1 hour after ingestion. Inside the outer shell is an inner core that utilizes a sophisticated drug delivery system, called OROS or osmotic release drug delivery system. It has an undigestible shell that surrounds a rate controlling membrane and a core of methylphenidate with a tiny sponge that slowly absorbs intestinal fluid which expands to push methylphenidate gradually through a tiny hole laser drilled on the end. This system delivers methylphenidate over 10 hours after the outer coat has dissolved. There is an initial peak concentration of methylphenidate 1 hour after ingestion, followed by a gradual rise for about 5 hours, and then a gradual decline over the next 6 hours. It is meant to mimic methylphenidate immediate-release preparations given 3 times daily, 4 hours apart and to provide effects that last 12 hours. Because of its complicated makeup, it has to be swallowed. It is not effective as designed if cut in half, crushed or chewed. It comes in 4 doses, 18mg (equal to 5mg methylphenidate given three times a day (tid) 4 hours apart), 27mg (7.5mg tid), 36mg (10mg tid) and 54mg (15mg tid). Concerta, like other long acting stimulants, is expensive, in the neighborhood of $375 per month. The parent company, Johnson and Johnson does participate in the Rx assist Patient Assistance Program which provides financial assistance for those who qualify.

Concerta does come in generic forms. There are now multiple manufacturers that make generic Concerta, called methylphenidate ER, but their use has been fraught with problems. When Concerta was originally marketed, there was only one Concerta option, and it worked very well and very predictably. When generics came out, there began to be widespread complaints about lack of efficacy. The history is complicated, but suffice it to say that generic versions of Concerta are not the same as brand name Concerta. They use a different delivery system, and while they may be similar, they often don't work in the same fashion as Concerta. Also, pharmacies will often switch between manufacturers in efforts to contain costs, and efficacy between generics is not necessarily equivalent. So for anyone taking Concerta or generics, if the medication seems to be ineffective where it once was working well, check with the pharmacist to see if there has been a change in manufacturer. Generic methylphenidate is considerably less expensive than Concerta, and comes as the same dosing as Concerta, as well as a 72mg option.

Cotempla XR-ODT: this is a recently released extended release methylphenidate preparation in a grape flavored orally disintegrating tablet designed to last 12 hours. There is an initial peak at about 2 hours, followed by a larger peak at 6 hours after ingestion, and then a gradual decline over the next 6 hours. It contains 25% immediate release and 75% extended release particles. Dosage forms are hard to remember 8.6mg, 17.3mg and 25.9mg, said to be equivalent to 10, 20 and 30mg of methylphenidate. It is produced by Neos Therapeutics and was first approved in 2017.

Daytrana: Manufactured by Noven Pharmaceuticals, Daytrana was initially approved in 2006; Daytrana is a transdermal patch that delivers methylphenidate throughout the day. It is applied to the hip area 2 hours before an effect is needed and removed 9 hours later, or can be removed sooner for shorter duration, or later if needed, so it allows some flexibility. Side effects are the same as with other methylphenidate preparations, plus skin reactions to the patch such as burning or itching. It comes as 10mg, 15mg, 20mg and 30mg strengths. The doses don't correlate well with other methylphenidate preparations, because the active drug doesn't pass through the gastrointestinal tract. The major disadvantage of Daytrana is the 2 hour delay in onset of action. Cost is about $320, but again, there are pharmaceutical coupons available to decrease the cost. There have been shortages of Daytrana, so it can at times be hard to find.

Focalin (dexmethylphenidate): Medications are molecules that have 3 dimensional structures, and their effect is based on binding to receptors in the body that recognize that structure, like a lock and key. There are many potential geometric forms possible for molecules with the same atomic structure, and in nature, often there exist molecules that come as a mix of geometric forms that are mirror images of each other, similar to right and left hands. Receptor sites in the body only recognize one image, and the other will usually have less or no activity and may cause side effects. These are called enantiomers, and come as left (s) or right (d) versions. Most medicines are a mixture of both enantiomers. Medicines can be developed that have only the active enantiomer, the theory being that it will be more effective and with fewer side effects than the parent compound. This is the case for example with escitalopram and citalopram, or with albuterol and xopenex. Focalin is the active d-enantiomer of methylphenidate, which is a 50/50 racemic mixture of the l- and d- enantiomers, the intent being fewer side effects than the racemic methylphenidate.

Focalin comes as an immediate release preparation that lasts usually 4 hours, so is given 2 or 3 times per day, 4 hours apart. Because it is the more active enantiomer, the recommended dose is ½ of the usual methylphenidate dose. Practically speaking however, the lower dose of Focalin is often not as effective as the higher dose of methylphenidate, so dosage may need to be increased to be effective. It comes as 2.5mg, 5mg and 10mg tablets. There is also an extended release Focalin XR preparation. It uses the Spheroidal Oral Drug Absorption System (SODAS) technology to enable extended release. It is a 50/50 mixture of immediate release beads of dexmethylphenidate, and enteric coated delayed release beads. It is designed to be equivalent to regular Focalin given twice per day 4 hours apart. Focalin XR comes as 5–40mg in 5mg increments. It is produced by Novartis Pharmaceuticals. Focalin was initially approved in 2001 and Focalin XR in 2005. There are now generic forms of both Focalin and Focalin XR called dexmethylphenidate, and they come in the same dosage forms. The XR capsule preparation can be opened and the contents sprinkled onto food such as applesauce or pudding, but should not be chewed.

Jornay PM: Recently released, Jornay PM's niche in the methylphenidate market is for those who struggle with ADHD symptoms in the morning before morning stimulant medication takes effect. It is a delayed release preparation that is designed to be given the night before, with release of medication 10–12 hours after ingestion, and provides symptom relief throughout the day, approximately 12 hours. It is approved for use in those 6 and older, and is produced by Ironshore Pharmaceuticals. Capsules can be opened and sprinkled for those who can't swallow the capsules. It is available in 20mg, 40mg, 60mg, 80mg and 100mg. Because of different pharmacokinetic profiles, it is recommended when switching from other methylphenidate preparations, to not switch based on mg equivalence, but to start Jornay PM with the 20mg dose and titrate upwards as needed. Cost is about $450, and pharmaceutical coupons are available.

Metadate CD: Controlled dosage, made by UCB pharmaceuticals, Metadate CD was first approved in 2001. It uses Diffucaps technology to provide sustained release of methylphenidate over 8 hours with 30% of the total dose made up of immediate release beads and 70% extended release beads. It mimics the effect of 2 doses of methylphenidate IR (immediate release) given 4 hours apart. So 20mg Metadate CD would be similar to the effects of two 10mg short acting methylphenidate tablets given 4 hours apart. Peak concentration occurs 1½ hours after the dose, with sustained levels until 6–8 hours post dose, followed by gradual diminishing levels. It comes as concentrations of 10–60mg in 10mg increments. The cost is high, ranging from about $250 to $400 per month depending on concentration, but there is a generic available (methylphenidate HCL Extended Release capsules) that is considerably less expensive. The capsule can be opened and the contents sprinkled over food like pudding or applesauce for those who can't swallow the capsule.

Metadate ER: Extended release tablet-wax matrix allowing slow release of stimulant as the tablet passes through the gastrointestinal tract. This is the original sustained release technology used in the no longer produced Ritalin SR, and is less reliable than newer technologies. It lasts 8 hours but takes 2–3 hours before peak effects. It comes now only as a 20mg strength, and is a tablet that should not be cut or crushed.

Methylin: A short acting methylphenidate preparation lasting 4 hours, it comes as a chewable version in strengths of 2.5mg, 5mg and 10mg, and a liquid preparation of 5mg/5ml and 10mg/5ml. Both come as generic methylphenidate chewables or solution in the same dosages.

Methylphenidate: This is the active ingredient in all methylphenidate preparations, the generic form of the original Ritalin preparation. It is short acting, lasting usually 4 hours. it comes as 5mg, 10mg and 20mg and is by far the least expensive methylphenidate preparation, costing about $30 per month. Because it is short acting, it generally is used 2–3 times per day.

Methylphenidate ER: This gets confusing. There are multiple different methylphenidate ER preparations that are generics for various brand name preparations, and they are not the same. Methylphenidate ER (or methylphenidate LA) comes as capsules that contain short acting and delayed release beads in a 50/50 ratio. This preparation is generic for Ritalin LA, and comes as 10mg, 20mg, 30mg 40mg and 60mg preparations. Then there are methylphenidate ER (or methylphenidate CD) capsules that mimic Metadate CD, meaning the immediate release and extended release beads are in a 30/70 ratio, and come as 10mg, 20mg, 30mg, 40mg, 50mg and 60mg. Finally, methylphenidate ER comes as a preparation that is generic for Concerta and comes as 18mg, 27mg, 36mg, 54mg and 72mg. Then, to add to the confusion there is the generic for Ritalin SR, Metadate ER and Methylin ER called Methylphenidate SR which used to come as 10mg and 20mg preparations, and is now available only as 20mg. Ritalin SR and Methylin ER are no longer available and these are usually less reliable than newer long acting preparations.

Quillivant XR: This uses LiquiXR technology to provide a combination of immediate release and extended release complexes, in a 20/80 ratio, similar to Concerta's ratio. It is meant to last up to 12 hours. Blood concentration peaks 5 hours after administration. It comes as 25mg/5ml, and comes with a syringe for accurate dosing. It is marketed by Pfizer and first became available in 2012, but became unavailable for a time because of shortages that were in part apparently due to damages to its manufacturing plant in Puerto Rico from Hurricane Maria. It is fruit flavored. It comes in volumes of 60ml, 120ml, 150ml and 180ml and cost appears to be the same regardless of volume.

Quillichew ER: This is a long acting chewable cherry flavored preparation of methylphenidate. It comes as 30% immediate release methylphenidate mixed with 70% extended release beads that are protected from crushing when chewed. Like Quillivant XR, peak serum concentration is 5 hours after ingestion. It comes as 20mg and 30mg scored tablets, and a 40mg unscored tablet. It was first released in 2016, but as with Quillivant XR there were shortages. Both are now available as of this writing (2020).

Ritalin: The original methylphenidate medication, it was first synthesized by a Swiss chemist, Leandro Panizzon, in 1944, and first marketed as Ritalin by Ciba pharmaceuticals, now Novartis. It was named Ritaline after the developer's wife Marguerite, nicknamed Rita, who took the medicine before playing tennis to help with low blood pressure.[36] It is short acting with an expected duration of efficacy of 4 hours, and is usually taken 2–3 times per day. It is relatively low cost, but costs at least twice the equivalent generic methylphenidate. It comes in strengths of 5mg, 10mg and 20mg.

Ritalin LA: It contains methylphenidate released from beads, 50% immediate and 50% delayed and enteric coated, using the same SODAS technology as Focalin XR. It is designed to mimic 2 doses of short acting methylphenidate given 4 hours apart. Because of its higher proportion of short acting methylphenidate, it may give better results in the morning than other long acting preparations like Concerta or Metadate CD. It comes in strengths of 10mg, 20mg, 30mg, and 40mg, and does come as a generic (see Methylphenidate ER). It can be sprinkled for those who can't swallow the capsule. It is produced by Novartis pharmaceutical, and was first approved in 2002.

Ritalin-SR: The first of the longer lasting methylphenidate preparations, it was first marketed in 1984. It was designed to mimic twice daily regular Ritalin, by utilizing a wax matrix with slow release technology. There is no immediate release component, so it takes longer to work. The brand name is no longer available, and is equivalent to Metadate ER 20mg.

Amphetamine Preparations

Amphetamine preparations increase dopamine and norepinephrine levels in the synaptic space by inhibiting transporters of each, thereby decreasing reuptake. Neurotransmitters after release into the synaptic space are quickly cleared by binding to transporters and then reabsorbed. Amphetamine medicines interfere with this process. Amphetamine also increases the release of dopamine into the synaptic space and also may inhibit the breakdown of the 2 molecules.[35] Amphetamine preparations are generally felt to be twice as potent as methylphenidate, so dosing recommendations would be half of the recommended methylphenidate doses. Weight based dosing is 0.15 to 0.3mg/kg per 4 hour increments, and a maximum of 1mg/kg/day, or a maximum per day of 30mg (70mg for Vyvanse). As with methylphenidate, there are multiple different amphetamine preparations on the market that vary as far as length of time of efficacy, and how the medication is delivered. Side effects are similar to methylphenidate side effects with possibly higher rates of appetite suppression, weight loss and sleep problems. Amphetamine preparations are in part metabolized by the CYP2D6 enzymes, so concomitant use with CYP2D6 inhibitors can increase serum levels of amphetamine, increasing toxicity (see section on SSRIs, chapter 12 for details), and variations in amphetamine metabolism occur between individuals. Also, acidifying agents such as vitamin C (especially grapefruit juice) can decrease amphetamine levels, and alkalinizing agents (bicarbonate for example) may increase levels.

Adderall: This is a preparation of 4 different enantiomers of amphetamine, d-amphetamine and l-amphetamine in a ratio of 3:1. They are both pharmacologically active but have slightly different effects, and the combination is felt to be better than the individual enantiomers. Originally marketed as Obetrol to treat obesity, the name was changed to Adderall and marketed for ADHD in 1996. Adderall may provide effects for 4–8 hours depending on dose, and may need to be given twice per day, 4–8 hours apart. It comes as scored tablets of 5mg, 7.5mg, 10mg, 12.5mg, 15mg, 20mg and 30mg, and there are generic preparations available (dextroamphetamine and amphetamine mixed salts) that are usually less expensive. Adderall is approved for children as young as 3 years old in low dosages, although use in that age is controversial.

Adderall XR: Initially approved in 2001, Adderall XR are capsules that contain a 50/50 mixture of immediate release Adderall and delayed release beads that are designed to give similar effects as taking Adderall IR twice per day, with effects lasting up to 12 hours. The capsules can be opened and contents sprinkled onto applesauce or pudding for those who can't swallow capsules. Children usually metabolize Adderall faster than adults, so effects may not last as long (this is true of most medicines). It is approved for use in children 6 years and older. Adderall XR comes as 5mg, 10mg, 15mg, 20mg, 25mg and 30mg. There are multiple manufacturers of generic Adderall XR (amphetamine and dextroamphetamine mixed salts ER or amphetamine salt combo XR).

Adzenys SR-ODT: This was initially FDA approved in 2017. Developed by NEOS Therapeutics, Adzenys XR-ODT is an extended release orange flavored orally disintegrating tablet (meaning it melts in your mouth), approved for use 6 years and above. It is made up of microparticles of amphetamine, 50% immediate release and 50% enteric coated extended release. It is a mixture of d- and l-amphetamine in a 3:1 ratio. Effects are similar to the corresponding doses of Adderall XR, and it is available as 3.1mg, 6.3mg, 9.4mg, 12.5mg, 15.7mg and 18.8mg. These strengths are supposedly bio equivalent to Adderall XR 5–30mg respectively. There are no generic preparations, and cost is high, about $350 per month, although there are pharmaceutical coupons available.

Adzenys ER: This is the same as the ODT version, but in an orange flavored liquid form, 1.25mg/ml. Conversion to Adderall XR equivalence is the same as for Adzenys SR-ODT, with 3.1mg (2.5ml) equal to 5mg XR, 6.3mg (5ml) equal to 10mg Adderall XR and so on. It comes in 450ml bottles, at a cost of about $700. This would be the dose for the equivalent of 30mg Adderall XR, so for those with lower doses, the cost would be proportionally less over time.

Desoxyn: This is methamphetamine hydrochloride. It lasts 6–8 hours, and comes as 5mg tablets only. Because of its high abuse potential it is not prescribed widely, but is approved for treatment of ADHD in children 6 and above. Dosage is 5–10mg 1–2 times per day. It is quite expensive, even as generic.

Dexedrine (dextroamphetamine): Dexedrine is the d-isomer of dextroamphetamine sulfate. It is no longer available as a brand name, only generic, and comes as 5 and 10mg scored tablets. It is a short acting preparation with duration of action of 4 hours. It was originally marketed by Smith, Kline and French in 1952.

Dexedrine Spansules: This is a sustained release capsule that contains granules of dextroamphetamine sulfate, with some immediate release and the rest designed to be released slowly over a prolonged period. It is similar to short acting dextroamphetamine given twice 4 hours apart, with expected duration of efficacy 6–8 hours. Dexedrine spansules do come as generics which are considerably less expensive. Dexedrine spansules were FDA approved in 1976. They are available as 5mg, 10mg and 15mg spansules.

Dextrostat: Dextroamphetamine sulfate is the same as Dexedrine. The Dextrostat brand name is no longer available.

Dynavel XR: FDA approved in 2015 for children 6 and above and marketed by Tris Pharma, Dynavel XR is an extended release bubble gum flavored liquid preparation containing a 3.2:1 ratio of d- to l-amphetamine. It has an immediate release component, and an extended release component that uses ion exchange resin technology to deliver continuous release throughout the day, with effects lasting up to 13 hours. It comes as a suspension of amphetamine (base equivalent), 2.5mg/ml, which would be dosed the same as 4mg of Adderall XR. Reviews have reported efficacy, but there are complaints about the taste. It comes in variable sized bottles of 60ml, 90ml, 120ml, 180ml and 240ml with cost proportional to volume. It is expensive, but there are available pharmaceutical coupons to lower the price. There is no generic version of Dynavel XR.

Evekeo: FDA approved in 2015 and marketed by Arbor Pharmaceuticals, Evekeo is a 50/50 mix of d- and l-amphetamine (as opposed to the 3:1 mixture in Adderall and others). It is a short acting, 4 hour amphetamine preparation, and because of the different isomer ratio than Adderall may have fewer side effects in some. It comes as 5 and 10mg scored tablets, is brand name only and is approved for children aged 3 and above. It has recently been released as an oral disintegrating tablet (Evekeo ODT) as well.

Mydayis: Marketed by Shire Pharmaceutical, the same company that makes Adderall and Vyvanse, Mydayis is designed to last throughout the day, up to 16 hours, and is made up of immediate release beads, and 2 delayed release beads, one for continued release midday and one for evening. It contains d-amphetamine and l-amphetamine salts in a ratio of 3:1, similar to Adderall. It is marketed as being helpful for those where Adderall XR wears off too quickly. Effects start within 2–4 hours and last up to 16 hours. It is approved for ages 13 and older. Dosing is not similar to other amphetamine products on a 1mg per milligram basis because of different amphetamine base compensations and differing pharmacokinetic profiles. Dosing recommendations are to start 12.5mg, increase weekly to a maximum dose of 50mg. It can be sprinkled if needed. Doses above 50mg have been shown to provide no additional benefit, and in adolescents doses higher than 25mg have not been evaluated. It comes as 12.5mg, 25mg, 37.5mg and 50mg capsules. Although, as expected, it is expensive, it is surprisingly less expensive than other long acting stimulants, with an average monthly cost of about $300, and with pharmaceutical coupons available.

Procentra Oral Solution: a bubble gum flavored oral solution of dextroamphetamine (the d-isomer of amphetamine sulfate), comes as 5mg/5ml. It is distributed by FSC Laboratories. It is similar in efficacy and duration to Dexedrine (dextroamphetamine) tablets. It does come as a generic preparation as well, and is very expensive, especially for a short acting preparation.

Vyvanse: Approved by the FDA in 2007, Vyvanse is marketed by Shire Pharmaceuticals. It contains lisdexamfetamine dimesylate, which is a pro-drug that is converted to dextroamphetamine in the blood. Duration of efficacy is 10–12 hours. It comes as a capsule the contents of which can be sprinkled, in doses ranging from 10–70mg in 10mg increments, and chewables ranging from 10–60mg. Comparability to Adderall XR is not exact, but a close approximation of efficacy is 30mg Vyvanse is similar to 10mg Adderall XR, 50mg of Vyvanse is similar to 20mg Adderall XR, and 70mg is close to 30mg Adderall XR. One theoretical advantage of Vyvanse is that since it is a prodrug, it may have less abuse potential than Adderall. There may be fewer side effects with Vyvanse compared to Adderall XR, but in practice, results are variable about which works better and level of side effects.

Zenzedi: Zenzedi is a brand name dextroamphetamine that is made by Arbor pharmaceuticals, with the advantage that it comes in multiple dosage forms, 2.5mg, 5mg, 7.5mg, 10mg, 15mg, 20mg, and 30mg. Effects are the same as Dexedrine (dextroamphetamine) with a duration of 4–6 hours. Because of its multiple dosage forms, it allows for tighter titration of dose, and because it is short acting, allows more flexibility in dosing throughout the day, but requires multiple doses to provide full day coverage. The tradeoff is that it is very expensive.

Table 11.1 Available Methylphenidate and Amphetamine Preparations

Medications	Contents	Length of Efficacy	How Supplied	Cost*
Short Acting methylphenidate	**pills**			
Dexmethylphenidate		4 hrs	2.5, 5, 10mg	1
Focalin		4 hrs	2.5, 5, 10mg	2
Methylphenidate		4 hrs	5, 10, 20mg	1
Ritalin		4 hrs	5, 10, 20mg	1–2
	Chewables/liquid			
Methylin		4 hrs	2.5, 5, 10mg chewable, 5 and 10mg/5ml	4–5 / 2
methylphenidate		4 hrs	2.5, 5, 10mg chewable, 5 and 10mg/5ml	1–2 / 3
Intermediate Acting	**Tablet**			
Metadate ER		8 hrs	20mg	1
	Capsules			
Dexmethylphenidate ER		8 hrs	5, 10, 15, 20, 25, 30, 35, 40mg	2

Medications	Contents	Length of Efficacy	How Supplied	Cost*
Focalin XR		8 hrs	5, 10, 15, 20, 25, 30, 35, 40mg	5+
Metadate CD		8 hrs	10, 20, 30, 40, 50, 60mg	4–5
Methylphenidate ER 30/70		8 hrs	10, 20, 30, 40, 50, 60mg	2
Methylphenidate ER 50/50		8 hrs	10, 20, 30, 40, 60mg	2
Ritalin LA		8 hrs	10, 20, 30, 40, 60mg	5
Long Acting	**Tablets**			
Concerta		12 hrs	18, 27, 36, 54mg	5
Methylphenidate ER		12 hrs	18, 27, 36, 54, 72mg	3–4
	capsules			
Adhansia XR		16 hrs	25, 35, 45, 55, 70, 85mg	5
Aptensio XR		12 hrs	10, 15, 20, 30, 40, 50, 60mg	4
Jornay PM		12 hrs	20, 40, 60, 80, 100mg	5+
	ODT			
Contempla XR-ODT		12 hrs	8.6, 17.3, 25.9mg	5
	Chewable			
Quillichew ER		12 hrs	20, 30, 40mg	4–5
	Liquid			
Quillivant XR		12 hrs	25mg/5ml in 60, 120, 150, 180ml bottles	4
	Patch			
Daytrana		9–11 hrs	10, 15, 20, 30mg	5
Short Acting amphetamine	**pills**			
dextroamphetamine		4 hrs	5, 10mg	2
Evekeo		4 hrs	5, 10mg	4
Zenzedi		4 hrs	5, 10, 20mg	2
			2.5, 7.5, 15, 20, 30mg	5
	Chewables/liquid			
Procentra oral solution		4 hrs	5mg/5ml	5+
dextroamphetamine		4 hrs	5mg/5ml	3–4
	ODT			
Evekeo ODT		4 hrs	5, 10, 15, 20mg	1

Medications	Contents	Length of Efficacy	How Supplied	Cost*
Intermediate Acting	**Tablet**			
Adderall		6–8 hrs	5, 7.5, 10, 12.5, 15, 20, 30mg	4–5
Amphetamine salt combo (generic Adderall)		6–8 hrs	5, 7.5, 10, 12.5, 15, 20, 30mg	1
Desoxyn (methamphetamine)		6–8 hrs	5mg	5++
methampthetamine		6–8 hrs	5mg	3
	capsules			
Dexedrine Spansules		8 hrs	5, 10, 15mg	5+
Dextroamphetamine ER			5, 10, 15mg	2
Long Acting	**ODT**			
Adzenys SR-ODT		12 hrs	3.1, 6.3, 9.4, 12.5, 15.7, 18.8mg	5
	capsules			
Adderall XR		12 hrs	5, 10, 15, 20, 25, 30mg	4
Amphetamine salt combo XR		12 hrs	5, 10, 15, 20, 25, 30mg	2
Mydayis		16 hrs	12.5, 25, 37.5, 50mg	4
Vyvanse		12 hrs	10, 20, 30, 40, 50, 60, 70mg	4–5
	Chewable			
Vyvanse		12 hrs	10, 20, 30, 40, 50, 60mg	4–5
	Liquid			
Adzenys ER		12 hrs	1.25mg/ml	4–5+ depending on amount
Dynavel XR		13 hrs	2.5mg/ml in 60, 90, 120, 180 and 240ml bottles	3–5+

See text for details of each preparation.
*Costs: 1=0–$50, 2=50–100, 3=100–200, 4=200–300, 5=300–400, 5+ is >$400. Costs vary widely amongst pharmacies, areas of the country and whether pharmaceutical or pharmacy coupons are available. Estimates obtained from GoodRx.

Bibliography

1. Off-label use of drugs in children. *Pediatrics.* 2014. doi:10.1542/peds.2013-4060.
2. Sachs AN, Avant D, Lee CS, Rodriquez W MD. Pediatric information in drug product labeling. *JAMA.* 2012;307(18):1914–1915.
3. ADHD: Clinical Practice Guideline for the Diagnosis, Evaluation, and Treatment of Attention-Deficit/Hyperactivity Disorder in Children and Adolescents. *Pediatrics.* October2011. http://pediatrics.aappublications.org/content/early/2011/10/14/peds.2011-2654.abstract.
4. Methylphenicate hydrochloride extended release tablets (generic Concerta) made by Mallinckrodt and Kudco. *FDA Bull.* 2016;(10-17-2016, 11–14-2016, 11-13-2016).
5. Spencer RC, Devilbiss DM, Berridge CW. The cognition-enhancing effects of psychostimulants involve direct action in the prefrontal cortex. *Biol Psychiatry.* 2015;77(11):940–950. doi:10.1016/j.biopsych.2014.09.013.
6. Faraone SV, Biederman J, Morley CP, Spencer TJ. Effect of stimulants on height and weight: a review of the literature. *J Am Acad Child Adolesc Psychiatry.* 2008;47 (9):994–1009. doi:10.1097/CHI.ObO13e31817eOea7.
7. Harstad EB, Weaver AL, Katusic SK, et al. ADHD, stimulant treatment, and growth: A longitudinal study. *Pediatrics.* 2014;134(4):e935–e944. doi:10.1542/peds.2014-0428.
8. Kurlan R.Tourette's syndrome: Are stimulants safe? *Curr Neurol Neurosci Rep.* 2003;3(4):285–288. doi:10.1007/s11910-003-0004-2.
9. Molina BSG, Howard AL, Swanson JM, et al. Substance use through adolescence into early adulthood after childhood-diagnosed ADHD: Findings from the MTA longitudinal study. *J Child Psychol Psychiatry.* January 2018. doi:10.1111/jcpp.12855.
10. Association AP, ed. *Diagnostic and Statistical Manual of Mental Disorders (DSM-5).* 5th ed. Washington DC; 2013.
11. Chang Z, Lichtenstein P, Halldner L, et al. Stimulant ADHD medication and risk for substance abuse. *J Child Psychol Psychiatry.* 2014;55(8):878–885. doi:10.1111/jcpp.12164.
12. Spencer TJ, Brown A, Seidman LJ, et al. Effect of Psychostimulants on brain structure and function in ADHD: A qualitative literature review of MRI-based neuroimaging studies. *J Clin Psychiatry.* 2013;74(9):902–917. doi:10.4088/JCP.12r08287.
13. Ivanov I, Murrough JW, Bansal R, Hao X, Peterson BS. Cerebellar morphology and the effects of stimulant medications in youths with Attention Deficit-Hyperactivity Disorder. *Neuropsychopharmacology.* 2014;39(3):718–726. doi:10.1038/npp.2013.257.
14. Frodl T, Skokauskas N. Meta-analysis of structural MRI studies in children and adults with attention deficit hyperactivity disorder indicates treatment effects. *Acta Psychiatr Scand.* 2012;125(2):114–126. doi:10.1111/j.1600-0447.2011.01786.x.
15. Barkley RA. *Attention-Deficit Hyperactivity Disorder a Handbook for Diagnosis and Treatment.* 4th ed. (Barkley RA, ed.) 356–379. Guilford Press; 2015.
16. Hennissen L, Bakker MJ, Banaschewski T, et al. Cardiovascular effects of stimulant and non-stimulant medication for children and adolescents with ADHD: A systematic review and meta-analysis of trials of methylphenidate, amphetamines and atomoxetine. *CNS Drugs.* 2017. doi:10.1007/s40263-017-0410-7.

17. Martinez-Badia J, Martinez-Raga J. Who says this is a modern disorder? The early history of attention deficit hyperactivity disorder. *World J Psychiatry.* 2015;5 (4):379–386. doi:10.5498/wjp.v5.i4.379.

18. Cooper WO, Habel LA, Sox CM, et al. ADHD medications and serious cardiovascular events in children and youth. doi:10.1056/NEJMoa1110212.

19. Schelleman H, Bilker WB, Strom BL, et al. Cardiovascular events and death in children exposed and unexposed to ADHD agents. *Pediatrics.* 2011;127(6):1102–1110. doi:10.1542/peds.2010-3371.

20. Hansen E, Poole TA, Nguyen V, et al. Prevalence of ADHD symptoms in patients with congenital heart disease. *Pediatr Int.* 2012;54(6):838–843. doi:10.1111/j.1442-200X.2012.03711.x.

21. Berger S. Attention deficit hyperactivity disorder medications in children with heart disease. *Curr Opin Pediatr.* 2016;28(5). https://journals.lww.com/co-pedia trics/Fulltext/2016/10000/Attention_deficit_hyperactivity_disorder.7.aspx.

22. Heart W, Receiving D. Recommendations for cardiovascular evaluation and monitoring of children and adolescents receiving medications for ADHD. Caring for Children with ADHD: A Resource Toolkit for Clinicians, 2nd ed. American Academy of Pediatrics. 2012.

23. Bartlik B, Harmon G, Kaplan P. Use of methylphenidate in a patient with glaucoma and attention-deficit hyperactivity disorder: A clinical dilemma. *Arch Gen Psychiatry.* 1997;54(2):188–189. http://dx.doi.org/10.1001/archpsyc.1997. 01830140100018.

24. Pliszka S. Practice parameter for the assessment and treatment of children and adolescents with Attention-Deficit/Hyperactivity Disorder. *J Am Acad Child Adolesc Psychiatry.* 2007;46(7):894–921. doi:10.1097/chi.0b013e318054e724.

25. Arnold LE. Methylphenidate vs. Amphetamine: Comparative Review. *J Attention Disorders.* Jan.; 2000. doi:10.1177/108705470000300403.

26. Midha KK, McKay G, Rawson MJ, Korchinski ED, Hubbard JW. Effects of food on the pharmacokinetics of methylphenidate. *Pharm Res.* 2001. doi:10.1023/ A:1010987212724.

27. Guideline CP. ADHD: Clinical practice guideline for the diagnosis, evaluation, and treatment of Attention-Deficit/Hyperactivity Disorder in children and adolescents. *Pediatrics.* 2011;128(5):1007–1022. doi:10.1542/peds.2011-2654.

28. Panther SG, Knotts AM, Odom-Maryon T, Daratha K, Woo T, Klein TA. Off-label prescribing trends for ADHD medications in very young children. *J Pediatr Pharmacol Ther.* 2017. doi:10.5863/1551-6776-22.6.423.

29. Wigal T, Greenhill L, Chuang S, et al. Safety and tolerability of methylphenidate in preschool children with ADHD. *J Am Acad Child Adolesc Psychiatry.* 2006;45(11):1294–1303. doi:10.1097/01.chi.0000235082.63156.27.

30. Visser SN, Danielson ML, Bitsko RH, et al. Trends in the parent-report of health care provider-diagnosed and medicated Attention-Deficit/Hyperactivity Disorder: United States, 2003–2011. *J Am Acad Child Adolesc Psychiatry.* 2014;53 (1):34–46.e2. doi:https://doi.org/10.1016/j.jaac.2013.09.001.

31. Lakhan SE, Kirchgessner A. Prescription stimulants in individuals with and without attention deficit hyperactivity disorder: Misuse, cognitive impact, and adverse effects. *Brain Behav.* 2012. doi:10.1002/brb3.78.

32. Giovannitti JA, Thoms SM, Crawford JJ. Alpha-2 adrenergic receptor agonists: A review of current clinical applications. *Anesth Prog.* 2015;62(1):31–38. doi:10.2344/0003-3006-62.1.31.

33. Ming X, Mulvey S, Mohanty S, Patel V. Safety and efficacy of clonidine and clonidine extended-release in the treatment of children and adolescents with attention deficit and hyperactivity disorders. *Adolesc Health Med Ther*. 2011;105. doi:10.2147/AHMT.S15672.

34. Kollins SH, Jain R, Brams M, et al. Clonidine extended-release tablets as add-on therapy to psychostimulants in children and adolescents with ADHD. *Pediatrics*. 2011;127(6):e1406 LP–e1413. http://pediatrics.aappublications.org/content/127/6/e1406.abstract.

35. Faraone SV. The pharmacology of amphetamine and methylphenidate: Relevance to the neurobiology of attention-deficit/hyperactivity disorder and other psychiatric comorbidities. *Neurosci Biobehav Rev*. 2018;87(February):255–270. doi:10.1016/j.neubiorev.2018.02.001.

36. Myers RL. *The 100 Most Important Chemical Compounds: A Reference Guide*. ABC-CLIO; 2007.

12 Medications for Conditions Associated with ADHD

J. Dennis Odell and George Wootton

While any discussion of ADHD treatment necessarily involves a discussion of ADHD medications, with the frequent association of other conditions there are often additional treatments that are important to consider and be aware of. Each condition has its unique treatment recommendations, but there are often overlapping indications for many of the medications used. And while medications are ideally specific to the diagnoses, oftentimes medications may be beneficial for the symptoms, regardless of diagnosis. For example, stimulant medications improve symptoms of hyperactivity in those with ADHD, but also may improve hyperactivity in those with autism, fetal alcohol syndrome and developmental or intellectual disabilities. We can't cover all of the medications that might be used in treating ADHD and all of the associated conditions, but there are a few classes of medications that need to be included to address the commonly seen other problems, specifically antidepressants and antipsychotics. Treatment guidelines and typical doses are discussed, but as with any medication, specific recommendations need to be under the direction and monitoring of the prescribing clinician.

The most common coexisting conditions that are often treated with medications are mood disorders and anxiety. These are extremely common with an estimated lifetime prevalence of symptoms causing severe impairment or distress of over 20% in children and adolescents.[1] Generally, if symptoms are mild, it is appropriate to treat mood disorders and anxiety with monitoring and consideration of counselling with appropriate therapists, and especially with youth, skilled providers who have experience with pediatric and adolescent therapeutic practices. But if symptoms persist, or are more severe, the combination of counselling and medication can be quite beneficial. Often mood disorders and anxiety are treated by the primary care physician, but if symptoms are severe, or there are worrisome other problems such as substance abuse, psychosis or significant suicidality, consultation with mental health providers including child, adolescent and adult psychiatrists is normally recommended.[2]

Selective Serotonin Reuptake Inhibitors

Selective serotonin reuptake inhibitors (SSRIs) are the most commonly used and usually the first choice of medications used to treat anxiety, depression and OCD, especially in children. Prior to the development of SSRIs, medicines available to treat mood disorders came with a lot of potentially dangerous side effects, limiting their use. SSRIs on the other hand are relatively safe and have far fewer side effects than older antidepressants, and so dramatically altered the treatment options for mood disorders. The name comes from their mechanism of action, where they increase the levels of the neurotransmitter serotonin in the synaptic space by inhibiting or blocking the reuptake of serotonin after it has been secreted. Serotonin is one of the chemical messengers or neurotransmitters in the brain that affects mood, and medications that treat mood disorders will usually target at least serotonin.

SSRIs currently available in the US include fluoxetine (Prozac), sertraline (Zoloft), citalopram (Celexa), escitalopram (Lexapro), paroxetine (Paxil), and fluvoxamine (Luvox). Prozac was the first of the SSRIs to be marketed, starting in 1987. Although they all work by increasing serotonin levels, there are differences between them in how long they last, dosage considerations and how they interact with other medicines. Unlike the experience with stimulant medications, the research from which to derive treatment recommendations for use of SSRIs and other medicines used to treat mood disorders in children is relatively sparse. Although there is probably not much difference in efficacy of the various SSRIs, the FDA has approved only fluoxetine (for ages 8–18) and escitalopram (ages 12–17) for use in the treatment of depression in children and adolescents. Fluoxetine has the best evidence for improvement in treating depression, and may be the best first option in medication treatment.[3] For anxiety and OCD, fluoxetine (ages 7–17), fluvoxamine (ages 8–17) and sertraline (ages 6–17) are approved for use in children and adolescents, and other SSRIs are used off label.

Pertinent to this discussion about SSRIs and to many other medications is the mode of metabolism. Most drugs are metabolized or broken down by enzymes produced from the so-called cytochrome P450 genes that are primarily located in cells in the liver. There are multiple variations (polymorphisms) that affect the function of these enzymes and the rate at which various drugs are metabolized. Also, drugs that use the same metabolic pathway may compete for receptor sites, also affecting the rate of metabolism. Cytochrome P450 genes are named CYP, followed by the group number, subfamily letter and gene number, for example CYP27A1.[4]

Awareness of which enzyme system is utilized by a particular drug can help in understanding potential side effects. With so many potential polymorphisms at each genetic site (there are approximately 60 CYP450 genes in humans), each individual may have a unique combination of enzymes affecting how they metabolize and respond to different drugs. These can now be identified through lab testing (genotyping), and in complicated situations where multiple drugs are needed to treat an individual, or where a person has not responded as expected, or had multiple unexpected side effects, running that test that identifies the individual's metabolic profile can be done. Needless to say this is an expensive test, but where medication costs can run into the thousands of dollars per year, the cost may be worth the expense.

Fluoxetine (Prozac) has the most studies demonstrating efficacy for depression, anxiety and OCD. Fluoxetine is unique amongst SSRIs in having a very long half-life of at least several days (the time it takes for ½ of the drug to be eliminated). This means it takes a long time, up to a month or more, to achieve a steady state, and can take a long time to disappear when discontinuing. This can be an advantage when one is prone to forgetting doses because of fewer withdrawal effects, but a disadvantage if there are significant side effects, as they take longer to resolve when discontinuing the medicine. It also means it may take longer to see positive effects. It is metabolized by the CYP2D6 enzyme, which comes with a number of known polymorphisms that affect rate of elimination.[5] As with atomoxetine discussed in the last chapter, some are slow metabolizers of fluoxetine because they have a relative dysfunction of the CYP2D6 enzyme, and some break it down faster than expected. Fluoxetine also inhibits the function of the CYP2D6 enzymes, so if an individual is also taking any other drug that is similarly metabolized it will result in higher than expected drug levels of that drug. So for example, adding fluoxetine to someone already taking atomoxetine will increase atomoxetine levels, so the dosage would need to be adjusted. Fluoxetine effects are increased (and there is more toxicity) when taken concurrently with opioids, other antidepressants and ibuprofen. Fluoxetine efficacy is decreased when taken with certain medicines used to treat seizures, and by cyproheptadine. Fluoxetine may increase the levels and toxicity of many other medications taken concurrently, including some pain medications, medicines used to prevent clotting, atomoxetine, dextromethorphan (the DM in over the counter cough medicines), other antidepressants, and others. So it is important when taking fluoxetine and any of the SSRIs to be aware of potential interactions with other medications that may affect efficacy and side effects. Information on potential drug interactions can be obtained from the prescribing physician, pharmacist, and online sites such as WebMD and drugs.com. Fluoxetine comes as a liquid preparation (20mg/5ml), tablets (10mg, 20mg, 60mg) or capsules (10mg, 20mg and 40mg). Dosage range is 10–60mg.

Sertraline (Zoloft) also has demonstrated efficacy in treating anxiety, OCD and depression in children and adolescents as well as adults. Sertraline has a significantly shorter half-life than fluoxetine of 26 hours. It is metabolized by multiple CYP enzymes, so is not as affected by the presence of other medications, but still may affect the efficacy and toxicity of other medicines taken with it.[6] Recommended dosage range is quite wide, 25–200mg, so it may take some time to get to higher doses if needed. Also, withdrawal symptoms can occur with sudden discontinuation, so the dosage needs to be tapered if going off the medication. Sertraline comes as a liquid preparation of 100mg/5ml (20mg/ml), or scored tablets of 25mg, 50mg and 100mg.

Citalopram (Celexa) is an SSRI that is not currently approved for use in pediatric patients, so its use is off label. Citalopram is usually well tolerated, and may be less activating than some of the other SSRIs. Its half-life is about 35 hours. One concern about citalopram is its higher risk of increasing the QTc interval (prolonged QT syndrome). The QT interval is a measurement on standard electrocardiograms, and if it is excessively prolonged carries the risk of causing dangerous arrhythmias of the heart. This is particularly a risk for those with a genetically based prolonged QT syndrome, which is rare, and with those taking other medications that have the same side effect. Because of this risk, the dosage limit on citalopram is 40mg, and less if there are other risk factors. This can be a problem with other SSRIs, but less than with citalopram.[7] It is metabolized by multiple CYP enzymes, but especially CYP2C19, and so may interact with other medicines using the same system, such as omeprazole (Prilosec). Dosage range is 20–40mg, and citalopram comes as a solution of 10mg/5ml and tablets of 10mg, 20mg and 40mg.

Escitalopram (Lexapro): citalopram is a mixture of 2 molecules that are mirror images of each other, like right and left hands, called enantiomers. One of the enantiomers, the left handed or s-enantiomer is far more active and effective than the other. Escitalopram is a formulation of citalopram that has only the more active enantiomer, thus the name escitalopram. It is approved for treatment of depression in adolescents. It has a half-life of about 30 hours, similar to the other SSRIs besides fluoxetine. It is approved for use in the treatment of adolescents with depression, but is also used for anxiety disorders and OCD off label. It is metabolized by the same CYP enzymes as citalopram, but appears to have less of a risk of QT prolongation. It comes as a solution of 5mg/5ml and 5mg, 10mg and 20mg tablets. Recommended dosage is 10–20mg.

Paroxetine (Paxil): Paroxetine is not currently approved for use in children or adolescents. The efficacy for treating depression in that age range is unproven, but there is some evidence of benefit with anxiety. However, because of a higher risk of suicidal behavior in those under 18, and safety concerns, its use in that population is discouraged. It is partially metabolized by the CYP2D6, with the same implications for drug interactions as fluoxetine. Paroxetine can be sedating. Paroxetine comes in multiple different dosage forms, oral suspension 10mg/5ml, tablets of 10mg, 20mg, 30mg and 40mg, capsule of 7.5mg, and extended-release tablets of 12.5mg, 25mg and 37.5mg. Dosage range is 10–60mg depending on what is being treated.

Fluvoxamine (Luvox): fluvoxamine is approved for use for treating OCD in children 8 years of age and older, and is used also for treating anxiety disorders and depression. Its half-life is relatively short compared with other SSRIs, about 15–22 hours, so is best dosed twice per day. It is metabolized by the CYP2D6 and 1A2, and has many drug interactions. Dosage is 25–200mg in children, usually divided twice per day, and maximum dose 300mg in adolescents and adults. Behavioral activation has been reported to be common especially in children on fluvoxamine, with symptoms that include increased activity, impulsivity, insomnia, and decreased inhibition. Symptoms usually resolve over time or respond to decreased dose, and the risk is decreased with slower titration of dose with increasing dose only every 2–4 weeks.[8] It comes as tablets of 25mg, 50mg and 100mg and extended release capsules of 100 and 150mg.

Treatment strategies: Doses in children should start low initially to minimize side effects. Dose is increased slowly, and the individual treated for at least 4–6 weeks at effective dose before assessing efficacy. Prescribers should avoid the temptation to increase the dose too quickly. Because of frequent early significant potential side effects such as activation and suicidal ideation, monitoring is recommended weekly in the first 4 weeks, and biweekly afterwards, until stable.[9] If there is no or incomplete response, the dosage should be pushed gradually to the maximum recommended dose. The treatment response rate is about 60% with an initial SSRI. If there is an inadequate response, if not already being done, working with an effective counselor with cognitive behavior therapy or other effective therapies is recommended. Switching to another SSRI can sometimes be effective, or considering another class of antidepressant such as venlafaxine.[10] Psychiatry referral should also be considered if incomplete improvement is achieved.

SSRI side effects: SSRIs were designed to be specific in their mechanism of action, and to limit side effects. Compared to previous antidepressants, they have been felt to be much safer. Unlike the previously used tricyclic antidepressants and others, overdosing on SSRIs is not nearly as dangerous. As a group, SSRIs are usually well tolerated, but there are a number of side effects to be aware of. Common side effects include gastrointestinal symptoms such as nausea, diarrhea and abdominal pain, headaches, fatigue, nervousness, sleep disturbances and sexual dysfunction, and the differences between the SSRIs for common side effects are modest. Several of the SSRIs (fluoxetine, paroxetine and fluvoxamine) exhibit a phenomenon called nonlinear kinetics, meaning the concentration of the drug in plasma rises disproportionally as the dose is increased. This, in combination with differences in CYP metabolism and effects of other medications that are being taken, results in widely different medication responses and side effect profiles amongst individuals taking SSRIs. There are several side effect categories to be aware of with all SSRIs.

Activation syndrome: symptoms consist of emotional arousal or behavioral activation, including irritability, aggressive behavior, disinhibition, agitation, restlessness, emotional lability and anxiety. It most often appears during the first 2–3 weeks after starting the medication. It is usually dose related, and may be associated with raising the dose too rapidly, and may be more prevalent in the "slow metabolizers". It is associated with age, with higher risk in younger children, with rates in children estimated at approximately 10%. It appears to occur more frequently in those with intellectual disability, Tourette syndrome and autism spectrum disorders.[11] In some, it is possible this represents a milder version of activation of manic symptoms in those with unrecognized bipolar disorder if there are symptoms of grandiose thinking and euphoria. Symptoms often improve by lowering the dose.

Suicidal ideation: All SSRIs and other medicines used to treat depression carry a "black box" warning, which is the strictest warning put in drug labels by the FDA when there is evidence of potentially serious harm from the medicine. The warning, which was put in place in 2004 by the FDA, states that there is an increased risk of suicidality in children, adolescents and young adults with the use of these medications. The increased risk appears to be in a small subset of youth treated with antidepressants, in the neighborhood of 2 per 100 treated with antidepressants compared with placebo. The warning includes the recommendation that individuals being treated with SSRIs and other antidepressants be monitored for suicidal thoughts and intent. However, for most treated with SSRIs, the actual suicide risk appears to be considerably less. Prior to 1990, suicide rates for youth had been increasing for several decades. Starting in 1990, with the more widespread use of SSRIs, the suicide rate dropped until 2003, only to start to rise again when antidepressant use declined again as a consequence of the black box warning. There were justifiable concerns that the black box warnings had made physicians and patients hesitant to prescribe and take antidepressants, meaning many with depression and other mood disorders were left untreated by medications. [12] Starting in 2010, suicide rates in teens have started to increase again. One factor found to possibly explain the current rise in suicide rates is the use of smart phones and social media, with more hours of use correlated to higher risk of mental health issues.[13]

Serotonin syndrome: Serotonin syndrome is caused by taking medications that cause excessively high levels of serotonin, either too high of a dose of a single medication like SSRIs, or more commonly the combination of multiple medications that affect serotonin levels. Symptoms include agitation, confusion, headache, rapid pulse and high blood pressure, muscle stiffening, sweating and diarrhea. More severe symptoms may include high fever, seizures, arrhythmias, and coma. Drugs that can increase serotonin levels and that should be used with caution in combination include all antidepressants, anti-migraine medications like imitrex, any opioid pain medications, lithium, medicines for vomiting (Zofran), and some over the counter medications (dextromethorphan), herbal medicines (St John's wort), and illicit drugs (cocaine).

Other considerations: Abrupt discontinuation of SSRI medications should be avoided as there are frequently withdrawal symptoms. This is less of a problem with fluoxetine because of the long half-life. Symptoms include agitation, anxiety, dizziness, headaches, muscle aches and flu like symptoms. The medications should be tapered gradually if weaning off of an SSRI. Also, SSRIs may impair clotting, and should be used with caution in the presence of other medications that increase the risk of bleeding, such as NSAIDs like ibuprofen and aspirin. There is some risk of switching from depression to mania in those with undiagnosed bipolar disorder. There is some risk of hyponatremia (low sodium or salt level in the blood), especially in the elderly, and generally the risk is highest in the first month.[14]

Other Antidepressants

SNRIs: Serotonin-norepinephrine reuptake inhibitors (SNRIs) are another class of medicines used to treat depression, anxiety and other mood disorders. They are considered second line treatments for these disorders, after SSRIs.[15] Like SSRIs, they block the reuptake of serotonin in the synapse, but also block the reuptake of another neurotransmitter, norepinephrine, increasing the levels of both. Drugs in this class include venlafaxine (Effexor) and duloxetine (Cymbalta) and others. Side effects are similar to SSRIs, and the same cautions apply. Additionally, discontinuation symptoms appear to be particularly severe with these medicines, so the dose should be tapered slowly when discontinuing. Elevated blood pressure is a potential side effect that needs to be monitored, and in children there can be effects on slowing weight gain and height. They are both metabolized by CYP enzymes, particularly CYP2D6, so there are potential interactions with multiple other medications. As a class they are considered as effective as SSRIs in adults, but there is less evidence supporting their use in children and adolescents. [15] None are approved for use in children or adolescents. Effexor XR is an extended release preparation and dosage range is 37.5mg to 225mg once daily, and comes as 37.5mg, 75mg, 150mg capsules, and tablets of the same strength plus 225mg. The generic venlafaxine also comes as tablets of multiple strengths, but must be given three times per day. Duloxetine (Cymbalta) comes as 20mg, 30mg and 60mg capsules, and dosage range is usually 20–60mg, with maximum dose of 120mg. These medicines have been used effectively to help chronic pain syndromes, especially when associated with depression and anxiety.

Tricyclic antidepressants: Tricyclic antidepressant medications such as imipramine, desipramine, and clomipramine have some efficacy in the child and adolescent population, and used to be the primary antidepressants used in pediatrics prior to the development of SSRIs. Clomipramine has been shown to be efficacious for the treatment of repetitive behaviors and stereotypies (repetitive, fixed movements that serve no obvious purpose) in some individuals with autism and obsessive compulsive disorder. Imipramine is now a second line medication in treating nocturnal enuresis. Desipramine has an indication for treating depression in children 13 and older. Use of these medications has decreased since newer medications with fewer side effects and risks have come into favor. The most alarming potential adverse effect is their ability to induce cardiac arrhythmias at relatively low doses.

Antipsychotic medications

Antipsychotic medications are generally prescribed under the direction of psychiatrists. But because they are used often, and at times primary care providers and other clinicians are involved in the care of those taking these medications, or may prescribe them, some understanding of their place in ADHD management is warranted. Although psychotic behaviors are relatively rare in the pediatric population, use of antipsychotic medications is often used to address severe behavior, agitation, and aggression seen in pediatric patients. There are many reasons antipsychotic use has increased. Greater acceptability of psychotropic medication use in children, increased knowledge and awareness of the potential for reducing serious behaviors, limited access to non-pharmacologic treatments, demand for quick and affordable treatments, inadequate provider time and limited treatment options for at risk and vulnerable populations such as children in foster care or juvenile detention facilities are all likely causes.[16]

Between 2007 and 2010 the most common diagnosis associated with pediatric use of atypical antipsychotic use was ADHD,[17] and a significant percentage of prescriptions for antipsychotic medications are for youth with ADHD.[18] Extreme behaviors are difficult to treat through typical non-pharmacologic therapy. Often families find themselves lacking access to highly skilled providers able to address these behaviors without medication. Increasing consensus exists that antipsychotic medication should be the treatment of last resort, after parenting skills training and other behavioral treatments have been tried. In this situation the potential risks of antipsychotic medications may outweigh the immediate risk to safety from aggressive behavior. Both typical (first generation) and atypical (second generation) antipsychotic medications (SGAs) have been used for these purposes. Use of typical antipsychotic medications has been limited because they have a higher likelihood of causing extrapyramidal effects, but second generation antipsychotics carry a higher risk of metabolic side effects.

Atypical antipsychotics (SGAs): Five atypical antipsychotics currently have FDA-approved indications for use in children and adolescents: risperidone (Risperdal), aripiprazole (Abilify), olanzapine (Zyprexa), paliperidone

(Invega), and quetiapine (Seroquel). Antipsychotics act by postsynaptic blockade of brain dopamine D2 receptors (a subtype of dopamine receptors), blocking the effects of dopamine in those specific areas. The exception is aripiprazole, which is a D2 partial agonist, meaning dopamine effects are blunted but not completely blocked. SGAs differ from the first generation antipsychotics in that they also block serotonin 5-HT2A receptors, and this property has been the explanation for the lower risk of extrapyramidal side effects. The extrapyramidal system is part of the neurologic motor system that regulates involuntary movements and coordination, and so called extrapyramidal symptoms or side effects refer to neurologic effects affecting this system. Antipsychotic medication use carries a risk of extrapyramidal side effects including inducing movement disorders such as parkinsonism (mimicking Parkinson's disease), dystonia (abnormal repetitive uncontrollable muscle movements), akathisia (restlessness), which are sometimes permanent (tardive dyskinesia).

Most cautions related to use of atypical antipsychotic medications in children and adolescents are class related. Side effects may include sedation, lethargy, akathisia, extrapyramidal symptoms, increased appetite, and metabolic risks such as extreme weight gain, metabolic syndrome and diabetes. Although rare with SGAs, neuroleptic malignant syndrome can occur. For prescribers it is also important to understand that, although there is data supporting the efficacy of atypical antipsychotic use on severe behavior, there is little longitudinal research on the neurologic effects associated with this class of medication in the pediatric and adolescent populations. As a general guideline with these medications, start low and go slow. As with antidepressants, it may take many weeks before maximal response is seen.

Monitoring: Due to the potential risks associated with use of this class of medication, careful monitoring should be considered both as a premedication work-up and for medication management. Although the likelihood of identifying a metabolic abnormality that may be causing the concerning behavior is small, a baseline evaluation can be helpful in case of abnormalities appearing once treatment has started. Recommendations for monitoring are scattered in the literature although specific and research based recommendations are difficult to find. The monitoring schedule below comes largely from *Practice Parameter for the Use of Atypical Antipsychotic Medications in Children and Adolescents* published by the American Academy of Child and Adolescent Psychiatry, August 2011.[19]

For asymptomatic clients screening guidelines for patients on SGAs is recommended:

- Weight, height, BMI and waist circumference checked at baseline, at 1 month, 3 months, 6 months, and annually
- Blood pressure and pulse checked at baseline, 1 month, 3 months, and annually

- Fasting plasma glucose and fasting lipid profile (HDL, LDL, TG, total cholesterol) checked at -baseline, at 3 months, 6 months and annually.
- Hemoglobin A1C and prolactin levels should be considered if symptoms of concern are present.
- Electrocardiogram should be considered if high doses are used.

Since some atypical antidepressants can have an effect on red and white blood cells, a complete blood count at baseline, at 12 weeks, and annually may provide helpful information. Thyroid screening is also suggested at baseline since hyper and hypothyroid symptoms can mimic ADHD and behavioral symptoms. Some of the most concerning short and long-term side effects associated with these agents are movement disorders. Careful screening for movement disorders should be done at baseline and every 6–12 months. Use of a standardized rating scale such as the Abnormal Involuntary Movement Scale (AIMS) is suggested.

Specific Medications – Risperidone (Risperdal): Risperidone was the first SGA to be approved for use in children and adolescents and is the SGA with the most methodologically stringent evidence in this population. It is approved to treat those who are over 13 years for schizophrenia, over 10 to treat bipolar I disorder, and ages 5–17 for irritability associated with autism. Starting dosages vary depending on the condition but can be as low as 0.125mg at bedtime. The highest recommended dose is 6mg but only for Bipolar disorder and schizophrenia. Typical dose range is 1–4mg per day. An additional concern with risperidone is elevation of prolactin levels which may cause early breast development and galactorrhea among other adverse effects, and monitoring prolactin levels should be considered.

Aripiprazole (Abilify): Aripiprazole is called an atypical atypical antipsychotic because of its partial dopamine (D2) agonist effect. It is approved for treatment of agitation in children ages 6–18 for treating Tourette syndrome and autism related agitation, for 10 and older for treating bipolar 1, and over 13 for treating schizophrenia. Dosing can start at 2mg and go as high as 30mg, with typical dose range of 2.5–15mg per day. It is also used to treat major depressive disorder. Common side effects include weight gain, nausea, constipation, dizziness, sleep problems, headache and agitation.

Olanzapine (Zyprexa): Olanzapine has an approval for treating both schizophrenia and manic phases of bipolar 1 disorder. Doses start at 2.5mg and can increase up to 20mg. It is approved for use as adjunct therapy for depressive episodes in bipolar 1 disorder in those over 10 years old, and as a primary agent for schizophrenia and bipolar 1 for those 10 years old and above. Olanzapine has a relatively high likelihood of causing metabolic side effects, especially weight gain and high blood sugar, but may have a lower risk of extrapyramidal effects than other SGAs.

Paliperidone (Invega): Paliperidone is approved for treatment of schizophrenia for those 12 and above. Dosing starts at 3mg and can go as high as

12mg. Paliperidone is the active metabolite of risperidone. This suggests they should act similarly although differences in receptor binding suggest they may have differences in action. Common side effects include sedation, restlessness and weight gain.

Quetiapine (Seroquel): Quetiapine has a wide dosing range and a good safety profile. It has been approved for treating schizophrenia in youth 13 years of age and older and manic episodes associated with bipolar disorder in youth 10 years of age and older. Dosing starts at 25mg at bedtime and typical range is 100–600mg per day.[20] Because of its sedating properties it is also helpful for insomnia.

Conclusion

While the mainstay of medication treatment for ADHD is stimulant medications, because of the wide variety of other conditions associated with ADHD and the frequently incomplete efficacy of stimulants alone, multiple other treatment modalities including other medication options are often part of the therapeutic regimen. Antidepressant medications and atypical antipsychotic medications are widely used in those with ADHD, and familiarity with the issues and side effects related to these is an essential part of ADHD management.

Bibliography

1. Merikangas KR, He JP, Burstein M, et al. Lifetime prevalence of mental disorders in U.S. adolescents: Results from the National Comorbidity Survey Replication—Adolescent Supplement (NCS-A). *J Am Acad Child Adolesc Psychiatry.* 2010;49(10):980–989. doi:10.1016/j.jaac.2010.05.017.

2. Cheung AH, Zuckerbrot RA, Jensen PS, Laraque D, Stein REK. Guidelines for Adolescent Depression in Primary Care (GLAD-PC): Part II. Treatment and ongoing management. *Pediatrics.* 2018;141(3).

3. Cipriani A, Zhou X, Del Giovane C, et al. Comparative efficacy and tolerability of antidepressants for major depressive disorder in children and adolescents: A network meta-analysis. *Lancet.* 2016;388(10047):881–890. doi:10.1016/S0140-6736(16)30385-3.

4. Cytochrome p450. NIH US National Library of Medicine, Genetics Home Reference website. https://ghr.nlm.nih.gov/primer/genefamily/cytochromep450.

5. Margolis JM, O'Donnell JP, Mankowski DC. SE and RSO. (R)-, (S)-, and racemic fluoxetine N-demethylation by human cytochrome P450 enzymes. *Drug Metab Dispos.* 28( ):1187–1191.

6. Obach RS, Cox LM, Tremaine LM. Sertraline is metabolized by multiple cytochrome P450 enzymes, monoamine oxidases, and glucuronyl transferases in human: An in vitro study. *Drug Metab Dispos.* 2005;33(2):262–270. doi:10.1124/dmd.104.002428.

7. Beach SR, Kostis WJ, Celano CM, et al. Meta-analysis of selective serotonin reuptake inhibitor-associated QTc prolongation. *J Clin Psychiatry*. 2014;75(5): e441–449. doi:10.4088/JCP.13r08672.

8. Reinblatt SP, dosReis S, Walkup JT, Riddle MA. Activation adverse events induced by the selective serotonin reuptake inhibitor fluvoxamine in children and adolescents. *J Child Adolesc Psychopharmacol*. 2009;19(2):119–126. doi:10.1089/cap.2008.040.

9. McVoy M, Findling RL, ed. *Clinical Manual of Child and Adolescent Psychopharmacology*. 3rd ed. American Psychiatric Association Publishing; 2017.

10. Brent D, Emslie G, Clarke G, et al. Switching to another SSRI or to venlafaxine with or without cognitive behavioral therapy for adolescents with SSRI-resistant depression: The TORDIA randomized controlled trial. *JAMA*. 2008;299(8):901–913. doi:10.1001/jama.299.8.901.

11. Amitai M, Chen A, Weizman A, Apter A. SSRI-induced activation syndrome in children and adolescents—What is next? *Curr Treat Options Psychiatry*. 2015;2 (1):28–37. doi:10.1007/s40501-015-0034-9.

12. McCain JA. Antidepressants and suicide in adolescents and adults: A public health experiment with unintended consequences? *P T*. 2009;34(7):355–378.

13. Twenge JM, Joiner TE, Rogers ML, Martin GN. Increases in depressive symptoms, suicide-related outcomes, and suicide rates among U.S. adolescents after 2010 and links to increased new media screen time. *Clin Psychol Sci*. 2017;6(1):3–17. doi:10.1177/2167702617723376.

14. Lien YHH. Antidepressants and hyponatremia. *Am J Med*. 2018;131(1):7–8. doi:10.1016/j.amjmed.2017.09.002.

15. Garland, EJ, Kutcher S, Virani A, Elbe D. Update on the use of SSRIs and SNRIs with children and adolescents in clinical practice. *J Can Acad Child Adolesc Psychiatry*. 2016;25(1):4–10.

16. Harrison JN, Cluxton-Keller F, Gross D. Antipsychotic medication prescribing trends in children and adolescents. *J Pediatr Heal Care Off Publ Natl Assoc Pediatr Nurse Assoc Pract*. 2012;26(2):139–145. doi:10.1016/j.pedhc.2011.10.009.

17. Sohn M, Moga DC, Blumenschein K, Talbert J. National trends in off-label use of atypical antipsychotics in children and adolescents in the United States. *Medicine (Baltimore)*. 2016;95(23):e3784. doi:10.1097/MD.0000000000003784.

18. Birnbaum ML, Saito E, Gerhard T, et al. Pharmacoepidemiology of antipsychotic use in youth with ADHD: Trends and clinical implications. *Curr Psychiatry Rep*. 2013;15(8):382. doi:10.1007/s11920-013-0382-3.

19. Findling RL. Practice parameter for the use of atypical antipsychotic medications in children and adolescents. *J Am Acad Child Adolesc Psychiatry*. 2011;August.

20. Centers for Medicare & Medicaid Services (Institution/Organization). Atypical antipsychotic medications: Use in pediatric patients. *Medicaid Services*. 2014; (July):1–6. https://cms.gov/Medicare-Medicaid-Coordination/Fraud-Prevention/Medicaid-Integrity-Education/Pharmacy-Education-Materials/Downloads/atyp-antipsych-pediatric-factsheet11-14.pdf.

13 Behavior Therapy

J. Dennis Odell and Camille Odell

The emphasis for treatment for ADHD is often on medication, because of so much evidence of benefit, relative ease of administration, and often rather dramatic results. However, it has been demonstrated that medication without other treatment modalities often doesn't result in improved long-term outcomes.[1] Best treatment practices include counselling or behavior therapy by itself or in addition to medication. American Academy of Pediatrics guidelines recommend behavior therapy as the first line of treatment in children under 6, with addition of medication only if symptoms do not improve and are sufficiently severe to warrant additional treatment. The same guidelines also recommend behavior therapy as part of long-term interventions for ADHD.[2]

There are difficulties with these recommendations however, because in many communities access to qualified therapy providers is limited, and insurance coverage is often spotty. There are many different therapy options, and understanding how to go about finding the best therapist and type of therapy for an individual can be very challenging. Although there is evidence that certain types of behavior therapy are indeed effective for treating core ADHD symptoms, many therapeutic options that are available do not have a research basis for efficacy. The child with ADHD will often develop compensatory behaviors for dealing with the challenges that come with having ADHD, and these may be maladaptive, with potential significant behavior problems, and comorbid conditions such as depression, anxiety and oppositional behavior. Each of these can also benefit from therapy, but specifics will differ than the interventions used for ADHD core symptoms. The following is a brief review of some of the therapy options for those with ADHD. Selecting which is the best fit will be determined by the therapist in conjunction with the family, but hopefully this review will provide some background on some of the options that are available.

Classroom Interventions

One of the primary sources of help available for all children and adolescents is going to be the school/educational services. Almost universal in comments from teachers regarding their students with ADHD is the observation that they have so much potential, but success is limited by their inability to stay focused, or by their behavior or seeming lack of motivation. ADHD can be conceptualized in part as a difficulty not so much in understanding what to do, but in doing what they know. But additionally, as reviewed previously, they may also struggle with executive function skills that impact organization and goal driven behaviors, and also may have learning disabilities. Those with learning disabilities may qualify for an Individualized Education Program (IEP) and all the resources available in the school system to help with learning problems. Most schools also have behavioral specialists, who can implement behavioral plans, and sometimes therapy within the school system to help with behavioral problems that are impacting school learning. Developing a behavior action plan using teacher directed rewards, time out, daily report cards or point systems in conjunction with the family can be implemented. There are many educational programs available for working with students with ADHD in the school environment that teachers and school therapists may have access to.

For those who need it, occupational therapy services can also be utilized when there needs to be environmental accommodations or specific help for sensory-motor issues that may be adversely affecting learning. Through a 504 plan, accommodations can be made specific to the individual to help within the classroom setting and at home. Study skills classes designed to teach organization and good study habits, and classes that provide extra help for completing assignments and understanding classroom material and concepts are often helpful accommodations. Just as with any therapy, having a teacher who understands what ADHD is and the challenges that accompany it, and has experience working with students with ADHD makes a huge difference. Coordination of these services with the help of community providers such as primary care medical providers, behavior therapists, occupational therapists and the family as part of the team can provide a network of support. If ADHD is conceptualized as a specific set of symptoms that are most prominent in certain environments that stretch the individual's capacity to attend and stay focused, one corollary is that adjusting the environment as much as possible to accommodate the individuals difficulties will be beneficial.

A monograph that provides helpful recommendations for working with school issues related to ADHD is *Teaching Children with Attention Deficit Hyperactivity Disorder: Instructional Strategies and Practices 2008*.[3] It is public domain, available online and can be reprinted. It provides information and suggestions for academic instruction, behavioral interventions and classroom accommodations. Teaching strategies include structured lessons with clearly elaborated expectations regarding learning and behavior. Outlining materials and resources needed, providing simple instructions, being predictable, limiting distractions and closely monitoring performance and providing help when needed are often helpful. Providing tracking sheets or some form of communication with parents is helpful to be sure the student is keeping up with assignments. Timed tests are often frustrating for the ADHD student, and minimizing these or providing extra time or help if needed can decrease the students' anxiety. Breaking projects down into small components to minimize overwhelming tasks, and working in peer groups on projects can also help. Seating in the front of the classroom or near the teacher, and sometimes modifying homework assignments and test location may be appropriate. There are a variety of aids and accommodations available for specific academic problems, and school personnel have the experience and resources available to provide these for individual students who are struggling.

Parent Training

As previously stated, adults with ADHD who have successful outcomes will usually attribute that good outcome in large part to having parents and/or teachers who supported them in spite of the challenges. Helping and supporting parents in their roles in raising ADHD children is critical in that success. Most of us teach appropriate behaviour in our children by utilizing consequences. If a 2-month-old child smiles at a parent, the parent smiles back, and that behavior is reinforced. If a child doesn't respond to a parental demand, there are usually consequences that make it clear parental demands must be met. However, for those with ADHD, behavior is often not changed by consequences. They may understand the consequences well, but do not use that knowledge in the decision-making process at the time. Parenting when consequences aren't meaningful becomes very difficult, and often parents become frustrated with trying to deal with their child's unmanageable behaviors. Parenting strategies may then become ineffective or maladaptive. One of the most effective therapies for helping children with ADHD is behavior parent training that is meant to provide successful parenting strategies for the ADHD child and to decrease the conflict that is often present. Many studies have demonstrated the efficacy of behavior parent training programs in improving symptoms of ADHD and in parent satisfaction regarding treatment outcomes.[4]

Individual therapy for the child with ADHD is often not as effective as parent training, as they often don't generalize what they learn in a once a week session with a therapist to life situations. The point of parent training is to target specific behaviors, to develop intervention strategies that the family can work on over the week, and then to review results the following session and refine the treatment plan. Usually this will start with a review of diagnoses and symptoms of concern and developing a clear understanding of what is causing the behavioral difficulties and how ADHD symptoms contribute. Undesirable behaviors are often present as the child's way of avoiding a task they don't want to do, such as homework or chores. Or there may be aggressive behaviors that are present when their personal space is invaded by a sibling or peer, or behavior meant to get attention from parents or peers. Some behaviors may be triggered by fear in certain settings, such as anxiety about social settings that could lead to ridicule, performance anxiety, or fear or irritability related to sensory issues (especially with those with autism or anxiety disorders).

Understanding the behavioral triggers leads to treatment strategies to help parents to work with the individual child to develop more appropriate behavioral responses. This involves teaching positive reinforcement techniques, selective ignoring and time out strategies, and consistent and reasonable consequences when needed for inappropriate behavior. Recognizing good or appropriate behavior when it happens, and decreasing negative interactions is emphasized. Also part of the treatment process is working on building a strong positive relationship with caregivers, as often this has been severely affected by the child's behaviors and parental responses. Setting clear goals on areas to be treated with expected treatment outcomes, and closely monitoring progress is also part of the process. Goals need to be reasonable, and realistically achievable to avoid frustration. In developing treatment plans, it is important to prioritize the problem behaviors well, as many areas of conflict may not be worth the effort to change, and simultaneously fighting too many battles is overwhelming for parents and the child. Finding appropriate reinforcers/rewards or use of time out techniques can be challenging, and often parents and therapists need to be creative in determining rewards and consequences that help shape behavior.

Goals to be considered might include behavioral concerns such as fighting with siblings or peers, aggressive behaviors, arguing with parents or teachers, or not following rules such as homework, mealtime and bedtime routines. Academic concerns are frequent and goals might include helping with organization, getting homework done in a reasonable time, and turned in, getting ready for school consistently. This can be helped by 504 or IEP accommodations at school to make homework assignments achievable, tracking sheets or communication methods available to monitor progress, and to provide school supports to help achieve learning goals.

Behavior parent training can be done as group therapy, or on an individual basis. Group sessions add the advantage of seeing what works for other families facing similar challenges, and mutual feedback and support, but has the disadvantage of not being able to address specific individual problems, or to adjust the therapy based on individual response and needs and time commitments. Some programs will combine group therapy and individual therapy. Behavior parent training programs are usually short term, 8–12 weeks, with follow up therapy as indicated. There is much variability in the types of programs available, but most critical is working with a therapist that the family trusts, with a sense of mutual respect as opposed to feeling judged, and with someone who has the training and expertise to provide the appropriate interventions. The decision on where to go to find the best therapist for the individual can be helped by consulting with the referring primary care medical provider, by school personnel, community and religious networks, and online reviews.

Cognitive Behavior Therapy

Individual psychotherapy may be very beneficial for those with ADHD, in helping to understand the disorder, to develop coping strategies to deal with the challenges and frustrations that often come with the ADHD diagnosis, to help with improving social interactions, to help the individual in working with school systems and programs, to help with family issues, and with associated problems such as depression and anxiety, and a myriad of other ADHD associated difficulties. Different types of therapies are available to the clinician. In young children, often play therapy is utilized. For older children, adolescents and adults, cognitive behavior therapy (CBT) has been touted to be beneficial, at times for the core ADHD symptoms but also to address comorbid conditions.

Cognitive behavior based therapies may differ in content, but share core features. CBT is meant to be a short-term goal driven intervention. It is based on the principal that there is a connection and interaction between a person's thoughts, emotions and behavior. CBT teaches the individual to develop the tools and skills to deal with unwanted emotions and thoughts when they occur. Analyzing the basis for those thoughts and emotions, and understanding their root cause in relationship to underlying diagnoses allows development of treatment strategies. Therapy includes learning to recognize the basis for negative thoughts and feelings, putting those feelings into proper perspective, and developing strategies to reshape the negative thinking into more positive terms. The therapist helps the individual learn the skills to deal with those thoughts and emotions, who then works on implementation over the ensuing week. Specific expected situations that may occur are anticipated with plans on then implementing new skills and strategies. The intent is to practice during the week the skills learned during the CBT session, and to then review results during the following session, and to gradually focus in on and internalize successful strategies.

CBT is a practical problem-solving approach to current concerns. The eventual goal is to help the individual to be able to have the skills to problem solve using techniques learned in CBT sessions without the need of the therapist. CBT is known to be effective in the treatment of a variety of psychiatric conditions, especially anxiety, depression and OCD, but may also be beneficial for the core symptoms of ADHD and executive function deficits. CBT may be done on an individual basis, or there are also group programs. Important in the success of CBT are the therapeutic skills of the therapist and the commitment of the individual.

Acceptance and Commitment Therapy

Another widely used behavioral therapeutic option is acceptance and commitment therapy (ACT) which uses a more mindfulness approach. Rather than trying to change negative thinking and emotions, ACT therapy emphasizes recognizing and observing the thought, accepting it, and then defusing it using mindfulness techniques. An important component of ACT therapy is the process of identifying values, or what is important to the individual over the lifetime, such as type of career, service, specific relationships, and health, and then using those core values to determine how to respond and react to stressors or thoughts that may impede progress. Mindfulness refers to being able to pay attention to what is happening now without judgment, and actively choosing what happens next. It teaches psychological flexibility in responding to intrusive thoughts and emotions. Rather than having a specific goal that is achieved, the focus is on recognizing and taking action towards your core values in any situation. Instead of trying to get rid of an emotion or thought, the emphasis is on noticing it, connecting with it and accepting its presence but without having it become overwhelming. The primary goal is not symptom reduction but observance and recognition, but as a byproduct of treatment, symptom reduction occurs. The individual learns that he/she can live with a particular symptom, and it is not as bad as perceived, allowing one to move on and not be stuck trying to battle the negative emotions. It is designed to reduce avoidant behavior and improve value driven acceptance.

ACT training is widely used, and studies suggest it can be helpful for any condition that involves negative thinking and emotions. This includes anxiety and depression, rumination, functional pain syndromes such as chronic fatigue syndrome, fibromyalgia, chronic migraines and gastro-intestinal pain. It has also been used to treat the core symptoms of ADHD and to help focus. As with other therapies, it may be accessed in individual or group settings, and is now becoming available in web based programs. Related but structured differently are various mindfulness programs that have become popular in treating ADHD.

Social Skills Training

Children and adolescents who have ADHD often struggle with social interactions with peers, siblings and with caregivers and other adults. Some of this is due to behaviors that are disruptive or irritating due to core features of hyperactive and impulsive behaviors. But those with ADHD may also struggle in understanding how their behaviors are perceived by others, and not recognize that their behaviors are making interactions with others challenging. Understanding social cues often does not come naturally for those with ADHD, especially in those with associated autism spectrum symptoms. Behavioral responses to frustrations can be impulsive and aggressive, and tantruming in younger children and inappropriate or overly reactive responses in older youth and adults can be common. Developing the ability to read other people's emotions and intents is an important developmental goal, and impairment in that ability can cause significant awkwardness in developing social relationships, especially during early adolescence when communication becomes much more complicated with the wider use of teasing and sarcasm. It is common for those with ADHD to be frustrated in wanting to have close friends but not understanding why their behaviors may be pushing others away. Associated oppositional behavior and conduct problems make the difficulties greater, and poor self-esteem is frequent.

Social skills training is a process that helps the individual to gain insight in how to interact in a positive way in the social environment. Although social awareness may be impaired in some with ADHD, it can be taught. This is often done in a group setting, and may involve role playing where each individual gets to comment on what they perceive is happening in a certain scenario, and what they conceptualize the role player is thinking and should do. It forces the student to try to put themselves in someone else's place and to try to understand what they are thinking and feeling. In the group setting comes the realization that others may perceive the situation differently, and allows one to have the opportunity to look at others' perspectives. Basics of social interactions are emphasized, such as eye contact, how to read facial expressions, listening skills, sharing, taking turns, how to respond appropriately when frustrated, and how to handle different social situations. These sessions are usually enjoyable for the participants, so can be beneficial when individuals may resist traditional behavioral therapy.

For those with significant impulsive response styles, social skills training may be of less benefit without the addition of medication or other skills training. For these the difficulties with social interactions may be more due to reactive behaviors despite knowing the appropriate responses, rather than ignorance of the appropriate response. Unless they have the ability to stop and think about the situation, responses may continue to be counterproductive, in spite of knowing the better responses. For social skills training to be effective, it is important to be able to practice these tools in real social settings. Involving parents and teachers to reinforce and practice these measures in the home and school settings is important. Teachers and caregivers will have their own feelings, often negative, about how a child or adolescent is behaving, and reflecting on how they are reacting to that behavior gives insight into how others are responding. Turning their reactions to a positive and supportive position and creating judgment free environments can help model the reactions that other children and adolescents will have. When a child's day consists of mostly negative events, from frustration trying to keep up in school, negative comments from classmates and teachers, prolonged homework time and parental frustration, with associated frequent failure, and few or no friends, it is easy to see why poor self-esteem and relationship difficulties are so common. Being able to have supportive friends and care givers is critical for good long-term outcome.

Applied Behavior Analysis

Applied Behavior Analysis (ABA) is widely known for its use in treating autism spectrum disorders. Its use for autism originated with UCLA psychologist Ivar Lovaas in the 1970s and has been found to be effective for treating autism. But it can also be helpful in treating those with a wide variety of other conditions, including severe behavior problems associated with ADHD and oppositional defiant disorder. ABA is usually more intensive than traditional once or twice per week behavioral counselling. The intent is to extinguish unwanted or negative behaviors and to replace them with or encourage positive behaviors. It is based on the "operant conditioning" model of BF Skinner that says actions that result in reinforcement are more likely to be repeated, and actions followed by undesirable outcomes are less likely to be repeated. ABA is provided by licensed clinical therapists who have additional training and certification in applied behavior analysis. ABA therapy starts with a functional behavioral assessment where the therapist observes behavior in the home or school setting and identifies the antecedents and reinforcers that are causing maladaptive behaviors to persist. This information is used to develop a treatment plan. Like behavior therapy, positive behavior is emphasized and rewarded and negative behavior is treated by ignoring or sometimes punishing interventions. Clients are taught more appropriate solutions to get their needs met rather than using negative behaviors. Traditionally, discrete trial learning is utilized where a very specific behavior is targeted. Tasks are broken down into their smaller core components. If a behavior is requested and the appropriate response is given, a small but meaningful reward is given. If there is noncompliance the reward is not given, and the trial is repeated until the desired behavior is mastered. As additional skills are mastered, the task is generalized into other environments. Other techniques utilizing reinforcement may be used to help with developmental and social skills. Goals are measured and monitored, and continuous reevaluation is undertaken. ABA therapy may be administered in a one on one setting, or in settings in the child's environment such as home or school.

There are other programs and therapies geared towards helping the individual with ADHD. Programs to help with improving executive function skills, occupational therapy to help with activities of daily living and sensory issues, summer treatment programs or camps and others are all potentially helpful for different aspects of ADHD. For whatever treatment programs chosen, it is important that the therapist or provider has the background and training to provide the intervention, and preferably that therapies used have a proven track record of success for the targeted symptoms and population.

Bibliography

1. Currie J, Stabile M, Jones L. Do stimulant medications improve educational and behavioral outcomes for children with ADHD? *J Health Econ*. 2014;37:58–69. doi:10.1016/j.jhealeco.2014.05.002.
2. Guideline CP. ADHD: Clinical practice guideline for the diagnosis, evaluation, and treatment of attention-deficit/hyperactivity disorder in children and adolescents. *Pediatrics*. 2011;128(5):1007–1022. doi:10.1542/peds.2011-2654.
3. U.S. Department of Education, Office of Special Education and Rehabilitative Services, Office of Special Education Programs. *Teaching Children with Attention Deficit Hyperactivity Disorder: Instructional Strategies and Practices*. Washington, D.C. 2008.
4. Pelham WEJ, Fabiano GA. Evidence-based psychosocial treatments for attention-deficit/hyperactivity disorder. *J Clin Child Adolesc Psychol*. 2008;37(1):184–214. doi:10.1080/15374410701818681.

14 Other Interventions for ADHD

J. Dennis Odell

In an interesting and optimistic discussion on the nature of ADHD, Dr. Joel Nigg concludes that while ADHD carries a genetic or hereditary predisposition, there is a very large environmental component that actually modulates the outcome of those with genetic susceptibility. This is in part based on epigenetics, referring to biologic changes that affect the expression of any given gene, or in other words, it is a mechanism where environmental influences affect the expression of inherited DNA. ADHD is conceptualized as a disorder requiring both DNA-transmitted susceptibility and environmental influences that modulate the expression or regulation of ADHD related genes.[1] Genes themselves don't determine outcome, it is the interplay of genes and environmental influences that determines development. The corollary to this view is that adjusting environmental influences can play a major role in determining outcome, and there is reason to believe that optimizing the environment of the ADHD predisposed individual can significantly improve outcome. This also emphasizes the importance of early identification of problems and putting in place appropriate interventions as early as is feasible.

What types of interventions or environmental modifications are available? In previous chapters we have discussed classroom accommodations, therapy options and medication treatments. However, a small percentage of individuals with ADHD will not respond well to medication interventions, or will have unwanted side effects. More commonly, many are uncomfortable taking medication themselves or having their children take medications for ADHD. And not uncommonly, medication alone, although helpful, will not provide complete resolution of concerns. Different therapy options such as psychotherapy, behavioral therapy, occupational and sometimes speech therapy all have their place in treatment of ADHD and associated conditions, but may be hard to access, and have variable success rates in treating ADHD symptoms. This chapter will try to address what other interventions may be helpful, and if there is evidence for other interventions besides medication and therapy options described in previous chapters.

Diet

A healthy diet is a standard recommendation for good health, and prevention of a plethora of medical conditions, such as heart disease, diabetes, hypertension and so on. There is also good evidence that healthy diets are helpful in prevention and treatment of ADHD. Optimal food and nutrient intake is clearly important during pregnancy for the health of the newborn, and there has been recognized an association between obesity and increased risk of ADHD, autism and behavioral problems in the resulting offspring.[2] Diet has always been a controversial part of ADHD management. Given the many effects of an inadequate diet on growth, development and behavior, and the complexity of additives in our foods, it makes some sense to consider dietary changes as a possible solution to some ADHD symptoms.

One very popular diet that was used widely in the past was the Feingold Diet. Benjamin Feingold was a pediatrician and allergist who practiced in California after World War II. He hypothesized that the apparent rise in behavioral problems in children could be attributed to the dramatic change that occurred at that time in the usual diets, from more fresh and unprocessed foods before the war to an abundance of cheaper prepackaged and non-perishable foods that contained additives including preservatives, food dyes and artificial flavors. Also noted at that time were the adverse interactions of aspirin and the potentially allergenic tartrazine (yellow food coloring). So he developed a diet meant to eliminate the offending agents with the goal of improving ADHD like behaviors that were felt to be due to an overabundance of food additives. The diet is quite restrictive and very difficult to adhere to, and eliminates artificial food dyes, flavoring, preservatives and sweeteners, and salicylate (aspirin) containing foods (such as apples, raisins, oranges and many other fruits, nuts and vegetables), and chemical additives such as monosodium glutamate, sodium benzoate, sulfites and nitrites. Especially popular in the 1970s and 1980s, the diet was widely recommended as an effective treatment for ADHD. However, most research at the time did not support the benefits of the Feingold diet, and it has gradually fallen out of favor. Although Dr. Feingold passed away in 1982, the Feingold Association remains an active entity espousing dietary solutions to ADHD and other behavior problems.

Dietary solutions for treatment of ADHD were felt to be not valid up until recently as early research failed to demonstrate significant results. However, in the past decade there seems to have been a resurgence in interest in the benefits of certain dietary changes and its effects on behavior. Options for dietary changes include adding certain foods or supplements to the diet, or the far more difficult restrictive diets that eliminate potentially harmful elements. One area that has received much attention recently is PUFAs, polyunsaturated fatty acids. These are an essential part of our diets because they are necessary for many important bodily and especially brain functions, and cannot be synthesized by mammals, meaning we have to consume them. Two important PUFAs are omega-3 and omega-6 fatty acids, so named because the first unsaturated carbon bond of the backbone structure is at the third or sixth carbon atom from the end. Up until the modern era, human diets typically consisted of equal parts omega-3 and omega-6 fatty acids. But with the industrial revolution, there began to be a marked shift in the relative ratios, where now typical diets are heavily weighted in favor of omega-6 fatty acids, about 10 times the amount of omega-3 fatty acids. This is due in large part to the heavy consumption of vegetable oils and the increased use of cereal grains for domestic livestock. [3] The concern is that excess intake of omega-6 fatty acids contributes to unhealthy inflammation, and omega-3 fatty acids can have positive health effects including beneficial effects on the risk of heart disease, cancer, Alzheimer's disease and others.

Researchers have looked at omega-3 fatty acid levels in children with ADHD and have found them to be low compared with control subjects. A number of studies have looked at results of treating children with ADHD with omega-3 supplementation and found modest improvement in ADHD symptoms.[4] Although both omega-3 and omega-6 fatty acids are important nutrients, the ratio appears to be important for optimal health. Decreasing omega-6 fatty acid intake can be accomplished by limiting processed foods and fast foods that utilize polyunsaturated vegetable oils such as soy oil, corn oil, sunflower, and cottonseed oils, and by utilizing olive oil for cooking, which does not contain much omega-3 or omega-6 fatty acids. Omega-3 fatty acid containing foods include wild salmon, mackerel, swordfish and sardines, omega-3 enriched eggs, grass fed meats rather than grain fed. Three servings of such foods a week will provide a reasonable amount of omega-3 fatty acids. If a diet is insufficient in omega-3 content, supplementing with fish oil can be considered. The dose for children is not well established, but general recommendations are to choose a supplement with both EPA and DHA (the critical omega-3 fatty acids), at a dose of about 1–2 grams per day. It should be noted that beneficial effects may take up to 6 months, so doing a fish oil trial or diet change requires much patience to see optimal results, and results are likely to be modest at best. Nonetheless there is evidence that omega-3 supplementation provides some benefits in those with ADHD, and should certainly be considered as an adjunctive intervention in addition to other therapies.

Iron supplementation has also been considered for ADHD therapy. Iron deficiency is known to have effects on behavior and cognitive function in children. A review of multiple studies on iron status and ADHD found evidence that iron stores as measured by serum ferritin levels are frequently decreased in those with ADHD compared to controls subjects.[5] Supplementing with iron is potentially harmful for those who are not iron deficient, but it is worthwhile to measure iron status in those with ADHD with serum blood count and ferritin levels, and treating with supplemental iron if iron stores are found to be low.

There are also some reports of zinc and magnesium deficiencies associated with ADHD symptoms. These studies are mostly from areas in the world where zinc and magnesium deficiencies are relatively common. Both are rare in the United States, but can occur with severely deficient diets, especially restricted vegetarian diets, or gastrointestinal conditions that affect absorption of nutrients, such as Crohn's disease or short bowel syndrome. Certain conditions such as alcohol abuse and sickle cell disease also increase the risk of mineral deficiencies. Both magnesium and zinc are incredibly important minerals that play significant roles in multiple body systems. Like iron deficiency, too much magnesium or zinc is harmful, so zinc and magnesium supplementation should only be done in those with documented deficiencies by blood tests.

Vitamin D is known for its importance in regulating calcium and phosphorus levels through its effects in the gut, bones and kidneys. But there is growing evidence that vitamin D has many other important functions, including a significant role in the developing fetal brain effecting the growth and development of nerve cells, structure and metabolism, and that dysfunction of the vitamin D network can adversely affect fetal brain development. Vitamin D deficiency during pregnancy and in infants and children has been linked to other disorders such as autism, schizophrenia and multiple sclerosis and current recommended doses of vitamin D supplementation are far too low to prevent vitamin D deficiency in many individuals.[6] Studies recommend vitamin D supplementation for everyone, but there is much debate about whether low vitamin D levels during pregnancy and during infancy and childhood can increase the risk for development of a variety of neurodevelopmental disorders including ADHD. Vitamin D is easily obtained by direct exposure to the sun. But because of decreased exposure due to skin cancer concerns and current life styles, and decreased sun exposure especially in the winter, vitamin D deficiency is very common in the United States. Given the very high prevalence of vitamin D deficiency and the potential for improvement in a variety of health measures by normalizing vitamin D levels, it seems prudent to at least measure vitamin D levels during pregnancy, and for anyone with ADHD and related disorders, and to provide sufficient vitamin D supplementation for those whose levels are found to be low.

L-Carnitine is an amino acid that is necessary for fatty-acid metabolism and energy production. Some L-carnitine is naturally synthesized in the body, but most is obtained from our diet, especially animal based foods. It has been used for many conditions such as certain heart problems, vascular conditions and muscle disorders. Actual carnitine deficiency is rare, and can be caused by a number of different rare genetic conditions or syndromes. There have been only a few small studies looking at supplementation of carnitine and ADHD, and results have been mixed, with evidence suggesting it may be most helpful for those with the inattentive type of ADHD.[7]

Anecdotally, we have seen a few patients with documented mild carnitine deficiencies who have benefitted from carnitine supplementation.

What about restricted diets and ADHD? In the United States most eating habits do not conform to current dietary recommendations, with most diets too low in vegetables, fruits, dairy and oils, and too high in added sugars, saturated fats and salt intake, as well as too many calories.[8] As previously mentioned, obesity is a big concern for those with ADHD, and in part from the impulsiveness it is probably no surprise that typical eating patterns for most individuals with ADHD are unhealthy. Stimulant medication especially can aggravate dietary concerns. Along with the rest of Americans, aligning our diets with dietary guidelines is an important general health measure. But what about food allergies and sensitivities for those with ADHD? Dietary manipulations have been touted as beneficial for treatment of ADHD, including the above mentioned Feingold diet.

First, it is important to distinguish between food allergies and food sensitivities. Food allergies are an immune response to a particular food. They occur almost immediately after ingesting the offending agent, and symptoms can include local swelling, hives, vomiting and diarrhea and in severe cases respiratory difficulties, throat swelling and shock. These can usually be detected by standard allergy testing that can be obtained from medical allergists, and because of potential serious reactions, require complete avoidance of the identified substance and availability of emergency measures such as epinephrine in case of accidental exposure.

Food sensitivities or food intolerance are far more common, and generally less severe. There can be multiple causes. For example, lactase deficiency is an acquired loss of the enzyme lactase that breaks down the milk sugar lactose, and absence of this enzyme results in abdominal discomfort, diarrhea, bloating and cramping. Celiac disease is an autoimmune reaction to gluten, resulting in a multitude of symptoms. But one can also have a gluten intolerance related to less specific and severe symptoms on exposure to gluten. Usually those with food sensitivities can tolerate some of the product, but increased exposure results in increased symptoms, and symptoms can at times be vague and confusing. Sometimes it is the food additives in foods, not the food itself that causes the problems. Especially packaged foods often contain multiple additives, the names of which most of us can't pronounce, that can cause potential reactions. The American Academy of Pediatrics has published concerns about a number of food additives including artificial food colors that can affect childhood behavior. Other food additives or contaminants of concern include Bisphenols (from plastic containers and beverage cans), Phthalates (from food wrap and containers), Perfluorochemicals (PFCs) and nitrates and nitrites used as preservatives and color enhancers.[9]

Elimination diets should start with any food that causes obvious symptoms, or with the more common offending agents. High amounts of sugar are frequently blamed for causing hyperactivity and behavior problems. In spite of anecdotal reports from every parent during holidays such as Halloween, evidence is not compelling that sugar itself is causing the hyperactivity. Nonetheless, the "junk food" associated with large amounts of sugar is useful to avoid if possible. Some are extremely sensitive to food dyes and preservatives such as sodium benzoate and Monosodium glutamate (MSG), so restricting those in the diet, if possible, can be helpful. Because milk intolerance is so common, trying a milk free diet can be worth considering. Other common offending foods are nuts, soy, wheat, and eggs. For most with ADHD, dietary changes may be good for their overall health, but will not result in significant behavioral improvement. But for some, results can be dramatic, and so may be worth trying. It is important to give dietary trials a long enough period to be effective, usually at least 2 weeks, and also they should be something that can be continued long term if effective. Usually it is helpful to have the whole family involved with diet changes, not just the one with ADHD. Overly restricted diets can have their own complications leading to nutritional deficiencies, so consultation with medical providers or nutritionists should be considered.

Exercise and Sleep

As with healthy diets, it seems obvious that exercise is good for those with ADHD, as it is for all of us. There are numerous studies touting the benefits of exercise for those with ADHD, and showing that amount of exercise correlates very well with academic performance. We all are aware that exercise is important for overall fitness, weight management, bone and cardiorespiratory health. Additional benefits are improved cognition and executive function, improved sleep and reduced risk for anxiety and depression. Current recommendations for exercise for children and adolescents are 1 hour per day of moderate to vigorous activity, to include aerobic, muscle strengthening and bone strengthening activities, with the expectation that this will improve strength and endurance, improve overall health and fitness, and improve motor skills, coordination and emotional well-being.[10] Evidence shows that it is helpful for ADHD as well, for core ADHD symptoms, executive function, social, emotional and behavior well-being.[11] And yet, especially in the ADHD population, most appear to get insufficient amounts of exercise. Reasons may be too much time spent on homework, addiction to videogames and other screen activity, lack of social structure to be able to join in group sports or activities, lack of desire for physical activity, obesity, and decreased availability of physical education classes in schools.

Just having free time not tied into school or chores is vital. Time spent in less structured activities, meaning time where adults are not telling them what to do, improves children's abilities to use their imaginations, problems solving skills and ability to set goals for themselves and reach them. But exercise also has direct beneficial effects on ADHD symptoms. Many with

ADHD struggle with team sports because of behavior or coordination challenges. Baseball is probably the worst sport for most children with ADHD. Time spent on the field can be very boring to the ADHD child, with severe consequences to the team if the ADHD fielder isn't paying attention. And batting draws everyone's attention and focus to the individual batter, which if the outcome is poor can be a recipe for extreme anxiety. For many, individual sports such as running, swimming and racquet sports can be very fulfilling with less pressure to perform. Depending on the coach or teacher, certain sports like karate can be very beneficial because they teach self-discipline. And even in group organized sports such as football and basketball, some coaches can be incredibly motivating for participants with ADHD. Exercise doesn't have to be in organized sports of course. Jumping on the trampoline, bicycling, hiking or any activity that burns up calories will be beneficial.

Sleep problems and interventions were reviewed in chapter 9, but it is worth reiterating here that correction of sleep problems can go a long way towards helping improve the symptoms of ADHD. Creating an environment conducive to sleeping by minimizing electronic device distractions in the bedroom (no TVs), avoiding any screen time for an hour before bedtime, turning off cell phones, getting adequate exercise during the day, consistency with bedtime rituals and mealtimes can improve sleep patterns and behavior problems that are due to insufficient sleep. To make long-term improvements in diet, exercise and sleep generally requires whole family involvement and commitment. These all require huge family commitments in time and effort, but can result in significant improvements in ADHD symptoms, and secondary problems such as mood disturbances, behavior problems, and general health concerns.

Biofeedback

Less proven, but nevertheless a recognized non medicine treatment for ADHD is biofeedback, neurofeedback and brain training. Individuals with ADHD have been found to demonstrate excessive cortical slowing that can be detected with electroencephalograms (EEGs). Biofeedback utilizing EEGs targets the areas of cortical slowing and through specific training activities, teaches the individual to focus, and trains those parts of the brain to be more active. Through active EEG monitoring and with the help of a therapist, the patient receives feedback on results, so that over time the individual develops the ability to recognize how to improve optimal brain activity and sustain attention, focus and self-control. This is usually done in 30 minute sessions and takes many sessions to see results. The results are affected heavily by the experience and expertise of the therapist.

Research studies have shown benefit of neurofeedback in measures of ADHD symptoms at least for the short term.[12] The results tend to be better for children than adults. Results may persist beyond the treatment sessions, but fade over time, but for the majority of those who have been treated with neurofeedback, results are positive if not dramatic. The down side is it takes a long time, usually 20–40 sessions or more, at an expense of thousands of dollars, and finding experienced practitioners can be challenging. Nonetheless it remains an option, whether to augment medication effects or as primary treatment for ADHD.

There are also a plethora of computer programs or aps designed to provide cognitive training, and improve performance for those with ADHD. Although there appears to be some promise for these, there is still much debate on their individual merits, and whether they provide long lasting benefit. To date, research has not demonstrated huge benefits, and again, many are expensive and require a large time commitment. There is certainly potential for these modalities to provide non medicinal interventions to help develop focusing and concentration skills and to improve academic performance. A list of some of the top computerized training programs for children with ADHD can be found on the attitudemag.com website.

Choosing the Right School

The biggest concern for most individuals with ADHD and their families is the school experience. Most of the behaviors of concern, stress and struggles occur related to school and learning activities. Finding the right fit can be extremely challenging, but is critically important, so doing some research is worth the effort. There are many educational options in most areas, including public schools, magnet schools, charter schools, private schools, online schools and home school. Which is best for an individual with ADHD will depend on local resources and family resources. Ideally children with ADHD will learn best in a one on one teaching environment, similar to the master and apprentice style of the middle ages. Any school setting that optimizes individual attention and learning experiences will improve learning and performance. This is likely true for everyone, but especially for those with ADHD. Experiential and hands on learning rather than learning by listening to lectures in a large classroom will be more suited to the typical learning style of many of those with ADHD. Schools have to be able to provide a safe environment conducive to learning. This includes providing safety from bullying and an environment that allows individuality and tolerance.

Years ago in our community we had a program that was started in our school district based on a Boys Town model. Teachers received special training, and the program entailed a learning track for students who fell through the cracks and exhibited poor school performance, but didn't qualify for resource help. The program included much smaller class sizes for these students, special classes to learn study skills, a tracking component so that teachers, parents and students were all aware of the curriculum, assignments and due dates, and extra help to be sure all assigned work was understood, and completed and turned in. This provided a needed structure for those students who were enrolled, and our patients with ADHD absolutely thrived in that environment. Grades skyrocketed, as did self-esteem. Many of the students who had been on medication to help with school and learning issues related to ADHD were able to discontinue the medications, and still succeed in school. It was a tremendously effective program, and well received, but eventually funding for the program dried up, and it was unfortunately discontinued.

Another example of a school intervention that was helpful was with a fourth grade student with ADHD. He had been treated with stimulant medication for the previous three years, and was doing pretty well in school. But his teacher in 4th grade made a bargain with him. He said he understood the student's need to fidget and be restless in the classroom, and he would allow him to be out of his seat, under his seat or on the floor, with the condition that at all times he had to be able to reach out and touch his desk. In addition he had to agree not to bother the other students. The other students, who already knew the child with ADHD well, were all informed of the accommodations, and were instructed not to be bothered if he was out of his seat. That year, we were able to take him off of medication, and he did well. The following year, his parents tried to have his 5th grade teacher implement the same accommodations, but were told that she wouldn't allow it, and regrettably, he had to go back on medication.

Public schools are usually the best resource for helping students with ADHD. They will have the ability to implement programs specific to the needs of the ADHD student, either through IEP or 504 plan mechanisms for those who qualify, and may have additional resources such as the availability of school counselors, study skill training, after school classes, social skills training, resource and special education programs and so on. They will usually have many who have training and expertise in helping those who struggle due to ADHD symptoms. So maximizing the learning experience in the school setting by being aware of the services the school provides and consulting with teachers, principal and counselors early and often can help to create an optimal learning environment there.

At times, the public school may not be a good fit for the student with ADHD and associated problems. Even though there may be many programs and options available for the student, the school may not have the resources to provide the optimal environment and individual attention for each student, and other options need to be researched. Private schools and charter schools may provide an environment more appropriate for some students, with potentially smaller class sizes, and more individual options. Some may be designed specifically for students with ADHD, or may have tracks such as the one mentioned above to help those with ADHD behaviors and learning challenges. They may be able to provide more individual attention and teaching opportunities than public schools have the resources for, as well as extra-curricular activities to enhance learning. Some may be able to provide different learning environments such as more hands on opportunities and experiential learning through projects and field trips.

Charter schools are publicly funded schools that operate independently under a contract or charter. The charter provides the goals and mission of the school, and is authorized by a governing agency (sponsor) that monitors compliance of the charter's rules and accountability. Charter school laws are present in most states, but the laws governing charter school requirements vary from state to state. Generally they are less restricted by standard public school rules and regulations but have to be accountable for meeting the standards set out in the original charter, or they can be shut down. There have been some problems reported where students who graduated from a non-accredited charter school did not receive credit for their classes. Charter schools receive their funding from state and local resources, just like traditional public schools, and money from the federal government for special education services. They may also raise funds from private donations. Charter schools may provide nontraditional and innovative approaches to education that are significantly different than regular public school offerings.

Because they are publicly funded schools, charter schools are required to provide services to all students, including those with disabilities, but they may not have the same resources as other public schools in the school district, and some schools may try to discourage a student with disabilities from enrolling because they lack the appropriate resources. Other concerns about charter schools are that they may dilute funding sources from the school district, and may be overly selective in which students they admit.[13]

Magnet schools are schools within a school district that focus on specific themes, such as performing arts, science and technology, languages through immersion, and others. Like other public schools, there is no tuition, and they are open to any students, and are subject to the same requirements of other public schools in the district. They provide an additional option for schooling, especially for those who have already developed or hope to develop specific career goals.

Another rapidly expanding option is online schools. These can be helpful as a way to get additional academic instruction in areas that may not be provided by the local public schools, or as a means of doing home schooling but with the structure and grading of a school program. There is also potential concern that diplomas of online schools may not be accepted by certain colleges, and of course there is wide variability in the education provided by online schools. But this is a rapidly expanding area of education, and another option for those who are not finding public schools to be a good fit. States vary on whether students in home school programs have access to community public school extracurricular activities such as sports programs, and services. Some may allow dual enrollment in home school programs and public school.

Homeschooling regulations also vary widely from state to state. Homeschooling is legal in all 50 states, but requirements on oversight vary. Some states require parents to meet specific educational qualifications, such as a high school diploma, but most do not. Some also require that certain subjects be taught. There may be options to do part-time enrollment in public schools as well as homeschool, and the student may be able to participate in extracurricular activities offered in the school district as well. There are many regulations in place regarding the requirements for homeschooling and accountability, so it is very important to be aware of the state and local rules. A good resource to help with understanding the intricacies of homeschooling and individual state rules is the Coalition for Responsible Home Education (responsiblehomeschooling.org).

Bibliography

1. Nigg JT. *Getting Ahead of ADHD*. Guilford Press; 2017.
2. Andersen CH, Thomsen PH, Nohr EA, Lemcke S. Maternal body mass index before pregnancy as a risk factor for ADHD and autism in children. *Eur Child Adolesc Psychiatry*. 2018;27(2):139–148. doi:10.1007/s00787-017-1027-6.
3. Kris-Etherton PM, Taylor DS, Yu-Poth S, et al. Polyunsaturated fatty acids in the food chain in the United States. *Am J Clin Nutr*. 2000;71(1):179S–188S. http://dx.doi.org/10.1093/ajcn/71.1.179S.
4. Hawkey E, Nigg JT. Omega-3 fatty acid and ADHD: blood level analysis and meta-analytic extension of supplementation trials. *Clin Psychol Rev*. 2014;34(6):496–505. doi:10.1016/j.cpr.2014.05.005.
5. Wang Y, Huang L, Zhang L, Qu Y, Mu D. Iron status in attention-deficit/hyperactivity disorder: A systematic review and meta-analysis. *PLoS One*. 2017;12(1):e0169145. doi:10.1371/journal.pone.0169145.
6. Biswas S, Kanwal B, Jeet C, Seminara RS. Fok-I, Bsm-I, and Taq-I variants of vitamin D receptor polymorphism in the development of autism spectrum disorder: A literature review. *Cureus*. 2018;10(8):e3228. doi:10.7759/cureus.3228.
7. Kotsi E, Kotsi E, Perrea DN. Vitamin D levels in children and adolescents with attention-deficit hyperactivity disorder (ADHD): a meta-analysis. *Atten Defic Hyperact Disord*. October2018. doi:10.1007/s12402-018-0276-7.
8. U.S. Department of Health and Human Services and U.S. Department of Agriculture. *2015–2020 Dietary Guidelines for Americans*. 8th ed. December 2015. Available at http://health.gov/dietaryguidelines/2015/guidelines/.
9. Trasande L, Shaffer RM, Sathyanarayana S. Food additives and child health. *Pediatrics*. 2018;142(2). http://pediatrics.aappublications.org/content/142/2/e20181410.abstract.
10. USDHHS. Physical activity guidelines for Americans. *ODPHP Publ No U0036*. 2008;53(4):41–42. doi:10.1161/CIRCOUTCOMES.118.005263.
11. Hoza B, Martin CP, Pirog A, Shoulberg EK. Using physical activity to manage ADHD symptoms: The state of the evidence. *Curr Psychiatry Rep*. 2016;18(12):113. doi:10.1007/s11920-016-0749-3.
12. Coeytaux RR, Maslow GR, Davis N, et al. Nonpharmacologic treatments for attention-deficit / hyperactivity disorder: A systematic review. *Pediatrics*. 2018;141(6).
13. Prothera A.What are Charter Schools. *Educ Week*. 2018;(Aug. 9).

Appendix

Resources

The following is a select list of resources for further reading and information.

Books

1 Barkley, Russell A. *Attention-Deficit Hyperactivity Disorder: A Handbook for Diagnosis and Treatment.* Fourth Edition. Guilford Press 2015. The gold standard for reference text on ADHD and its impact across the lifespan, heavily referenced, and authored by multiple specialists, edited by Russell Barkley.

2 Reiff, Michael I. *ADHD: What Every Parent Needs to Know.* Second Edition. American Academy of Pediatrics 2011. Written as a practical guide for parents with multiple contributors and edited by Michael Reiff.

3 Barkley, Russell A. *Taking Charge of ADHD. Third Edition: The Complete, Authoritative Guide for Parents.* Guilford Press 2013. A comprehensive guide for parents.

4 Hallowell, Edward M and Ratey, John J. *Driven to Distraction: Recognizing and Coping with Attention Deficit Disorder.* Anchor Books 2011. A very readable discussion of ADHD for those with the condition, using in depth case studies.

5 Brown, Thomas E. *Outside the Box. Rethinking ADD/ADHD in Children and Adults.* American Psychiatric Association Publishing 2017. Provides a discussion and reevaluation of ADHD, core difficulties, causes and interventions in light of current research.

6 Armstrong, Thomas. *The Myth of the ADHD Child. 101 Ways to Improve Your Child's Behavior and Attention Span Without Drugs, Labels, or Coercion.* Tarcher Perigree 2017. Disputes current medical conceptualization of ADHD and provides 101 practical strategies to various problems encountered in those with ADHD.

7   Nigg, Joel T. Getting Ahead of ADHD. What Next-Generation Science Says about Treatments that Work and How You Can Make Them Work for your Child. Guilford Press 2017. Explores ADHD in light of current research, especially epigenetics, and the implications for new and innovative treatments.

8   *Diagnostic and Statistical Manual of Mental Disorders Fifth Edition DSM-5.* American Psychiatric Association 2015. The most recent edition of the definitive resource describing mental health conditions.

9   Rief, Sandra F. *The ADHD Book of Lists: A Practical Guide for Helping Children and Teens with Attention Deficit Disorders.* Second Edition. Jossey-Bass 2013. A comprehensive guide to ADHD for parents and teachers, particularly helpful for lists of strategies to help with behavior and educational difficulties for those with ADHD.

10 Rief, Sandra F. *The ADD/ADHD Checklist: A Practical Reference for Parents and Teachers.* Second Edition. Jossey-Bass 2008. Directed towards teachers and parents, provides general information about ADHD and related conditions, and reviews practical interventions for helping the individual with ADHD at home and in the school environment.

11 *Caring for Children with ADHD: A Resource Toolkit for Clinicians.* Second Edition. American Academy of Pediatrics 2011. DVD outlining AAP recommendations regarding evaluation and treatment of those with ADHD, including multiple resources. Designed for clinicians.

12 Silver, Larry B. *The Misunderstood Child. Understanding and Coping with Your Child's Learning Disabilities.* Fourth Edition. Harmony 2006. A reference guide for parents on identifying and addressing specific learning disabilities.

13 Clark Lynn. *SOS for Parents. A Practical Guide for Handling Common Everyday Behavior Problems.* Fourth Edition. SOS Programs and Parents Press 2017. A parent education program for improving child behaviors and emotional adjustment.

14 Hechtman, Lily. *Attention Deficit Hyperactivity Disorder. Adult Outcome and its Predictors.* Oxford University Press 2016. A comprehensive review of the best long-term outcome studies on ADHD.

15 Brooks, Robert and Goldstein, Sam. *Raising Resilient Children. Fostering Strength, Hope, and Optimism in Your Child.* McGraw Hill 2001. Discusses the qualities of resilience and the abilities required in overcoming adversity, and how to promote resilience in our children.

Internet Resources

ADHD

https://www.additudemag.com The official web site for the *ADDitude* magazine, this is a very useful source of information about ADHD and associated issues, with informational articles, questions and answers and dis-cussions. Advisory board includes many of the most prominent ADHD experts.

https://chadd.org The official website for CHADD (Children and Adults with Attention-Deficit/Hyperactivity Disorder), serves as a clearinghouse for evidence based information on ADHD, organizes local support groups for families affected by ADHD, and advocates for public policies in response to needs faced by those affected by ADHD.

https://www.understood.org Designed for parents, provides well-resear-ched practical information on learning and attention issues.

https://secure.myadhd.com A centralized resource service that helps clinicians, teachers and patients exchange clinical information based on rating scales to help diagnose and monitor ADHD.

https://add.org website for Attention Deficit Disorder Association (ADDA). Provides resources and information for adults with ADHD.

Autism

https://www.autismspeaks.org Advocacy, dissemination of information on autism, and research support for autism, built from the merging of the autism coalition for research and education, the national alliance for autism research and cure autism now.

https://www.autism-society.org The official site for the Autism Society of America founded by Dr. Bernard Rimland and Dr. Ruth Sullivan.

https://www.autism.com The website for the autism Research Institute, established by Dr. Bernard Rimland.

Learning Disabilities

www.ldonline.org Provides up to date information on learning disabilities and ADHD. It is the official website for the National Joint Committee on Learning Disabilities and is an educational service of public television station WETA in Washington, D.C.

https://ldaamerica.org The website for the Learning Disabilities Associa-tion of America, with multiple resources for those with learning disabilities and ADHD.

https://www.ncld.org The website for the National Center for Learning Disabilities.

https://council-for-learning-disabilities.org The website for The Council for Learning Disabilities; provides information on evidence based research and practices related to the education of those with learning disabilities.

https://dyslexiaida.org Site for the International Dyslexia Association with information on reading disabilities and specifically dyslexia.

Tourette Syndrome

https://tourette.org Home of the Tourette Association of America.

General Health and Mental Health

https://www.medicalhomeportal.org A reliable source of information about children and youth with special health care needs for families, physicians, medical home providers, other professionals and caregivers. A resource for information about chronic medical conditions and where to find local and national resources.

https://www.healthyplace.com Provides information on mental health disorders for consumers and mental health providers.

http://www.aap.org The official website for the American Academy of Pediatrics with information for consumers and pediatric care professionals.

https://healthychildren.org Sponsored by the American Academy of Pediatrics with reviews of multiple health conditions including ADHD.

https://www.verywellmind.com Provides information about mental health for consumers.

https://www.nimh.nih.gov The National Institute of Mental Health Information Resource Center website with information on multiple mental health disorders including a section on ADHD.

https://www.cdc.gov Information website for the Center for Disease Control, the nation's health protection agency, with information on multiple health conditions including ADHD.

https://www.webmd.com General health website with information on multiple health conditions.

https://www.aacap.org The official website for the American Academy of Child and Adolescent Psychiatry. It provides multiple resources, and has a specific ADHD Resource Center for families and professionals.

https://medlineplus.gov Produced by the National Library of Medicine, it is the National Institutes of Health website for patients and families with up to date reliable information about multiple health topics including ADHD.

https://www.parentcenterhub.org The Center for Parent Information and Resources, it is the resource website for parent training and information centers and community parent resource centers that provide services for families of children with disabilities. It is funded by the Office of Special Education Programs at the US Department of Education.

https://health.ucdavis.edu/mindinstitute The University of California Davis Medical Investigation of Neurodevelopmental Disorders emphasizes research and dissemination of information on the spectrum of neurodevelopmental disorders including autism and ADHD among others.

Index

Page numbers in **bold** indicate Tables.